A MATHEMATICAL PRIMER FOR SOCIAL STATISTICS

Quantitative Applications in the Social Sciences

A SAGE PUBLICATIONS SERIES

Quantitative Applications in the Social Sciences

A SAGE PUBLICATIONS SERIES

To the memory of my mother, Diana,
the real mathematician in the family.

Sara Miller McCune founded SAGE Publishing in 1965 to support the dissemination of usable knowledge and educate a global community. SAGE publishes more than 1000 journals and over 800 new books each year, spanning a wide range of subject areas. Our growing selection of library products includes archives, data, case studies and video. SAGE remains majority owned by our founder and after her lifetime will become owned by a charitable trust that secures the company's continued independence.

Los Angeles | London | New Delhi | Singapore | Washington DC | Melbourne

A MATHEMATICAL PRIMER FOR SOCIAL STATISTICS

Second Edition

John Fox

McMaster University

Quantitative Applications in the Social Sciences, Volume 159

SAGE

Los Angeles | London | New Delhi
Singapore | Washington DC

Los Angeles | London | New Delhi
Singapore | Washington DC

FOR INFORMATION:

SAGE Publications, Inc.

2455 Teller Road

Thousand Oaks, California 91320

E-mail: order@sagepub.com

SAGE Publications Ltd.

1 Oliver's Yard

55 City Road

London EC1Y 1SP

United Kingdom

SAGE Publications India Pvt. Ltd.

B 1/I 1 Mohan Cooperative Industrial Area

Mathura Road, New Delhi 110 044

India

SAGE Publications Asia-Pacific Pte. Ltd.

18 Cross Street #10-10/11/12

China Square Central

Singapore 048423

Acquisitions Editor: Helen Salmon

Editorial Assistant: Elizabeth Cruz

Production Editor: Natasha Tiwari

Copy Editor: QuADS Prepress Pvt. Ltd.

Typesetter: Hurix Digital

Proofreader: Theresa Kay

Indexer: Integra

Cover Designer: Candice Harman

Marketing Manager: Victoria Velasquez

Copyright ©2021 by SAGE Publications, Inc.

Printed in the United States of America

Library of Congress Cataloging-in-Publication Data

Names: Fox, John, 1947-author. | Sage (Firm)
Title: A mathematical primer for social statistics / John Fox, McMaster University.
Other titles: Quantitative applications in the social sciences.

Description: Second Edition. | Los Angeles : SAGE 2020. | Series: Quantitative applications in the social sciences | First edition published 2009. | Includes bibliographical references.

Identifiers: LCCN 2020031287 | ISBN 9781071833209 (Paperback : acid-free paper) | ISBN 9781071833247 (ePub) | ISBN 9781071833230 (ePub) | ISBN 9781071833223 (ePub)

Subjects: LCSH: Social sciences-Mathematics. | Social sciences-Statistical methods.

Classification: LCC H61.25 .F69 2020 | DDC 519.5-dc23

LC record available at https://lccn.loc .gov/2020031287

This book is printed on acid-free paper.
20 21 22 23 24 10 9 8 7 6 5 4 3 2 1

CONTENTS

SERIES EDITOR'S INTRODUCTION

The statistical sophistication of articles published in major social science journals has been increasing steadily over time. However, because the mathematical knowledge that social science students bring to their graduate statistics training has not always kept pace, the skills needed to fully understand, critique, and replicate these methods may be lacking. *A Mathematical Primer for Social Statistics* (2nd ed.) provides the missing foundation for those who need it and fills in the gaps for those whose training is spotty or out-of-date.

The *Primer*'s author, John Fox, is a well-known and respected expert in statistical methods. The mathematical concepts and skills needed to learn advanced social statistical methods are thus well-known to him. But perhaps as importantly, so are the areas of particular weakness among social scientists. The *Primer* is designed to address these weaknesses very specifically in order to provide the background social scientists need for the statistical methods they are likely to use. The scope is similar to that of the math camps that precede the beginning of PhD programs in economics and some political science, public policy, and sociology programs.

The *Primer* (2nd ed.) is organized around bodies of mathematical knowledge central to learning and understanding advanced statistics: the basic "language" of linear algebra, differential and integral calculus, probability theory, common probability distributions, and statistical estimation and inference. The volume concludes showing the application of mathematical concepts and operations to the familiar case, linear least-squares regression. Compared to the first edition of the *Primer*, published a decade ago, the second edition gives much more attention to visualization. It also covers some new topics—for example, an introduction to Markov-chain Monte Carlo methods. Also included is a companion website with materials that will enable readers to use the R statistical computing environment to reproduce and expand on computations presented in the volume.

The *Primer* would make an excellent text to accompany a math camp or a course designed to provide foundational mathematics needed to understand advanced statistics. It would also serve as a valuable reference for those who have completed their formal training but are still interested in learning new statistical methods. For example, those preparing to learn factor analysis or principal components analysis might benefit from a review of eigenvalues and eigenvectors (Chapter 2). Those about to dive into generalized linear models might usefully review the exponential family of distributions (Chapter 5). In the process of working through an advanced text, readers might consult the *Primer* when they encounter a topic for which they need a quick refresher—for example, a Kronecker product (Chapter 1), a Lagrange multiplier (Chapter 3), or the likelihood ratio test (Chapter 6). A detailed Table of Contents as well as an Index help readers navigate the topics covered in the *Primer*, large and small.

Generations have learned from Professor Fox's many texts. In addition to the *Primer*, there are several others in the QASS Series: *Multiple and Generalized Nonparametric Regression* (Book 131); *Nonparametric Simple Regression: Smoothing Scatterplots* (Book 130); and *Regression Diagnostics*, 2nd ed. (Book 79). The *Primer* is thus in excellent company and will serve the needs of generations to come.

—*Barbara Entwisle*
Series Editor

ACKNOWLEDGMENTS

I am grateful to Barbara Entwisle, the academic editor of the Sage QASS series, and to several (originally anonymous) referees for their helpful comments and suggestions:

Scott Basinger, *University of Houston*

Victor Ferreros, *Walden University*

Scott Liebertz, *University of South Alabama*

I am also grateful to Helen Salmon, my editor at SAGE, for her continuing help and encouragement. Finally, I'd like to acknowledge support for this work from the Social Sciences and Humanities Research Council of Canada.

PREFACE

Statistics is not mathematics. Math is central to the development, communication, and understanding of statistics, but applied statistics—the kind of statistics of most interest to social scientists—is not about proving abstract theorems but about analyzing data.

Typical introductory statistics courses taught to social science students use only very basic mathematics—arithmetic, simple formulas, and the interpretation of graphs. There are good reasons for this: Most social science students have weak backgrounds in mathematics. Even more important, however, the fundamental goals of a basic statistics course (or at least what in my opinion should be the fundamental goals) are to convey the role of statistical methods in collecting and summarizing data along with the essential ideas of statistical inference. Accomplishing these goals is sufficiently challenging without drowning the big ideas in a sea of equations. I believe, incidentally, that this is the case even for students who have strong foundations in mathematics.

Once beyond the introductory level, and perhaps a second course in applied regression analysis, the situation changes: Insufficient grounding in mathematics makes it difficult to proceed in applied statistics. The good news, however, is that a relatively modest background in intermediate-level mathematics suffices for the study of a great deal of statistics. Often, all that is needed is an understanding of basic mathematical ideas, familiarity with some important facts, and an ability to read and perhaps manipulate equations. This book aims to provide that basic background.

The book originated in online appendices that I wrote for the second edition of my applied regression text (Fox, 2008, which is now in a third edition, Fox, 2016). I felt initially that some readers might prefer a printed and bound copy of the appendices to downloading them from the internet. It then occurred to me that the appendices might prove more generally useful, and ultimately I augmented them with material that was not directly relevant to my applied regression text but that is important to other statistical methods that are widely employed in the social sciences. The book, therefore, includes material not in the original appendices, and this second edition of the book includes material not in the first edition (see page xvii below).

The book covers three areas of mathematics that are of central importance to applied statistics:

- Chapters 1 and 2 takes up matrices, linear algebra, and vector geometry. Matrices, which are rectangular arrays of numbers, are a natural representation of most statistical data, and consequently, the arithmetic and algebra of matrices is the natural language for developing most statistical methods. Beyond the basic level, matrices are omnipresent in statistics, and therefore, some acquaintance with matrices is necessary for reading statistical material. The closely related areas of linear algebra and its visual representation, vector geometry, are also central to the development and understanding of many statistical methods.

- Chapter 3 introduces the basic ideas of differential and integral calculus. Here, the emphasis is on fundamental concepts and simple methods. Differential calculus is frequently used in statistics for optimization problems—that is, minimization and maximization: Think, for example, of the method of *least* squares or of *maximum*-likelihood estimation. Integral calculus figures prominently in probability theory, which is fundamentally tied to statistical modeling and statistical inference. Although the presentation of calculus in this book is elementary, I do cover topics important to statistics, such as multivariable and matrix calculus, that, while not fundamentally difficult, are often deferred to advanced treatments of the subject.

- Chapters 4, 5, and 6 develop probability theory, describe probability distributions important to statistics, and introduce statistical theory, including asymptotic distribution theory, the properties of estimators, the centrally important method of maximum likelihood, and the basics of Bayesian statistical inference. The ideas in these chapters feature prominently in applied statistics, and indeed, the three chapters represent a kind of "crash course" in some of the fundamentals of mathematical statistics.

- Chapter 7 illustrates the use of the preceding mathematics in applied statistics by briefly developing the seminal statistical method of linear least-squares regression and deriving some of its properties.

It is, all told, remarkable how far one can get in applied statistics with a modicum of mathematics—the modicum that this book supplies. This is the resource that I wish I had when I started to study statistics seriously. I hope that it will prove helpful to you, both on initial reading and as a reference.

What's New in the Second Edition

Although the material has been reorganized, the contents of the first edition of the book are included in the second edition, with small additions and modifications. There are as well a few more substantial additions to the book:

- Chapter 2 includes new material on visualizing quadratic forms using ellipses and on the QR matrix decomposition.

- Chapter 3 on calculus includes a new introduction to numerical optimization.

- Ellipses are also used in Chapter 5 to represent contours of the bivariate-normal distribution and in Chapter 7 to visualize properties of simple and multiple least-squares regression.

- Chapter 6 includes a new introduction to Markov-chain Monte Carlo (MCMC) methods for approximating probability distributions, methods that are central to modern Bayesian statistics.

- The QR and singular-value decompositions are applied in Chapter 7 to the numerically stable computation of least-squares regression coefficients.

Notation

Specific notation is introduced at various points in the text. Throughout the text, I adhere to the following general conventions, with few exceptions. [Examples are shown in brackets.]

- Known scalar constants (i.e., individual numbers, including subscripts) are represented by lowercase italic letters [a, b, x_i].

- Observable scalar random variables are represented by uppercase italic letters [X, Y_i]. Where it is necessary to make the distinction, *specific values* of random variables are represented as constants [x, y_i].

- Scalar parameters are represented by lowercase Greek letters [α, β, γ_2]. (See the Greek alphabet in Table 1.) Their estimators are generally denoted by "corresponding" italic characters [A, B, C_2], or by Greek letters with "hats" [$\widehat{\alpha}, \widehat{\beta}, \widehat{\gamma}_2$].

Table 1   The Greek Alphabet With Roman "Equivalents"

Greek Letter			Roman Equivalent	
Lowercase	Uppercase		Phonetic	Other
α	A	alpha	a	
β	B	beta	b	
γ	Γ	gamma	g, n	c
δ	Δ	delta	d	
ε	E	epsilon	e	
ζ	Z	zeta	z	
η	H	eta	e	
θ	Θ	theta	th	
ι	I	iota	i	
κ	K	kappa	k	
λ	Λ	lambda	l	
μ	M	mu	m	
ν	N	nu	n	
ξ	Ξ	xi	x	
o	O	omicron	o	
π	Π	pi	p	
ρ	P	rho	r	
σ	Σ	sigma	s	
τ	T	tau	t	
υ	Υ	upsilon	y, u	
ϕ	Φ	phi	ph	
χ	X	chi	ch	x
ψ	Ψ	psi	ps	
ω	Ω	omega	o	w

- Unobservable scalar random variables are also represented by lowercase Greek letters [ε_i].

- Vectors (one-dimensional "lists" of numbers) and matrices (rectangular tables of numbers) are represented by boldface characters— lowercase for vectors [$\mathbf{x}_1$, $\boldsymbol{\beta}$], uppercase for matrices [$\mathbf{X}$, $\boldsymbol{\Sigma}$]. In a statistical context, Roman letters are used for constants and observable random variables [$\mathbf{y}$, $\mathbf{x}_1$, $\mathbf{X}$], and Greek letters are used for parameters and unobservable random variables [$\boldsymbol{\beta}$, $\boldsymbol{\Sigma}$, $\boldsymbol{\varepsilon}$]. It is occasionally convenient to show the order (number of rows and columns) of a vector or matrix below the matrix [$\underset{(n \times 1)}{\boldsymbol{\varepsilon}}$, $\underset{(n \times k+1)}{\mathbf{X}}$]. The order of an identity matrix is given by a subscript $[\mathbf{I}_n]$. A zero matrix or vector is represented by a boldface zero $[\mathbf{0}]$; a vector of 1s is represented by a boldface $\mathbf{1}$, possibly subscripted with its number of elements $[\mathbf{1}_n]$. The transpose of a matrix is denoted by a prime $[\mathbf{X}']$, and vectors are column vectors (i.e., one-column matrices), unless they are explicitly transposed [column: $\mathbf{x}$; row: $\mathbf{x}'$].

- The symbol $\equiv$ can be read as "is defined by," or "is equal to by definition" $[\overline{X} \equiv (\sum X_i)/n]$.

- The symbol $\approx$ means "is approximately equal to" $[\pi \approx 3.14159]$.

- The symbol $\propto$ means "is proportional to" $[p(\alpha|D) \propto L(\alpha)p(\alpha)]$.

- The symbol $\sim$ means "is distributed as" $[\varepsilon_i \sim N(0, \sigma^2)]$.

- The operator $E(\ )$ denotes the expectation of a scalar, vector, or matrix random variable $[E(Y_i), E(\boldsymbol{\varepsilon}), E(\mathbf{X})]$.

- The operator $V(\ )$ denotes the variance of a scalar random variable or the variance–covariance matrix of a vector random variable $[V(\varepsilon_i), V(\mathbf{b})]$.

- Estimated variances or variance–covariance matrices are indicated by a circumflex ("hat") placed over the variance operator $[\widehat{V}(\varepsilon_i), \widehat{V}(\mathbf{b})]$.

- The operator $C(\ )$ gives the covariance of two scalar random variables or the covariance matrix of two vector random variables $[C(X, Y), C(\mathbf{x}, \mathbf{y})]$.

- The operators $\mathscr{E}(\ )$ and $\mathscr{V}(\ )$ denote asymptotic expectation and variance, respectively. Their usage is similar to that of $E(\ )$ and $V(\ )$ $[\mathscr{E}(B), \mathscr{E}(\mathbf{b}), \mathscr{V}(\widehat{\boldsymbol{\beta}}), \widehat{\mathscr{V}}(\mathbf{b})]$.

- Probability limits are specified by plim [plim $b = \beta$].

- Standard mathematical functions are shown in lowercase [$\cos W$ or $\cos(W)$, trace($\mathbf{A}$)]. The base of the log function is always specified explicitly [$\log_e L, \log_{10} X$], unless it is irrelevant [$\log 1 = 0$]. The exponential function $\exp(x)$ represents e^x.

- The summation sign $\sum$ is used to denote continued addition [$\sum_{i=1}^{n} X_i \equiv X_1 + X_2 + \cdots + X_n$]. Often, the range of the index is suppressed if it is clear from the context [$\sum_i X_i$], and the index may be suppressed as well [$\sum X_i$]. The symbol $\prod$ similarly indicates continued multiplication [$\prod_{i=1}^{n} p(Y_i) \equiv p(Y_1) \times p(Y_2) \times \cdots \times p(Y_n)$].

- The symbol ∂ denotes the partial derivative $[\partial f(x_1, x_2)/\partial x_1]$.

- To avoid awkward and repetitive phrasing in the statement of definitions and results, the words "if" and "when" are understood to mean "if and only if," unless explicitly indicated to the contrary. Terms are generally set in *italics* when they are introduced. ["Two vectors are *orthogonal* if their inner product is zero."]

Recommended Reading

The subjects addressed in this book—linear algebra, calculus, probability, and statistical theory—are larger than can be covered in depth in a 200-page book. It is my hope that the book will not only provide a basic background in these topics for students of social statistics, but also the foundation required to pursue the topics in greater depth, for example in the following sources.

There is a plethora of books on linear algebra and matrices. Most presentations develop the fundamental properties of vector spaces, but often, unfortunately, without explicit visual representation.

- Several matrix texts, including Healy (1986), Graybill (1983), Searle (1982), and Green and Carroll (1976), focus specifically on statistical applications. The last of these sources has a strongly geometric orientation.

- Davis (1965), who presents a particularly lucid and simple treatment of matrix algebra, includes some material on vector geometry (limited, however, to two dimensions).

- Namboodiri (1984) provides a compact introduction to matrix algebra (but not to vector geometry).

- Books on statistical computing, such as the classic text by Kennedy and Gentle (1980) and Monahan (2001), typically describe the implementation of matrix and linear-algebra computations on digital computers. Fieller (2016) presents a treatment of numerical matrix algebra that focuses on the R statistical computing environment.

There is an almost incredible profusion of introductory calculus texts, and I cannot claim to have read more than a few of them.

- Of these, my favorite brief treatment is Thompson and Gardner (1998), which was first published in the early 20th century, and which deals almost exclusively with functions of one independent variable.

- For a much more detailed introduction, including to multivariable calculus, see Stewart (2016), a very popular text that has appeared in many versions and editions.

Most more advanced treatments of calculus are either highly abstract or focus on applications in the physical sciences.

- For an extensive treatment of calculus of several variables with a social science (specifically, economic) orientation, see Binmore and Davies (2001).

- Nash (2014) provides an in-depth treatment of numerical optimization methods oriented toward the R statistical computing environment.

Almost any introductory text in mathematical statistics, and many econometric texts, cover probability theory, statistical distributions, and the foundations of statistical inference more formally and in greater detail than I do in this book, and there are also books that focus on each of these subjects.

- The text by Cox and Hinkley (1974) is a standard, if relatively difficult, treatment of most of the topics in Chapters 4, 5, and 6.

- A compact summary appears in Zellner (1983).

- Wonnacott and Wonnacott (1990) present insightful treatments of many of these topics at a much lower level of mathematical sophistication; I particularly recommend this source if you found the simpler parts of Chapter 4 too terse.

- A good, relatively accessible, discussion of asymptotic distribution theory appears in Theil (1971, Chapter 8).

- A general presentation of Wald, likelihood-ratio, and score tests can be found in Engle (1984).

- Lancaster (2004), Gelman and Hill (2007), and McElreath (2020) offer accessible introductions to Bayesian methods, while Gelman, Carlin, Stern, and Rubin (2013) present a more extensive treatment of the subject.

- Clear explanations of the Gibbs sampler and Hamiltonian Monte Carlo may be found in Casella and George (1992) and Neal (2011), respectively.

Website

I have prepared a website for the book, accessible at **https://tinyurl.com/ Math-Primer**, including errata (if any, as they come to my attention), and a variety of materials focussed on computations using the R statistical computing environment. For example, I use the **matlib** package for R to illustrate matrix and linear-algebra computations employed in the book, such as step-by-step demonstrations of Gaussian elimination and the construction of vector diagrams.

ABOUT THE AUTHOR

John Fox is Professor Emeritus of Sociology at McMaster University in Hamilton, Ontario, Canada, where he was previously the Senator William McMaster Professor of Social Statistics. Professor Fox received a PhD in sociology from the University of Michigan in 1972 and is the author of many articles and books on statistics, including *Applied Regression Analysis and Generalized Linear Models* (3rd ed., 2016), *Using the R Commander: A Point-and-Click Interface for R* (2018), *Regression Diagnostics* (2nd ed., 2019), and, with Sanford Weisberg, *An R Companion to Applied Regression* (3rd ed., 2019). He continues to work on the development of statistical methods and their implementation in software. Professor Fox is an elected member of the R Foundation for Statistical Computing and an associate editor of the *Journal of Statistical Software*.

CHAPTER 1. MATRICES, LINEAR ALGEBRA, AND VECTOR GEOMETRY: THE BASICS

Matrices provide a natural notation for much of statistics; the algebra of linear statistical models is linear algebra; and vector geometry is a powerful conceptual tool for understanding linear algebra and for visualizing many aspects of linear models. The purpose of this chapter is to present essential concepts and results concerning matrices, linear algebra, and vector geometry. The focus is on topics that are employed widely in social statistics, and the style of presentation is informal rather than mathematically rigorous: At points, results are stated without proof; at other points, proofs are outlined; often, results are justified intuitively. Readers interested in pursuing linear algebra at greater depth might profitably make reference to one of the many available texts on the subject, each of which develops in greater detail most of the topics presented here (see, e.g., the recommended readings in the Preface, page xx).

The first section of the chapter develops elementary matrix algebra. The second and third sections introduce vector geometry and vector spaces. The final section discusses the related topics of matrix rank and the solution of linear simultaneous equations.

1.1 Matrices

1.1.1 Introducing the Actors: Definitions

A *matrix* is a rectangular table of numbers or of numerical variables;[1] for example,

$$\underset{(4\times3)}{\mathbf{X}} = \begin{bmatrix} 1 & -2 & 3 \\ 4 & -5 & -6 \\ 7 & 8 & 9 \\ 0 & 0 & 10 \end{bmatrix} \tag{1.1}$$

---

[1] In this text, I restrict consideration to matrices composed of *real numbers*, but matrices can also have *complex numbers* as elements—that is, numbers of the form $a + bi$, where $i \equiv \sqrt{-1}$. Matrices with complex elements have few applications in statistics (e.g., in time-series analysis), although they are prominent in other fields, such as physics.

or, more generally,

$$
\mathop{\mathbf{A}}_{(m\times n)} =
\begin{bmatrix}
a_{11} & a_{12} & \cdots & a_{1n} \\
a_{21} & a_{22} & \cdots & a_{2n} \\
\vdots & \vdots & & \vdots \\
a_{m1} & a_{m2} & \cdots & a_{mn}
\end{bmatrix}
\tag{1.2}
$$

A matrix such as this with m rows and n columns is said to be of *order* m by n, written as $(m \times n)$. For clarity, I at times indicate the order of a matrix below the matrix, as in Equations 1.1 and 1.2. Each *entry* or *element* of a matrix may be subscripted by its row and column indices: a_{ij} is the entry in the ith row and jth column of the matrix $\mathbf{A}$. Individual numbers, such as the entries of a matrix, are termed *scalars*. Sometimes, for compactness, I specify a matrix by enclosing its typical element in braces; for example, $\mathop{\mathbf{A}}_{(m\times n)} = \{a_{ij}\}$ is equivalent to Equation 1.2.

A matrix consisting of one column is called a *column vector*; for example,

$$
\mathop{\mathbf{a}}_{(m\times 1)} =
\begin{bmatrix}
a_1 \\
a_2 \\
\vdots \\
a_m
\end{bmatrix}
$$

Likewise, a matrix consisting of one row is called a *row vector*,

$$
\mathbf{b}' = [b_1, b_2, \cdots, b_n]
$$

In specifying a row vector, I typically place commas between its elements for clarity.

The *transpose* of a matrix $\mathbf{A}$, denoted $\mathbf{A}'$, is formed from $\mathbf{A}$ so that the ith *row* of $\mathbf{A}'$ consists of the elements of the ith *column* of $\mathbf{A}$;[2] thus (using the

---

[2] Although in this book I'll consistently use a prime, as in $\mathbf{A}'$, to denote the matrix transpose, it's also common to use a superscript T, as in $\mathbf{A}^T$.

matrices in Equations 1.1 and 1.2),

$$\mathbf{X}'_{(3\times4)} = \begin{bmatrix} 1 & 4 & 7 & 0 \\ -2 & -5 & 8 & 0 \\ 3 & -6 & 9 & 10 \end{bmatrix}$$

$$\mathbf{A}'_{(n\times m)} = \begin{bmatrix} a_{11} & a_{21} & \cdots & a_{m1} \\ a_{12} & a_{22} & \cdots & a_{m2} \\ \vdots & \vdots & & \vdots \\ a_{1n} & a_{2n} & \cdots & a_{mn} \end{bmatrix}$$

The transpose of the transpose is the original matrix: $(\mathbf{A}')' = \mathbf{A}$. I adopt the common convention that a vector is a column vector (such as $\mathbf{a}$ above) unless it is explicitly transposed (such as $\mathbf{b}'$).

A *square matrix of order n*, as the term implies, has n rows and n columns. The entries a_{ii} (i.e., $a_{11}, a_{22}, \ldots, a_{nn}$) of a square matrix $\mathbf{A}$ comprise the *main diagonal* of the matrix. The sum of the diagonal elements is the *trace* of the matrix:

$$\text{trace}(A) \equiv \sum_{i=1}^{n} a_{ii}$$

For example, the square matrix

$$\mathbf{B}_{(3\times3)} = \begin{bmatrix} -5 & 1 & 3 \\ 2 & 2 & 6 \\ 7 & 3 & -4 \end{bmatrix}$$

has diagonal elements, $-5, 2$, and -4, and trace$(\mathbf{B}) = \sum_{i=1}^{3} b_{ii} = -5 + 2 - 4 = -7$.

A square matrix $\mathbf{A}$ is *symmetric* if $\mathbf{A} = \mathbf{A}'$, that is, when $a_{ij} = a_{ji}$ for all i and j. Consequently, the matrix $\mathbf{B}$ (above) is not symmetric, while the matrix

$$\mathbf{C} = \begin{bmatrix} -5 & 1 & 3 \\ 1 & 2 & 6 \\ 3 & 6 & -4 \end{bmatrix}$$

is symmetric. Many matrices that appear in statistical applications are symmetric—for example, correlation matrices, covariance matrices, and matrices of sums of squares and cross products.

An *upper-triangular matrix* is a square matrix with 0s below its main diagonal:

$$\mathbf{U}_{(n\times n)} = \begin{bmatrix} u_{11} & u_{12} & \cdots & u_{1n} \\ 0 & u_{22} & \cdots & u_{2n} \\ \vdots & \vdots & \ddots & \vdots \\ 0 & 0 & \cdots & u_{nn} \end{bmatrix}$$

To be clear, some of the elements on and above the main diagonal of $\mathbf{U}$ *may* be 0, but all of the elements below the diagonal *are* 0. Similarly, a *lower-triangular matrix* is a square matrix of the form

$$
\underset{(n\times n)}{\mathbf{L}} =
\begin{bmatrix}
l_{11} & 0 & \cdots & 0 \\
l_{21} & l_{22} & \cdots & 0 \\
\vdots & \vdots & \ddots & \vdots \\
l_{n1} & l_{n2} & \cdots & l_{nn}
\end{bmatrix}
$$

A square matrix is *diagonal* if all entries except those on its main diagonal are 0; thus,

$$
\underset{(n\times n)}{\mathbf{D}} =
\begin{bmatrix}
d_1 & 0 & \cdots & 0 \\
0 & d_2 & \cdots & 0 \\
\vdots & \vdots & \ddots & \vdots \\
0 & 0 & \cdots & d_n
\end{bmatrix}
$$

For compactness, I may write $\mathbf{D} = \mathrm{diag}(d_1, d_2, \ldots, d_n)$. A *scalar matrix* is a diagonal matrix all of whose diagonal entries are equal: $\mathbf{S} = \mathrm{diag}(s, s, \ldots, s)$. An especially important family of scalar matrices are the *identity matrices* $\mathbf{I}$, which have 1s on the main diagonal:

$$
\underset{(n\times n)}{\mathbf{I}} =
\begin{bmatrix}
1 & 0 & \cdots & 0 \\
0 & 1 & \cdots & 0 \\
\vdots & \vdots & \ddots & \vdots \\
0 & 0 & \cdots & 1
\end{bmatrix}
$$

I write $\mathbf{I}_n$ for $\underset{(n\times n)}{\mathbf{I}}$.

Two other special matrices are the family of *zero matrices*, $\mathbf{0}$, all of whose entries are 0, and the $\mathbf{1}$ vectors, all of whose entries are 1. I write $\mathbf{1}_n$ for the column vector of 1s with n entries; for example, $\mathbf{1}_4 = [1, 1, 1, 1]'$. Although the identity matrices, the zero matrices, and the $\mathbf{1}$ vectors are *families* of matrices, it is often convenient to refer to these matrices in the singular, for example, to "*the* identity matrix.'

A *partitioned matrix* is a matrix whose elements are organized into *submatrices*; for example,

$$
\underset{(4\times 3)}{\mathbf{A}} =
\left[
\begin{array}{cc|c}
a_{11} & a_{12} & a_{13} \\
a_{21} & a_{22} & a_{23} \\
a_{31} & a_{32} & a_{33} \\
\hline
a_{41} & a_{42} & a_{43}
\end{array}
\right]
=
\left[
\begin{array}{c|c}
\mathbf{A}_{11} & \mathbf{A}_{12} \\
(3\times 2) & (3\times 1) \\
\hline
\mathbf{A}_{21} & \mathbf{A}_{22} \\
(1\times 2) & (1\times 1)
\end{array}
\right]
$$

where the submatrix

$$\mathbf{A}_{11} \equiv \begin{bmatrix} a_{11} & a_{21} \\ a_{21} & a_{22} \\ a_{31} & a_{32} \end{bmatrix}$$

and $\mathbf{A}_{12}$, $\mathbf{A}_{21}$, and $\mathbf{A}_{22}$ are similarly defined. When there is no possibility of confusion, I omit the lines separating the submatrices. If a matrix is partitioned vertically but not horizontally, then I separate its submatrices by commas; for example, $\underset{(m \times n+p)}{\mathbf{C}} = \begin{bmatrix} \underset{(m \times n)}{\mathbf{C}_1} , & \underset{(m \times p)}{\mathbf{C}_2} \end{bmatrix}$.

1.1.2 Simple Matrix Arithmetic

Two matrices are *equal* if they are of the same order and all corresponding entries are equal (a definition used implicitly in the preceding section).

Two matrices may be *added* only if they are of the same order; then their sum is formed by adding corresponding elements. Thus, if $\mathbf{A}$ and $\mathbf{B}$ are of order $(m \times n)$, then $\mathbf{C} = \mathbf{A} + \mathbf{B}$ is also of order $(m \times n)$, with $c_{ij} = a_{ij} + b_{ij}$. Likewise, if $\mathbf{D} = \mathbf{A} - \mathbf{B}$, then $\mathbf{D}$ is of order $(m \times n)$, with $d_{ij} = a_{ij} - b_{ij}$. The *negative* of a matrix $\mathbf{A}$, that is, $\mathbf{E} = -\mathbf{A}$, is of the same order as $\mathbf{A}$, with elements $e_{ij} = -a_{ij}$. For example, for matrices

$$\underset{(2 \times 3)}{\mathbf{A}} = \begin{bmatrix} 1 & 2 & 3 \\ 4 & 5 & 6 \end{bmatrix}$$

and

$$\underset{(2 \times 3)}{\mathbf{B}} = \begin{bmatrix} -5 & 1 & 2 \\ 3 & 0 & -4 \end{bmatrix}$$

we have

$$\underset{(2 \times 3)}{\mathbf{C}} = \mathbf{A} + \mathbf{B} = \begin{bmatrix} -4 & 3 & 5 \\ 7 & 5 & 2 \end{bmatrix}$$

$$\underset{(2 \times 3)}{\mathbf{D}} = \mathbf{A} - \mathbf{B} = \begin{bmatrix} 6 & 1 & 1 \\ 1 & 5 & 10 \end{bmatrix}$$

$$\underset{(2 \times 3)}{\mathbf{E}} = -\mathbf{B} = \begin{bmatrix} 5 & -1 & -2 \\ -3 & 0 & 4 \end{bmatrix}$$

Because they are element-wise operations, matrix addition, subtraction, and negation follow essentially the same rules as the corresponding scalar arithmetic operations; in particular,

$$\mathbf{A} + \mathbf{B} = \mathbf{B} + \mathbf{A} \text{ (matrix addition is commutative)}$$
$$\mathbf{A} + (\mathbf{B} + \mathbf{C}) = (\mathbf{A} + \mathbf{B}) + \mathbf{C} \text{ (matrix addition is associative)}$$
$$\mathbf{A} - \mathbf{B} = \mathbf{A} + (-\mathbf{B}) = -(\mathbf{B} - \mathbf{A})$$
$$\mathbf{A} - \mathbf{A} = \mathbf{0}$$
$$\mathbf{A} + \mathbf{0} = \mathbf{A}$$
$$-(-\mathbf{A}) = \mathbf{A}$$
$$(\mathbf{A} + \mathbf{B})' = \mathbf{A}' + \mathbf{B}'$$

The *product* of a scalar c and an $(m \times n)$ matrix $\mathbf{A}$ is an $(m \times n)$ matrix $\mathbf{B} = c\mathbf{A}$ in which $b_{ij} = ca_{ij}$. Continuing the preceding examples:

$$\mathbf{F}_{(2 \times 3)} = 3 \times \mathbf{B} = \begin{bmatrix} -15 & 3 & 6 \\ 9 & 0 & -12 \end{bmatrix}$$

The product of a scalar and a matrix obeys the following rules:

$$c\mathbf{A} = \mathbf{A}c \text{ (commutative)}$$
$$\mathbf{A}(b + c) = \mathbf{A}b + \mathbf{A}c \text{ (distributes over scalar addition)}$$
$$c(\mathbf{A} + \mathbf{B}) = c\mathbf{A} + c\mathbf{B} \text{ (distributes over matrix addition)}$$
$$0\mathbf{A} = \mathbf{0}$$
$$1\mathbf{A} = \mathbf{A}$$
$$(-1)\mathbf{A} = -\mathbf{A}$$

where $b, c, 0, 1$, and -1 are scalars, and $\mathbf{A}, \mathbf{B}$, and $\mathbf{0}$ are matrices of the same order.

The *inner product* (or *dot product*) of two vectors (each with n entries), say $\mathbf{a}'_{(1 \times n)}$ and $\mathbf{b}_{(n \times 1)}$, denoted $\mathbf{a}' \cdot \mathbf{b}$, is a scalar formed by multiplying corresponding entries of the vectors and summing the resulting products:

$$\mathbf{a}' \cdot \mathbf{b} = \sum_{i=1}^{n} a_i b_i$$

For example,

$$[2, 0, 1, 3] \cdot \begin{bmatrix} -1 \\ 6 \\ 0 \\ 9 \end{bmatrix} = 2(-1) + 0(6) + 1(0) + 3(9) = 25$$

Although this example is for the inner product of a row vector with a column vector, both vectors may be row vectors or both column vectors, as long as the two vectors have the same number of elements.

Two matrices **A** and **B** are *conformable for multiplication* in the order given (i.e., **AB**) if the number of *columns* of the left-hand factor (**A**) is equal to the number of *rows* of the right-hand factor (**B**). Thus **A** and **B** are conformable for multiplication if **A** is of order $(m \times n)$ and **B** is of order $(n \times p)$, where m and p are unconstrained. For example,

$$\underset{(2\times3)}{\begin{bmatrix} 1 & 2 & 3 \\ 4 & 5 & 6 \end{bmatrix}} \underset{(3\times3)}{\begin{bmatrix} 1 & 0 & 0 \\ 0 & 1 & 0 \\ 0 & 0 & 1 \end{bmatrix}} \tag{1.3}$$

are conformable for multiplication but

$$\underset{(3\times3)}{\begin{bmatrix} 1 & 0 & 0 \\ 0 & 1 & 0 \\ 0 & 0 & 1 \end{bmatrix}} \underset{(2\times3)}{\begin{bmatrix} 1 & 2 & 3 \\ 4 & 5 & 6 \end{bmatrix}} \tag{1.4}$$

are not.

Let $\mathbf{C} = \mathbf{AB}$ be the *matrix product*; and let $\mathbf{a}'_i$ represent the ith *row* of **A** and $\mathbf{b}_j$ represent the jth *column* of **B**. Then **C** is a matrix of order $(m \times p)$ in which

$$c_{ij} = \mathbf{a}'_i \cdot \mathbf{b}_j = \sum_{k=1}^{n} a_{ik} b_{kj}$$

Here are some examples:

$$\underset{(2\times3)}{\begin{bmatrix} \Longrightarrow & & \\ 1 & 2 & 3 \\ 4 & 5 & 6 \end{bmatrix}} \underset{(3\times3)}{\begin{bmatrix} \Downarrow & & \\ 1 & 0 & 0 \\ 0 & 1 & 0 \\ 0 & 0 & 1 \end{bmatrix}}$$

$$= \underset{(2\times3)}{\begin{bmatrix} 1(1)+2(0)+3(0), & 1(0)+2(1)+3(0), & 1(0)+2(0)+3(1) \\ 4(1)+5(0)+6(0), & 4(0)+5(1)+6(0), & 4(0)+5(0)+6(1) \end{bmatrix}}$$

$$= \begin{bmatrix} 1 & 2 & 3 \\ 4 & 5 & 6 \end{bmatrix}$$

$$\underset{(1\times4)}{[\beta_0, \beta_1, \beta_2, \beta_3]} \underset{(4\times1)}{\begin{bmatrix} 1 \\ x_1 \\ x_2 \\ x_3 \end{bmatrix}} = \underset{(1\times1)}{[\beta_0 + \beta_1 x_1 + \beta_2 x_2 + \beta_3 x_3]}$$

$$\begin{bmatrix} 1 & 2 \\ 3 & 4 \end{bmatrix} \begin{bmatrix} 0 & 3 \\ 2 & 1 \end{bmatrix} = \begin{bmatrix} 4 & 5 \\ 8 & 13 \end{bmatrix} \qquad (1.5)$$

$$\begin{bmatrix} 0 & 3 \\ 2 & 1 \end{bmatrix} \begin{bmatrix} 1 & 2 \\ 3 & 4 \end{bmatrix} = \begin{bmatrix} 9 & 12 \\ 5 & 8 \end{bmatrix}$$

$$\begin{bmatrix} 2 & 0 \\ 0 & 3 \end{bmatrix} \begin{bmatrix} \frac{1}{2} & 0 \\ 0 & \frac{1}{3} \end{bmatrix} = \begin{bmatrix} 1 & 0 \\ 0 & 1 \end{bmatrix} \qquad (1.6)$$

$$\begin{bmatrix} \frac{1}{2} & 0 \\ 0 & \frac{1}{3} \end{bmatrix} \begin{bmatrix} 2 & 0 \\ 0 & 3 \end{bmatrix} = \begin{bmatrix} 1 & 0 \\ 0 & 1 \end{bmatrix}$$

In the first of these examples, the arrows indicate how the rows of the left-hand factor are multiplied into the columns of the right-hand factor.

Matrix multiplication is associative, $\mathbf{A(BC)} = \mathbf{(AB)C}$, and distributive with respect to addition:

$$(\mathbf{A}+\mathbf{B})\mathbf{C} = \mathbf{AC}+\mathbf{BC}$$
$$\mathbf{A}(\mathbf{B}+\mathbf{C}) = \mathbf{AB}+\mathbf{AC}$$

but it is not in general commutative: If $\mathbf{A}$ is $(m \times n)$ and $\mathbf{B}$ is $(n \times p)$, then the product $\mathbf{AB}$ is defined but $\mathbf{BA}$ is defined only if $m = p$ (cf., e.g., the matrices in 1.3 and 1.4 above). Even so, $\mathbf{AB}$ and $\mathbf{BA}$ are of different orders (and hence are not candidates for equality) unless $m = p$. And even if $\mathbf{A}$ and $\mathbf{B}$ are square, $\mathbf{AB}$ and $\mathbf{BA}$, though of the same order, are not necessarily equal (as illustrated in Equation 1.5). If it is the case that $\mathbf{AB} = \mathbf{BA}$ (as in Equation 1.6), then the matrices $\mathbf{A}$ and $\mathbf{B}$ are said to *commute* with one another. A scalar factor, however, may be moved anywhere within a matrix product: $c\mathbf{AB} = \mathbf{A}c\mathbf{B} = \mathbf{AB}c$.

The identity and zero matrices play roles with respect to matrix multiplication analogous to those of the numbers 1 and 0 in scalar algebra:

$$\underset{(m \times n)}{\mathbf{A}} \ \mathbf{I}_n = \mathbf{I}_m \underset{(m \times n)}{\mathbf{A}} = \mathbf{A}$$

$$\underset{(m \times n)}{\mathbf{A}} \underset{(n \times p)}{\mathbf{0}} = \underset{(m \times p)}{\mathbf{0}}$$

$$\underset{(q \times m)}{\mathbf{0}} \underset{(m \times n)}{\mathbf{A}} = \underset{(q \times n)}{\mathbf{0}}$$

A further property of matrix multiplication, which has no analog in scalar algebra, is that $\mathbf{(AB)}' = \mathbf{B'A'}$—the transpose of a product is the product of the transposes taken in the opposite order, a rule that extends to the product of several (conformable) matrices:

$$(\mathbf{AB}\cdots\mathbf{F})' = \mathbf{F}'\cdots\mathbf{B}'\mathbf{A}'$$

The *powers* of a square matrix are the products of the matrix with itself. That is, $\mathbf{A}^2 = \mathbf{AA}$, $\mathbf{A}^3 = \mathbf{AAA} = \mathbf{AA}^2 = \mathbf{A}^2\mathbf{A}$, and so on. If $\mathbf{B}^2 = \mathbf{A}$, then we call $\mathbf{B}$ a *square root* of $\mathbf{A}$, which we may write as $\mathbf{A}^{1/2}$. Unlike in scalar algebra, however, the square root of a matrix is not generally unique. Of course, even the scalar square root is unique only up to a change in sign: For example, $\sqrt{4} = \pm 2$.[3] If $\mathbf{A}^2 = \mathbf{A}$, then $\mathbf{A}$ is said to be *idempotent*. As in scalar algebra, and by convention, $\mathbf{A}^0 = \mathbf{I}$ (where the identity matrix $\mathbf{I}$ is of the same order as $\mathbf{A}$). The matrix inverse $\mathbf{A}^{-1}$ is discussed later in the chapter (Section 1.1.3), and is *not* $\{1/a_{ij}\}$.

For purposes of matrix addition, subtraction, and multiplication, the submatrices of partitioned matrices may be treated as if they were elements, as long as the factors are partitioned conformably. For example, if

$$\mathbf{A} = \left[\begin{array}{ccc|cc} a_{11} & a_{12} & a_{13} & a_{14} & a_{15} \\ a_{21} & a_{22} & a_{23} & a_{24} & a_{25} \\ a_{31} & a_{32} & a_{33} & a_{34} & a_{35} \end{array}\right] = \left[\begin{array}{cc} \mathbf{A}_{11} & \mathbf{A}_{12} \\ \mathbf{A}_{21} & \mathbf{A}_{22} \end{array}\right]$$

and

$$\mathbf{B} = \left[\begin{array}{ccc|cc} b_{11} & b_{12} & b_{13} & b_{14} & b_{15} \\ b_{21} & b_{22} & b_{23} & b_{24} & b_{25} \\ b_{31} & b_{32} & b_{33} & b_{34} & b_{35} \end{array}\right] = \left[\begin{array}{cc} \mathbf{B}_{11} & \mathbf{B}_{12} \\ \mathbf{B}_{21} & \mathbf{B}_{22} \end{array}\right]$$

then

$$\mathbf{A} + \mathbf{B} = \left[\begin{array}{c|c} \mathbf{A}_{11} + \mathbf{B}_{11} & \mathbf{A}_{12} + \mathbf{B}_{12} \\ \hline \mathbf{A}_{21} + \mathbf{B}_{21} & \mathbf{A}_{22} + \mathbf{B}_{22} \end{array}\right]$$

Similarly, if

$$\underset{(m+n \times p+q)}{\mathbf{A}} = \left[\begin{array}{cc} \mathbf{A}_{11} & \mathbf{A}_{12} \\ {\scriptstyle (m \times p)} & {\scriptstyle (m \times q)} \\ \mathbf{A}_{21} & \mathbf{A}_{22} \\ {\scriptstyle (n \times p)} & {\scriptstyle (n \times q)} \end{array}\right]$$

and

$$\underset{(p+q \times r+s)}{\mathbf{B}} = \left[\begin{array}{cc} \mathbf{B}_{11} & \mathbf{B}_{12} \\ {\scriptstyle (p \times r)} & {\scriptstyle (p \times s)} \\ \mathbf{B}_{21} & \mathbf{B}_{22} \\ {\scriptstyle (q \times r)} & {\scriptstyle (q \times s)} \end{array}\right]$$

---

[3] For another kind of matrix square root, see the discussion of the Cholesky decomposition in Section 2.2.2.

then

$$\mathbf{AB}_{(m+n\times r+s)} = \left[\begin{array}{c|c} \mathbf{A}_{11}\mathbf{B}_{11}+\mathbf{A}_{12}\mathbf{B}_{21} & \mathbf{A}_{11}\mathbf{B}_{12}+\mathbf{A}_{12}\mathbf{B}_{22} \\ \hline \mathbf{A}_{21}\mathbf{B}_{11}+\mathbf{A}_{22}\mathbf{B}_{21} & \mathbf{A}_{21}\mathbf{B}_{12}+\mathbf{A}_{22}\mathbf{B}_{22} \end{array} \right]$$

The Sense Behind Matrix Multiplication

The definition of matrix multiplication makes it simple to formulate systems of scalar equations as a single matrix equation, often providing a useful level of abstraction. For example, consider the following system of two linear equations in two unknowns, x_1 and x_2:

$$2x_1 + 5x_2 = 4$$
$$x_1 + 3x_2 = 5$$

These equations are linear because each additive term in the equation is either a constant (e.g., 4 on the right-hand side of the first equation) or the product of a constant and a variable (e.g., $2x_1$ on the left-hand side of the first equation). Each of the equations $2x_1 + 5x_2 = 4$ and $x_1 + 3x_2 = 5$ literally represents a line in two-dimensional (2D) coordinate space (see the review of the equations of lines and planes in Section 3.1.2). Writing the two scalar equations as a matrix equation,

$$\begin{bmatrix} 2 & 5 \\ 1 & 3 \end{bmatrix} \begin{bmatrix} x_1 \\ x_2 \end{bmatrix} = \begin{bmatrix} 4 \\ 5 \end{bmatrix}$$
$$\underset{(2\times 2)}{\mathbf{A}} \; \underset{(2\times 1)}{\mathbf{x}} \; = \; \underset{(2\times 1)}{\mathbf{b}}$$

where

$$\mathbf{A} = \begin{bmatrix} 2 & 5 \\ 1 & 3 \end{bmatrix}$$
$$\mathbf{x} = \begin{bmatrix} x_1 \\ x_2 \end{bmatrix}$$
$$\mathbf{b} = \begin{bmatrix} 4 \\ 5 \end{bmatrix}$$

The formulation and solution of systems of linear simultaneous equations is taken up subsequently (Section 1.4.2).

1.1.3 Matrix Inverses

In scalar algebra, division is essential to the solution of simple equations. For example,

$$6x = 12$$
$$x = \frac{12}{6} = 2$$

or, equivalently,

$$\frac{1}{6} \times 6x = \frac{1}{6} \times 12$$
$$x = 2$$

where $\frac{1}{6} = 6^{-1}$ is the scalar inverse of 6.

In matrix algebra, there is no direct analog of division, but most square matrices have a *matrix inverse*. The inverse of a square matrix $\mathbf{A}$ is a square matrix of the same order, written $\mathbf{A}^{-1}$, with the property that $\mathbf{AA}^{-1} = \mathbf{A}^{-1}\mathbf{A} = \mathbf{I}$.[4] If a square matrix has an inverse, then the matrix is termed *nonsingular*; a square matrix without an inverse is termed *singular*.[5] If the inverse of a matrix exists, then it is unique; moreover, if for a square matrix $\mathbf{A}$, $\mathbf{AB} = \mathbf{I}$, then necessarily $\mathbf{BA} = \mathbf{I}$, and thus $\mathbf{B} = \mathbf{A}^{-1}$.

For example, the inverse of the nonsingular matrix

$$\begin{bmatrix} 2 & 5 \\ 1 & 3 \end{bmatrix}$$

is the matrix

$$\begin{bmatrix} 3 & -5 \\ -1 & 2 \end{bmatrix}$$

as we can readily verify:

$$\begin{bmatrix} 2 & 5 \\ 1 & 3 \end{bmatrix} \begin{bmatrix} 3 & -5 \\ -1 & 2 \end{bmatrix} = \begin{bmatrix} 1 & 0 \\ 0 & 1 \end{bmatrix} \checkmark$$

$$\begin{bmatrix} 3 & -5 \\ -1 & 2 \end{bmatrix} \begin{bmatrix} 2 & 5 \\ 1 & 3 \end{bmatrix} = \begin{bmatrix} 1 & 0 \\ 0 & 1 \end{bmatrix} \checkmark$$

---

[4]As I will explain (Section 1.4.3), it is also possible to define *generalized inverses* for rectangular matrices and for square matrices that do not have conventional inverses.

[5]When mathematicians first encountered nonzero matrices without inverses, they found the existence of such matrices remarkable or "singular."

In scalar algebra, only the number 0 has no inverse. It is simple to show by example that there exist singular *nonzero* matrices: Let us hypothesize that **B** is the inverse of the matrix

$$\mathbf{A} = \begin{bmatrix} 1 & 0 \\ 0 & 0 \end{bmatrix}$$

But

$$\mathbf{AB} = \begin{bmatrix} 1 & 0 \\ 0 & 0 \end{bmatrix} \begin{bmatrix} b_{11} & b_{12} \\ b_{21} & b_{22} \end{bmatrix} = \begin{bmatrix} b_{11} & b_{12} \\ 0 & 0 \end{bmatrix} \neq \mathbf{I}_2$$

which contradicts the hypothesis, and **A** consequently has no inverse.

There are many methods for finding the inverse of a nonsingular square matrix. I will briefly and informally describe a procedure called *Gaussian elimination* (after the great German mathematician, Carl Friedrich Gauss, 1777–1855). Although there are methods that tend to produce more accurate numerical results when implemented on a digital computer, elimination has the virtue of relative simplicity, and has applications beyond matrix inversion (as we will see later in this chapter).

To illustrate the method of elimination, I will employ the matrix

$$\mathbf{A} = \begin{bmatrix} 2 & -2 & 0 \\ 1 & -1 & 1 \\ 4 & 4 & -4 \end{bmatrix} \tag{1.7}$$

Let us begin by adjoining to this matrix an identity matrix; that is, form the partitioned or *augmented* matrix

$$[\mathbf{A}, \mathbf{I}_3] = \begin{bmatrix} 2 & -2 & 0 & 1 & 0 & 0 \\ 1 & -1 & 1 & 0 & 1 & 0 \\ 4 & 4 & -4 & 0 & 0 & 1 \end{bmatrix}$$

Then let's attempt to reduce the original matrix to an identity matrix by applying operations of three sorts:

E_I: Multiply each entry in a row of the matrix by a nonzero scalar constant.

E_{II}: Add a scalar multiple of one row to another, replacing the other row.

E_{III}: Exchange two rows of the matrix.

E_I, E_{II}, and E_{III} are called *elementary row operations*.

Starting with the first row, and dealing with each row in turn, ensure that there is a nonzero entry in the diagonal position, employing a row interchange for a lower row if necessary. Then divide the row through by its diagonal element (called the *pivot*) to obtain an entry of 1 in the diagonal position. Finally, add multiples of the current row to the other rows so as to "*sweep out*" the nonzero elements in the pivot column. For the illustration:

1. Divide Row 1 by 2,

$$\begin{bmatrix} 1 & -1 & 0 & \frac{1}{2} & 0 & 0 \\ 1 & -1 & 1 & 0 & 1 & 0 \\ 4 & 4 & -4 & 0 & 0 & 1 \end{bmatrix}$$

2. Subtract the new Row 1 from Row 2,

$$\begin{bmatrix} 1 & -1 & 0 & \frac{1}{2} & 0 & 0 \\ 0 & 0 & 1 & -\frac{1}{2} & 1 & 0 \\ 4 & 4 & -4 & 0 & 0 & 1 \end{bmatrix}$$

3. Subtract $4 \times$ Row 1 from Row 3,

$$\begin{bmatrix} 1 & -1 & 0 & \frac{1}{2} & 0 & 0 \\ 0 & 0 & 1 & -\frac{1}{2} & 1 & 0 \\ 0 & 8 & -4 & -2 & 0 & 1 \end{bmatrix}$$

4. Move to Row 2; there is a 0 entry in Row 2, Column 2, so interchange Rows 2 and 3,

$$\begin{bmatrix} 1 & -1 & 0 & \frac{1}{2} & 0 & 0 \\ 0 & 8 & -4 & -2 & 0 & 1 \\ 0 & 0 & 1 & -\frac{1}{2} & 1 & 0 \end{bmatrix}$$

5. Divide Row 2 by 8,

$$\begin{bmatrix} 1 & -1 & 0 & \frac{1}{2} & 0 & 0 \\ 0 & 1 & -\frac{1}{2} & -\frac{1}{4} & 0 & \frac{1}{8} \\ 0 & 0 & 1 & -\frac{1}{2} & 1 & 0 \end{bmatrix}$$

6. Add Row 2 to Row 1,

$$\begin{bmatrix} 1 & 0 & -\frac{1}{2} & \frac{1}{4} & 0 & \frac{1}{8} \\ 0 & 1 & -\frac{1}{2} & -\frac{1}{4} & 0 & \frac{1}{8} \\ 0 & 0 & 1 & -\frac{1}{2} & 1 & 0 \end{bmatrix}$$

7. Move to Row 3; there is already a 1 in the pivot position; add $\frac{1}{2} \times$ Row 3 to Row 1,

$$\left[\begin{array}{ccc|ccc} 1 & 0 & 0 & 0 & \frac{1}{2} & \frac{1}{8} \\ 0 & 1 & -\frac{1}{2} & -\frac{1}{4} & 0 & \frac{1}{8} \\ 0 & 0 & 1 & -\frac{1}{2} & 1 & 0 \end{array}\right]$$

8. Add $\frac{1}{2} \times$ Row 3 to Row 2,

$$\left[\begin{array}{ccc|ccc} 1 & 0 & 0 & 0 & \frac{1}{2} & \frac{1}{8} \\ 0 & 1 & 0 & -\frac{1}{2} & \frac{1}{2} & \frac{1}{8} \\ 0 & 0 & 1 & -\frac{1}{2} & 1 & 0 \end{array}\right]$$

Once the original matrix is reduced to the identity matrix, the final columns of the augmented matrix contain the inverse, as we can verify for the example:

$$\left[\begin{array}{ccc} 2 & -2 & 0 \\ 1 & -1 & 1 \\ 4 & 4 & -4 \end{array}\right] \left[\begin{array}{ccc} 0 & \frac{1}{2} & \frac{1}{8} \\ -\frac{1}{2} & \frac{1}{2} & \frac{1}{8} \\ -\frac{1}{2} & 1 & 0 \end{array}\right] = \left[\begin{array}{ccc} 1 & 0 & 0 \\ 0 & 1 & 0 \\ 0 & 0 & 1 \end{array}\right] \checkmark$$

It is simple to explain why Gaussian elimination works: Each elementary row operation can be represented as multiplication on the left by an appropriately formulated square matrix. Thus, for example, to interchange the second and third rows, we can multiply on the left by[6]

$$\mathbf{E}_{\mathrm{III}} \equiv \left[\begin{array}{ccc} 1 & 0 & 0 \\ 0 & 0 & 1 \\ 0 & 1 & 0 \end{array}\right]$$

The elimination procedure applies a sequence of (say p) elementary row operations to the augmented matrix $\left[\underset{(n \times n)}{\mathbf{A}}, \mathbf{I}_n\right]$, which we can then write as

$$\mathbf{E}_p \cdots \mathbf{E}_2 \mathbf{E}_1 [\mathbf{A}, \mathbf{I}_n] = [\mathbf{I}_n, \mathbf{B}]$$

using $\mathbf{E}_i$ to represent the ith operation in the sequence. Defining $\mathbf{E} \equiv \mathbf{E}_p \cdots \mathbf{E}_2 \mathbf{E}_1$, we have $\mathbf{E}[\mathbf{A}, \mathbf{I}_n] = [\mathbf{I}_n, \mathbf{B}]$; that is, $\mathbf{E} \mathbf{A} = \mathbf{I}_n$ (implying that $\mathbf{E} = \mathbf{A}^{-1}$),

---

[6]*Reader:* Show how Types I (e.g., Step 1 in the example) and II (e.g., Step 3 in the example) elementary row operations can also be represented as multiplication on the left by suitably formulated square matrices, say $\mathbf{E}_{\mathrm{I}}$ and $\mathbf{E}_{\mathrm{II}}$.

and $\mathbf{EI}_n = \mathbf{B}$. Consequently, $\mathbf{B} = \mathbf{E} = \mathbf{A}^{-1}$. If $\mathbf{A}$ is singular, then it cannot be reduced to $\mathbf{I}$ by elementary row operations: At some point in the process, we will find that no nonzero pivot is available.

The matrix inverse obeys the following rules:

$$\mathbf{I}^{-1} = \mathbf{I}$$
$$(\mathbf{A}^{-1})^{-1} = \mathbf{A}$$
$$(\mathbf{A}')^{-1} = (\mathbf{A}^{-1})'$$
$$(\mathbf{AB})^{-1} = \mathbf{B}^{-1}\mathbf{A}^{-1}$$
$$(c\mathbf{A})^{-1} = c^{-1}\mathbf{A}^{-1}$$

(where $\mathbf{A}$ and $\mathbf{B}$ are order-n nonsingular matrices, and c is a nonzero scalar). If $\mathbf{D} = \text{diag}(d_1, d_2, \ldots, d_n)$, and if all $d_i \neq 0$, then $\mathbf{D}$ is nonsingular and $\mathbf{D}^{-1} = \text{diag}(1/d_1, 1/d_2, \ldots, 1/d_n)$; if any of the d_i are 0, then $\mathbf{D}$ is singular. Finally, the inverse of a nonsingular symmetric matrix is itself symmetric.

1.1.4 Determinants

Each square matrix $\mathbf{A}$ is associated with a scalar called its *determinant*, written as $\det \mathbf{A}$.[7] For a (2×2) matrix $\mathbf{A}$, the determinant is $\det \mathbf{A} = a_{11}a_{22} - a_{12}a_{21}$. For a (3×3) matrix $\mathbf{A}$, the determinant is

$$\det \mathbf{A} = a_{11}a_{22}a_{33} - a_{11}a_{23}a_{32} + a_{12}a_{23}a_{31}$$
$$- a_{12}a_{21}a_{33} + a_{13}a_{21}a_{32} - a_{13}a_{22}a_{31}$$

Although there is a general definition of the determinant of a square matrix of order n, I find it simpler to define the determinant implicitly by specifying the following properties (or *axioms*):

D1: Multiplying a row of a square matrix by a scalar constant multiplies the determinant of the matrix by the same constant.

D2: Adding a multiple of one row to another leaves the determinant unaltered.

D3: Interchanging two rows changes the sign of the determinant.

D4: $\det \mathbf{I} = 1$.

---

[7]A common alternative notation for $\det \mathbf{A}$ is $|\mathbf{A}|$.

Axioms D1, D2, and D3 specify the effects on the determinant of the three kinds of elementary row operations. Because the Gaussian elimination method described previously reduces a square matrix to the identity matrix, these properties, along with axiom D4, are sufficient for establishing the value of the determinant. Indeed, the determinant is simply the product of the pivot elements, with the sign of the product reversed if, in the course of elimination, an odd number of row interchanges is employed. For the illustrative matrix $\mathbf{A}$ in Equation 1.7 (on page 12), then, the determinant is $-(2)(8)(1) = -16$, because there was one row interchange (in Step 4) and the pivots were 2, 8, and 1 (Steps 1, 5, and 7). If a matrix is singular, then one or more of the pivots are zero, and the determinant is zero. Conversely, a nonsingular matrix has a nonzero determinant.

Some additional properties of determinants (for order-n square matrices $\mathbf{A}$ and $\mathbf{B}$) are as follows:

- $\det \mathbf{A}' = \det \mathbf{A}$.

- $\det(\mathbf{AB}) = \det \mathbf{A} \times \det \mathbf{B}$.

- If $\mathbf{A}$ is nonsingular, then $\det \mathbf{A}^{-1} = 1/\det \mathbf{A}$.

- If $\mathbf{A}$ is idempotent (recall, $\mathbf{A}^2 = \mathbf{A}$), then $\det \mathbf{A} = 1$ if $\mathbf{A}$ is nonsingular or 0 if it is singular.

The third result follows from second, along with the observations that $\mathbf{AA}^{-1} = \mathbf{I}_n$ and $\det \mathbf{I}_n = 1$. The fourth result also follows from the second. (*Reader:* Can you see why?)

In addition to their useful algebraic properties, determinants occasionally appear directly in statistical applications—for example, in the formula for the multivariate-normal distribution (see Section 5.2.5).

1.1.5   The Kronecker Product

Suppose that $\mathbf{A}$ is an $m \times n$ matrix and that $\mathbf{B}$ is a $p \times q$ matrix. Then the *Kronecker product* (named after the 19th-century German mathematician Leopold Kronecker) of $\mathbf{A}$ and $\mathbf{B}$, denoted $\mathbf{A} \otimes \mathbf{B}$, is defined as

$$\underset{(mp \times nq)}{\mathbf{A} \otimes \mathbf{B}} \equiv \begin{bmatrix} a_{11}\mathbf{B} & a_{12}\mathbf{B} & \cdots & a_{1n}\mathbf{B} \\ a_{21}\mathbf{B} & a_{22}\mathbf{B} & \cdots & a_{2n}\mathbf{B} \\ \vdots & \vdots & & \vdots \\ a_{m1}\mathbf{B} & a_{m2}\mathbf{B} & \cdots & a_{mn}\mathbf{B} \end{bmatrix}$$

The Kronecker product is sometimes useful in statistics for compactly representing patterned matrices. For example, suppose that

$$\Sigma = \begin{bmatrix} \sigma_1^2 & \sigma_{12} \\ \sigma_{12} & \sigma_2^2 \end{bmatrix}$$

is a (2×2) variance–covariance matrix (see Section 4.2.4). Then,

$$\mathbf{I}_3 \otimes \Sigma = \begin{bmatrix} 1 & 0 & 0 \\ 0 & 1 & 0 \\ 0 & 0 & 1 \end{bmatrix} \otimes \begin{bmatrix} \sigma_1^2 & \sigma_{12} \\ \sigma_{12} & \sigma_2^2 \end{bmatrix}$$

$$= \left[\begin{array}{cc|cc|cc} \sigma_1^2 & \sigma_{12} & 0 & 0 & 0 & 0 \\ \sigma_{12} & \sigma_2^2 & 0 & 0 & 0 & 0 \\ \hline 0 & 0 & \sigma_1^2 & \sigma_{12} & 0 & 0 \\ 0 & 0 & \sigma_{12} & \sigma_2^2 & 0 & 0 \\ \hline 0 & 0 & 0 & 0 & \sigma_1^2 & \sigma_{12} \\ 0 & 0 & 0 & 0 & \sigma_{12} & \sigma_2^2 \end{array} \right]$$

Such expressions arise naturally, for example, in multivariate statistics.

Many of the properties of the Kronecker product are similar to those of ordinary matrix multiplication; in particular,

$$\mathbf{A} \otimes (\mathbf{B} + \mathbf{C}) = \mathbf{A} \otimes \mathbf{B} + \mathbf{A} \otimes \mathbf{C}$$
$$(\mathbf{B} + \mathbf{C}) \otimes \mathbf{A} = \mathbf{B} \otimes \mathbf{A} + \mathbf{C} \otimes \mathbf{A}$$
$$(\mathbf{A} \otimes \mathbf{B}) \otimes \mathbf{D} = \mathbf{A} \otimes (\mathbf{B} \otimes \mathbf{D})$$
$$c(\mathbf{A} \otimes \mathbf{B}) = (c\mathbf{A}) \otimes \mathbf{B} = \mathbf{A} \otimes (c\mathbf{B})$$

where $\mathbf{B}$ and $\mathbf{C}$ are matrices of the same order, and c is a scalar. As well, like matrix multiplication, the Kronecker product is not commutative: In general, $\mathbf{A} \otimes \mathbf{B} \neq \mathbf{B} \otimes \mathbf{A}$. Additionally, for matrices $\underset{(m \times n)}{\mathbf{A}}$, $\underset{(p \times q)}{\mathbf{B}}$, $\underset{(n \times r)}{\mathbf{C}}$, and $\underset{(q \times s)}{\mathbf{D}}$,

$$(\mathbf{A} \otimes \mathbf{B})(\mathbf{C} \otimes \mathbf{D}) = \mathbf{AC} \otimes \mathbf{BD}$$

Consequently, if $\underset{(n \times n)}{\mathbf{A}}$ and $\underset{(m \times m)}{\mathbf{B}}$ are nonsingular matrices, then

$$(\mathbf{A} \otimes \mathbf{B})^{-1} = \mathbf{A}^{-1} \otimes \mathbf{B}^{-1}$$

because

$$(\mathbf{A} \otimes \mathbf{B})\left(\mathbf{A}^{-1} \otimes \mathbf{B}^{-1}\right) = (\mathbf{A}\mathbf{A}^{-1}) \otimes (\mathbf{B}\mathbf{B}^{-1}) = \mathbf{I}_n \otimes \mathbf{I}_m = \mathbf{I}_{(nm \times nm)}$$

Finally, for any matrices $\mathbf{A}$ and $\mathbf{B}$,

$$(\mathbf{A} \otimes \mathbf{B})' = \mathbf{A}' \otimes \mathbf{B}'$$

and for square matrices $\mathbf{A}$ and $\mathbf{B}$ of order m and n, respectively,

$$\text{trace}(\mathbf{A} \otimes \mathbf{B}) = \text{trace}(\mathbf{A}) \times \text{trace}(\mathbf{B})$$
$$\det(\mathbf{A} \otimes \mathbf{B}) = (\det \mathbf{A})^m (\det \mathbf{B})^n$$

1.2   Basic Vector Geometry

Considered algebraically, vectors are one-column (or one-row) matrices. Vectors also have the following geometric interpretation: The vector $\mathbf{x} = [x_1, x_2, \ldots, x_n]'$ is represented as a directed line segment extending from the origin of an n-dimensional coordinate space to the point defined by the entries (called the *coordinates*) of the vector. Some examples of geometric vectors in 2D and 3D space are shown in Figure 1.1.

The basic arithmetic operations defined for vectors have simple geometric interpretations. To add two vectors $\mathbf{x}_1$ and $\mathbf{x}_2$ is, in effect, to place the "tail" of one at the tip of the other. When a vector is shifted from the origin in this manner, it retains its length and orientation (the angles that it makes with respect to the coordinate axes); length and orientation serve to define a vector uniquely. The operation of vector addition, illustrated in two dimensions in Figure 1.2, is equivalent to completing a parallelogram in which $\mathbf{x}_1$ and $\mathbf{x}_2$ are two adjacent sides; the vector sum is the diagonal of the parallelogram, starting at the origin.

As shown in Figure 1.3, the difference $\mathbf{x}_1 - \mathbf{x}_2$ is a vector whose length and orientation are obtained by proceeding from the tip of $\mathbf{x}_2$ to the tip of $\mathbf{x}_1$. Likewise, $\mathbf{x}_2 - \mathbf{x}_1$ proceeds from $\mathbf{x}_1$ to $\mathbf{x}_2$.

The *length* of a vector $\mathbf{x}$, denoted by $||\mathbf{x}||$, is the square root of its sum of squared coordinates:

$$||\mathbf{x}|| = \sqrt{\sum_{i=1}^{n} x_i^2}$$

This result follows from the Pythagorean theorem in two dimensions,[8] as shown in Figure 1.4(a). The result can be extended one dimension at a time

---

[8]Recall that the Pythagorean theorem (named after the ancient Greek mathematician Pythagoras) states that the squared length of the hypotenuse (side opposite the right angle) in a right triangle is equal to the sums of squared lengths of the other two sides of the triangle.

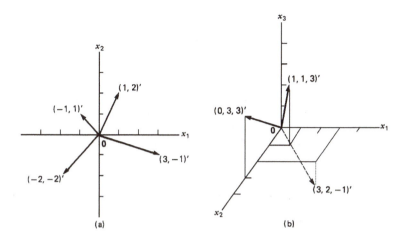

Figure 1.1 Examples of geometric vectors in (a) two-dimensional and (b) three-dimensional space. Each vector is a directed line segment from the origin ($\mathbf{0} = [0,0]'$ in two dimensions or $\mathbf{0} = [0,0,0]'$ in three dimensions) to the point whose coordinates are given by the entries of the vector.

to higher-dimensional coordinate spaces, as shown for a 3D space in Figure 1.4(b). The *distance* between two vectors $\mathbf{x}_1$ and $\mathbf{x}_2$, defined as the distance separating their tips, is given by $||\mathbf{x}_1 - \mathbf{x}_2|| = ||\mathbf{x}_2 - \mathbf{x}_1||$ (see Figure 1.3).

The product $a\mathbf{x}$ of a scalar a and a vector $\mathbf{x}$ is a vector of length $|a| \times ||\mathbf{x}||$, as is readily verified:

$$||a\mathbf{x}|| = \sqrt{\sum(ax_i)^2}$$

$$= \sqrt{a^2 \sum x_i^2}$$

$$= |a| \times ||\mathbf{x}||$$

If the scalar a is positive, then the orientation of $a\mathbf{x}$ is the same as that of $\mathbf{x}$; if a is negative, then $a\mathbf{x}$ is *collinear* with (i.e., along the same line as) $\mathbf{x}$ but in the opposite direction. The negative $-\mathbf{x} = (-1)\mathbf{x}$ of $\mathbf{x}$ is, therefore, a vector of the same length as $\mathbf{x}$ but of opposite orientation. These results are illustrated for two dimensions in Figure 1.5.

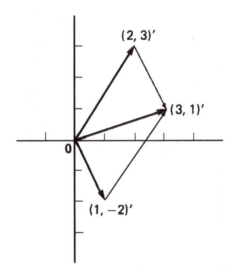

Figure 1.2   Vectors are added by placing the "tail" of one on the tip of the other and completing the parallelogram. The sum is the diagonal of the parallelogram starting at the origin.

1.3   Vector Spaces and Subspaces

The *vector space of dimension n* is the infinite set of all vectors $\mathbf{x} = [x_1, x_2, \ldots, x_n]'$; the coordinates x_i may be any real numbers. The vector space of dimension one is, therefore, the real line; the vector space of dimension two is the plane; and so on.

The *subspace* of the *n*-dimensional vector space that is *generated* by a set of *k* vectors $\{\mathbf{x}_1, \mathbf{x}_2, \ldots, \mathbf{x}_k\}$ is the subset of vectors $\mathbf{y}$ in the space that can be expressed as linear combinations of the generating set:

$$\mathbf{y} = a_1\mathbf{x}_1 + a_2\mathbf{x}_2 + \cdots + a_k\mathbf{x}_k$$

The set of vectors $\{\mathbf{x}_1, \mathbf{x}_2, \ldots, \mathbf{x}_k\}$ is said to *span* the subspace that it generates. Notice that each of $\mathbf{x}_1, \mathbf{x}_2, \ldots, \mathbf{x}_k$ is a vector, with *n* coordinates; that is, $\{\mathbf{x}_1, \mathbf{x}_2, \ldots, \mathbf{x}_k\}$ is a set of *k* vectors, *not* a vector with *k* coordinates.

A set of vectors $\{\mathbf{x}_1, \mathbf{x}_2, \ldots, \mathbf{x}_k\}$ is *linearly independent* if no vector in the set can be expressed as a linear combination of other vectors:

$$\mathbf{x}_j = a_1\mathbf{x}_1 + \cdots + a_{j-1}\mathbf{x}_{j-1} + a_{j+1}\mathbf{x}_{j+1} + \cdots + a_k\mathbf{x}_k \tag{1.8}$$

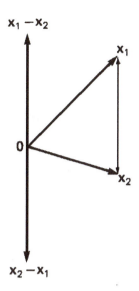

Figure 1.3   Vector differences $x_1 - x_2$ and $x_2 - x_1$.

(where some of the constants a_l can be zero). Equivalently, the set of vectors is linearly independent if there are no constants $b_1, b_2, \ldots, b_k$, not all zero, for which

$$b_1 x_1 + b_2 x_2 + \cdots + b_k x_k = \underset{(n \times 1)}{0} \tag{1.9}$$

Equation 1.8 or 1.9 is called a *linear dependency* or *collinearity*. If these equations hold, then the vectors comprise a *linearly dependent* set. By Equation 1.8, the zero vector is linearly dependent on every other vector, inasmuch as $0 = 0x$.

The *dimension* of the subspace spanned by a set of vectors is the number of vectors in its largest linearly independent subset. The dimension of the subspace spanned by $\{x_1, x_2, \ldots, x_k\}$ cannot, therefore, exceed the smaller of k and n. These relations are illustrated for a vector space of dimension $n = 3$ in Figure 1.6. Figure 1.6(a) shows the 1D subspace (i.e., the line) generated by a single nonzero vector x; Figure 1.6(b) shows the 1D subspace generated by two collinear vectors x_1 and x_2; Figure 1.6(c) shows the 2D subspace (the plane) generated by two linearly independent vectors x_1 and x_2; and Figure 1.6(d) shows the plane generated by three linearly dependent vectors x_1, x_2,

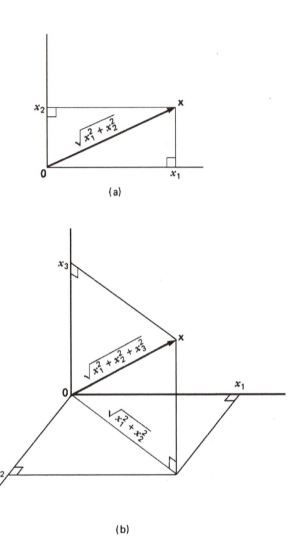

Figure 1.4   The length of a vector is the square root of its sum of squared coordinates, $||\mathbf{x}|| = \sqrt{\sum_{i=1}^{n} x_i^2}$. This result is illustrated in (a) two and (b) three dimensions.

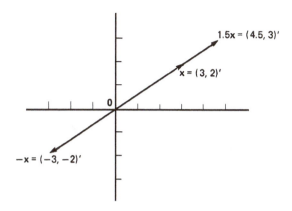

Figure 1.5 Product $a\mathbf{x}$ of a scalar and a vector, illustrated in two dimensions. The vector $a\mathbf{x}$ is collinear with $\mathbf{x}$; it is in the same direction as $\mathbf{x}$ if $a > 0$, and in the opposite direction from $\mathbf{x}$ if $a < 0$.

and $\mathbf{x}_3$, no two of which are collinear. In this last case, any one of the three vectors lies in the plane generated by the other two.

A linearly independent set of vectors $\{\mathbf{x}_1, \mathbf{x}_2, \ldots, \mathbf{x}_k\}$—such as $\{\mathbf{x}\}$ in Figure 1.6(a), $\{\mathbf{x}_1, \mathbf{x}_2\}$ in Figure 1.6(c), or (say) $\{\mathbf{x}_1, \mathbf{x}_3\}$ in Figure 1.6(d)— is said to provide a *basis* for the subspace that it spans. (*Reader:* What about Figure 1.6(b)?) Any vector $\mathbf{y}$ in this subspace can be written *uniquely* as a linear combination of the basis vectors:

$$\mathbf{y} = c_1\mathbf{x}_1 + c_2\mathbf{x}_2 + \cdots + c_k\mathbf{x}_k$$

The constants $c_1, c_2, \ldots, c_k$ are called the *coordinates of* $\mathbf{y}$ *with respect to the basis* $\{\mathbf{x}_1, \mathbf{x}_2, \ldots, \mathbf{x}_k\}$. Because $\mathbf{0} = 0\mathbf{x}_1 + 0\mathbf{x}_2 + \cdots + 0\mathbf{x}_k$, the zero vector is included in every subspace.

The coordinates of a vector with respect to a basis for a 2D subspace can be found geometrically by the parallelogram rule of vector addition, as illustrated in Figure 1.7. Finding coordinates algebraically entails the solution of

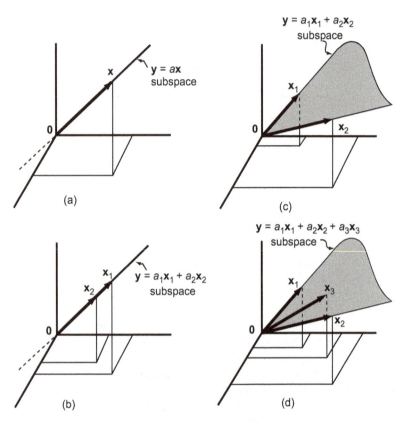

Figure 1.6 Subspaces generated by sets of vectors in three-dimensional space. (a) One nonzero vector generates a one-dimensional subspace (a line). (b) Two collinear vectors also generate a one-dimensional subspace. (c) Two linearly independent vectors generate a two-dimensional subspace (a plane). (d) Three linearly dependent vectors, two of which are linearly independent, generate a two-dimensional subspace. The lines in (a) and (b) extend infinitely, as do the planes in (c) and (d): The planes are drawn between x_1 and x_2 only for clarity.

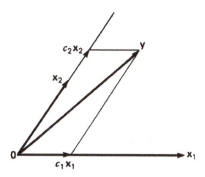

Figure 1.7   The coordinates of **y** with respect to the basis $\{\mathbf{x}_1, \mathbf{x}_2\}$ of a two-dimensional subspace can be found from the parallelogram rule of vector addition.

a system of linear simultaneous equations in which the c_js are the unknowns:

$$\underset{(n\times 1)}{\mathbf{y}} = c_1\mathbf{x}_1 + c_2\mathbf{x}_2 + \cdots + c_k\mathbf{x}_k$$

$$= [\mathbf{x}_1, \mathbf{x}_2, \ldots, \mathbf{x}_k] \begin{bmatrix} c_1 \\ c_2 \\ \vdots \\ c_k \end{bmatrix}$$

$$= \underset{(n\times k)(k\times 1)}{\mathbf{X} \quad \mathbf{c}}$$

When the vectors in $\{\mathbf{x}_1, \mathbf{x}_2, \ldots, \mathbf{x}_k\}$ are linearly independent, the matrix **X** is of *full column rank k*, and the equations have a unique solution. The concept of rank and the solution of systems of linear simultaneous equations are taken up later in this chapter (Section 1.4.2).

1.3.1   Orthogonality and Orthogonal Projections

Recall that the inner product of two vectors is the sum of products of their coordinates:

$$\mathbf{x} \cdot \mathbf{y} = \sum_{i=1}^{n} x_i y_i$$

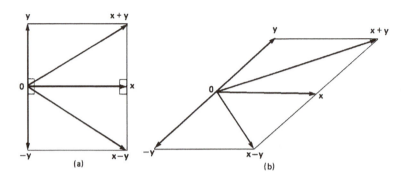

Figure 1.8   When two vectors $\mathbf{x}$ and $\mathbf{y}$ are orthogonal, as in (a), their inner product $\mathbf{x} \cdot \mathbf{y}$ is zero. When the vectors are not orthogonal, as in (b), their inner product is nonzero.

Two vectors $\mathbf{x}$ and $\mathbf{y}$ are *orthogonal* (i.e., perpendicular) if their inner product is zero. The essential geometry of vector orthogonality is shown in Figure 1.8. Although $\mathbf{x}$ and $\mathbf{y}$ lie in an n-dimensional space (which cannot be visualized directly when $n > 3$), they span a subspace of dimension two, which, by convention, I make the plane of the paper.[9] When $\mathbf{x}$ and $\mathbf{y}$ are orthogonal, as in Figure 1.8(a), the two right triangles with vertices $(\mathbf{0}, \mathbf{x}, \mathbf{x} + \mathbf{y})$ and $(\mathbf{0}, \mathbf{x}, \mathbf{x} - \mathbf{y})$ are congruent; consequently, $||\mathbf{x} + \mathbf{y}|| = ||\mathbf{x} - \mathbf{y}||$. Because the squared length of a vector is the inner product of the vector with itself $(\mathbf{x} \cdot \mathbf{x} = \sum x_i^2)$, we have

$$(\mathbf{x} + \mathbf{y}) \cdot (\mathbf{x} + \mathbf{y}) = (\mathbf{x} - \mathbf{y}) \cdot (\mathbf{x} - \mathbf{y})$$
$$\mathbf{x} \cdot \mathbf{x} + 2\mathbf{x} \cdot \mathbf{y} + \mathbf{y} \cdot \mathbf{y} = \mathbf{x} \cdot \mathbf{x} - 2\mathbf{x} \cdot \mathbf{y} + \mathbf{y} \cdot \mathbf{y}$$
$$4\mathbf{x} \cdot \mathbf{y} = 0$$
$$\mathbf{x} \cdot \mathbf{y} = 0$$

When, in contrast, $\mathbf{x}$ and $\mathbf{y}$ are not orthogonal, as in Figure 1.8(b), then $||\mathbf{x} + \mathbf{y}|| \neq ||\mathbf{x} - \mathbf{y}||$, and $\mathbf{x} \cdot \mathbf{y} \neq 0$.

The definition of orthogonality can be extended to matrices in the following manner: The matrix $\underset{(n \times k)}{\mathbf{X}}$ is orthogonal if each pair of its columns

---

[9]It is helpful to employ this device in applying vector geometry to statistical problems, where the subspace of interest can often be confined to two or three dimensions, even though the dimension of the full vector space is typically equal to the sample size n.

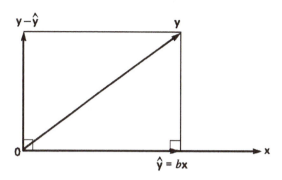

Figure 1.9 The orthogonal projection $\widehat{\mathbf{y}} = b\mathbf{x}$ of $\mathbf{y}$ onto $\mathbf{x}$.

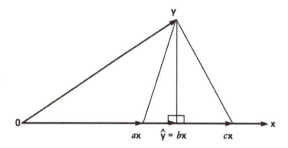

Figure 1.10 The orthogonal projection $\widehat{\mathbf{y}} = b\mathbf{x}$ is the point along the line spanned by $\mathbf{x}$ that is closest to $\mathbf{y}$.

is orthogonal—that is, if $\mathbf{X}'\mathbf{X}$ is diagonal.[10] The matrix $\mathbf{X}$ is *orthonormal* if $\mathbf{X}'\mathbf{X} = \mathbf{I}$.

The *orthogonal projection* of one vector $\mathbf{y}$ onto another vector $\mathbf{x}$ is a scalar multiple $\widehat{\mathbf{y}} = b\mathbf{x}$ of $\mathbf{x}$ such that $(\mathbf{y} - \widehat{\mathbf{y}})$ is orthogonal to $\mathbf{x}$. The geometry of orthogonal projection is illustrated in Figure 1.9. By the Pythagorean theorem (see Figure 1.10), $\widehat{\mathbf{y}}$ is the point along the line spanned by $\mathbf{x}$ that is closest to

---

[10]The i, jth entry of $\mathbf{X}'\mathbf{X}$ is $\mathbf{x}_i'\mathbf{x}_j = \mathbf{x}_i \cdot \mathbf{x}_j$, where $\mathbf{x}_i$ and $\mathbf{x}_j$ are, respectively, the ith and jth columns of $\mathbf{X}$. The ith diagonal entry of $\mathbf{X}'\mathbf{X}$ is likewise $\mathbf{x}_i'\mathbf{x}_i = \mathbf{x}_i \cdot \mathbf{x}_i$, which is necessarily nonzero unless $\mathbf{x}_i = \mathbf{0}$.

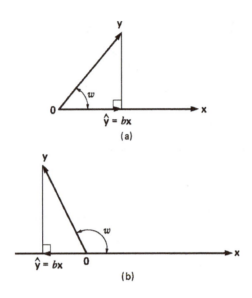

Figure 1.11   The angle w separating two vectors, $\mathbf{x}$ and $\mathbf{y}$: (a)
$0° < w < 90°$ (when b is positive); (b) $90° < w < 180°$
(when b is negative).

$\mathbf{y}$. To find b, we note that

$$\mathbf{x} \cdot (\mathbf{y} - \widehat{\mathbf{y}}) = \mathbf{x} \cdot (\mathbf{y} - b\mathbf{x}) = 0$$

Thus, $\mathbf{x} \cdot \mathbf{y} - b\mathbf{x} \cdot \mathbf{x} = 0$ and $b = (\mathbf{x} \cdot \mathbf{y})/(\mathbf{x} \cdot \mathbf{x})$.

The orthogonal projection of $\mathbf{y}$ onto $\mathbf{x}$ can be used to determine the angle
w separating two vectors, by finding its cosine. Because the cosine function
is symmetric around $w = 0$, it does not matter in which direction we measure an angle, and I will simply treat angles as positive.[11] I will distinguish
between two cases:[12] In Figure 1.11(a), the angle separating the vectors is
between $0°$ and $90°$; in Figure 1.11(b), the angle is between $90°$ and $180°$.

---

[11] The cosine and other basic trigonometric functions are reviewed in Section 3.1.5.

[12] By convention, we examine the smaller of the two angles separating a pair of vectors, and,
therefore, never encounter angles that exceed $180°$. Call the smaller angle w; then the larger
angle is $360° - w$. This convention is of no consequence because $\cos(360 - w) = \cos(w)$.

In the first instance,

$$\cos(w) = \frac{||\widehat{\mathbf{y}}||}{||\mathbf{y}||} = \frac{b||\mathbf{x}||}{||\mathbf{y}||} = \frac{\mathbf{x} \cdot \mathbf{y}}{||\mathbf{x}||^2} \times \frac{||\mathbf{x}||}{||\mathbf{y}||} = \frac{\mathbf{x} \cdot \mathbf{y}}{||\mathbf{x}|| \times ||\mathbf{y}||}$$

and, likewise, in the second instance,

$$\cos(w) = -\frac{||\widehat{\mathbf{y}}||}{||\mathbf{y}||} = \frac{b||\mathbf{x}||}{||\mathbf{y}||} = \frac{\mathbf{x} \cdot \mathbf{y}}{||\mathbf{x}|| \times ||\mathbf{y}||}$$

In both instances, the sign of b for the orthogonal projection of $\mathbf{y}$ onto $\mathbf{x}$ correctly reflects the sign of $\cos(w)$. When the vectors are orthogonal (not shown in the figure), $b = 0$, $\cos(w) = 0$, and $w = 90°$; when the vectors are collinear (also not shown), $\cos(w) = 1$, and $w = 0°$.

The orthogonal projection of a vector $\mathbf{y}$ onto the subspace spanned by a set of vectors $\{\mathbf{x}_1, \mathbf{x}_2, \ldots, \mathbf{x}_k\}$ is the vector

$$\widehat{\mathbf{y}} = b_1\mathbf{x}_1 + b_2\mathbf{x}_2 + \cdots + b_k\mathbf{x}_k$$

formed as a linear combination of the $\mathbf{x}_j$s such that $(\mathbf{y} - \widehat{\mathbf{y}})$ is orthogonal to each and every vector $\mathbf{x}_j$ in the set. The geometry of orthogonal projection for $k = 2$ is illustrated in Figure 1.12. The vector $\widehat{\mathbf{y}}$ is the point closest to $\mathbf{y}$ in the subspace spanned by the $\mathbf{x}_j$s.

Placing the constants b_j into a vector $\mathbf{b}$, and gathering the vectors $\mathbf{x}_j$ into an $(n \times k)$ matrix $\mathbf{X} \equiv [\mathbf{x}_1, \mathbf{x}_2, \ldots, \mathbf{x}_k]$, we have $\widehat{\mathbf{y}} = \mathbf{Xb}$. By the definition of an orthogonal projection,

$$\mathbf{x}_j \cdot (\mathbf{y} - \widehat{\mathbf{y}}) = \mathbf{x}_j \cdot (\mathbf{y} - \mathbf{Xb}) = 0 \quad \text{for } j = 1, \ldots, k \qquad (1.10)$$

Equivalently, $\mathbf{X}'(\mathbf{y} - \mathbf{Xb}) = \mathbf{0}$, or $\mathbf{X}'\mathbf{y} = \mathbf{X}'\mathbf{Xb}$. We can solve this matrix equation uniquely for $\mathbf{b}$ as long as the $(k \times k)$ matrix $\mathbf{X}'\mathbf{X}$ is nonsingular, in which case $\mathbf{b} = (\mathbf{X}'\mathbf{X})^{-1}\mathbf{X}'\mathbf{y}$ (see Section 1.4.2 on the solution of linear simultaneous equations). The matrix $\mathbf{X}'\mathbf{X}$ is nonsingular if $\{\mathbf{x}_1, \mathbf{x}_2, \ldots, \mathbf{x}_k\}$ is a linearly independent set of vectors, providing a basis for the subspace that it generates; otherwise, $\mathbf{b}$ is not unique.

The application of the geometry of orthogonal projections to linear least-squares regression is quite direct, and so I will explain it here (rather than in Chapter 7 on least-square regression). For example, suppose that the vector $\mathbf{x}$ in Figures 1.9 and 1.11 represents the explanatory ("independent") variable in a simple regression; the vector $\mathbf{y}$ represents the response ("dependent") variable; and both variables are expressed as deviations from their means, $\mathbf{x} = \{X_i - \overline{X}\}$ and $\mathbf{y} = \{Y_i - \overline{Y}\}$. Then $\widehat{\mathbf{y}} = b\mathbf{x}$ is the mean-deviation vector of fitted ("predicted") Y-values from the linear least-squares regression of Y

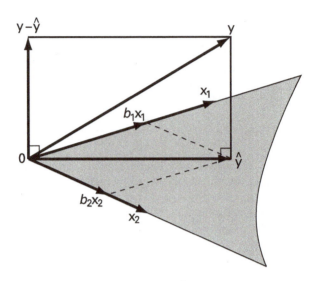

Figure 1.12   The orthogonal projection $\widehat{\mathbf{y}}$ of $\mathbf{y}$ onto the subspace (plane) spanned by $\mathbf{x}_1$ and $\mathbf{x}_2$.

on X; b is the slope coefficient for the regression; and $\mathbf{y} - \widehat{\mathbf{y}}$ is the vector of least-square residuals. By the Pythagorean theorem,

$$||\mathbf{y}||^2 = ||\widehat{\mathbf{y}}||^2 + ||\mathbf{y} - \widehat{\mathbf{y}}||^2$$

which shows the decomposition of the total sum of squares for Y into the regression and residual sums of squares—the so-called analysis of variance for the regression. The correlation r between X and Y is then the cosine of the angle w separating their mean-deviation vectors.

Suppose similarly that $\mathbf{y}$ is the mean-deviation vector for the response variable and that $\mathbf{x}_1$ and $\mathbf{x}_2$ are the mean-deviation vectors for two explanatory variables in a multiple regression. Then Figure 1.12 represents the linear least-squares regression of Y on X_1 and X_2; b_1 and b_2 are the partial regression coefficients for the two explanatory variables; $\widehat{\mathbf{y}}$ is the vector of mean-deviation fitted values for the multiple regression; the right triangle formed by the origin and the vectors $\mathbf{y}$ and $\widehat{\mathbf{y}}$ gives the analysis of variance for the multiple regression; and the cosine of the angle separating $\mathbf{y}$ and $\widehat{\mathbf{y}}$ is the multiple-correlation coefficient R for the regression—that is, the correlation between observed and fitted Y-values.

1.4 Matrix Rank and the Solution of Linear Simultaneous Equations

1.4.1 Rank

The *row space* of an $(m \times n)$ matrix $\mathbf{A}$ is the subspace of the n-dimensional vector space spanned by the m rows of $\mathbf{A}$ (treated as a set of vectors). The *rank* of $\mathbf{A}$ is the dimension of its row space, that is, the maximum number of linearly independent rows in $\mathbf{A}$. It follows immediately that $\text{rank}(\mathbf{A}) \leq \min(m,n)$.

For example, the row space of the matrix

$$\mathbf{A} = \begin{bmatrix} 1 & 0 & 0 \\ 0 & 1 & 0 \end{bmatrix}$$

consists of all vectors

$$\begin{aligned} \mathbf{x}' &= a[1,0,0] + b[0,1,0] \\ &= [a,b,0] \end{aligned}$$

for any values of a and b. This subspace is of dimension two, and thus $\text{rank}(\mathbf{A}) = 2$.

A matrix is said to be in *reduced row–echelon form* (*RREF*) if it satisfies the following criteria:

R1: All of its nonzero rows (if any) precede all of its zero rows (if any).

R2: The first nonzero entry (proceeding from left to right) in each nonzero row, called the *leading entry* in the row, is 1.

R3: The leading entry in each nonzero row after the first is to the right of the leading entry in the previous row.

R4: All other entries are 0 in a *column* containing a leading entry.

RREF is displayed schematically in the matrix in 1.11, where the asterisks represent elements of arbitrary value (i.e., they may be zero or nonzero):

$$\begin{bmatrix} 0 & \cdots & 0 & 1 & * & \cdots & * & 0 & * & \cdots & * & 0 & * & \cdots & * \\ 0 & \cdots & 0 & 0 & 0 & \cdots & 0 & 1 & * & \cdots & * & 0 & * & \cdots & * \\ \vdots & & \vdots & \vdots & \vdots & & \vdots & \vdots & \vdots & & \vdots & \vdots \\ 0 & \cdots & 0 & 0 & 0 & \cdots & 0 & 0 & 0 & \cdots & 0 & 1 & * & \cdots & * \\ 0 & \cdots & 0 & 0 & 0 & \cdots & 0 & 0 & 0 & \cdots & 0 & 0 & 0 & \cdots & 0 \\ \vdots & & \vdots & \vdots & \vdots & & \vdots & \vdots & \vdots & & \vdots & \vdots & \vdots & & \vdots \\ 0 & \cdots & 0 & 0 & 0 & \cdots & 0 & 0 & 0 & \cdots & 0 & 0 & 0 & \cdots & 0 \end{bmatrix} \begin{matrix} \\ \\ \text{nonzero} \\ \text{rows} \\ \\ \text{zero} \\ \text{rows} \end{matrix}$$

$$(1.11)$$

The rank of a matrix in **RREF** is equal to the number of nonzero rows in the matrix: The pattern of leading entries, each located in a column all of whose other elements are zero, ensures that no nonzero row can be formed as a linear combination of other rows.

A matrix can be placed in **RREF** by a sequence of elementary row operations, adapting the Gaussian elimination procedure described earlier in this chapter. For example, starting with the matrix

$$\begin{bmatrix} -2 & 0 & -1 & 2 \\ 4 & 0 & 1 & 0 \\ 6 & 0 & 1 & 2 \end{bmatrix}$$

1. Divide Row 1 by -2,

$$\begin{bmatrix} 1 & 0 & \frac{1}{2} & -1 \\ 4 & 0 & 1 & 0 \\ 6 & 0 & 1 & 2 \end{bmatrix}$$

2. Subtract $4 \times$ Row 1 from Row 2,

$$\begin{bmatrix} 1 & 0 & \frac{1}{2} & -1 \\ 0 & 0 & -1 & 4 \\ 6 & 0 & 1 & 2 \end{bmatrix}$$

3. Subtract $6 \times$ Row 1 from Row 3,

$$\begin{bmatrix} 1 & 0 & \frac{1}{2} & -1 \\ 0 & 0 & -1 & 4 \\ 0 & 0 & -2 & 8 \end{bmatrix}$$

4. Multiply Row 2 by -1,

$$\begin{bmatrix} 1 & 0 & \frac{1}{2} & -1 \\ 0 & 0 & 1 & -4 \\ 0 & 0 & -2 & 8 \end{bmatrix}$$

5. Subtract $\frac{1}{2} \times$ Row 2 from Row 1,

$$\begin{bmatrix} 1 & 0 & 0 & 1 \\ 0 & 0 & 1 & -4 \\ 0 & 0 & -2 & 8 \end{bmatrix}$$

6. Add $2\times$ Row 2 to Row 3,

$$\begin{bmatrix} 1 & 0 & 0 & 1 \\ 0 & 0 & 1 & -4 \\ 0 & 0 & 0 & 0 \end{bmatrix}$$

The rank of a matrix $\mathbf{A}$ is equal to the rank of its RREF $\mathbf{A}_R$, because a zero row in $\mathbf{A}_R$ can only arise if one row of $\mathbf{A}$ is expressible as a linear combination of other rows (or if $\mathbf{A}$ contains a zero row). That is, none of the elementary row operations alters the rank of a matrix. The rank of the matrix transformed to RREF in the example is thus 2. The RREF of a nonsingular square matrix is the identity matrix, and the rank of a nonsingular square matrix is therefore equal to its order. Conversely, the rank of a singular matrix is less than its order.

I have defined the rank of a matrix $\mathbf{A}$ as the dimension of its row space. It can be shown that the rank of $\mathbf{A}$ is also equal to the dimension of its *column space*—that is, to the maximum number of linearly independent columns in $\mathbf{A}$.

1.4.2 Linear Simultaneous Equations

A system of m linear simultaneous equations in n unknowns can be written in matrix form as

$$\underset{(m\times n)(n\times 1)}{\mathbf{A}\ \ \mathbf{x}} = \underset{(m\times 1)}{\mathbf{b}} \tag{1.12}$$

where the elements of the coefficient matrix $\mathbf{A}$ and the right-hand-side vector $\mathbf{b}$ are prespecified constants, and $\mathbf{x}$ is a vector of unknowns. Suppose that there is an equal number of equations and unknowns—that is, $m = n$. Then if the coefficient matrix $\mathbf{A}$ is nonsingular, Equation 1.12 has the *unique solution* $\mathbf{x} = \mathbf{A}^{-1}\mathbf{b}$.

Alternatively, $\mathbf{A}$ may be singular. Then $\mathbf{A}$ can be transformed to RREF by a sequence of (say, p) elementary row operations, representable as successive multiplication on the left by elementary-row-operation matrices:

$$\mathbf{A}_R = \mathbf{E}_p \cdots \mathbf{E}_2 \mathbf{E}_1 \mathbf{A} = \mathbf{E}\mathbf{A}$$

Applying these operations to both sides of Equation 1.12 produces

$$\mathbf{E}\mathbf{A}\mathbf{x} = \mathbf{E}\mathbf{b} \tag{1.13}$$
$$\mathbf{A}_R\mathbf{x} = \mathbf{b}_R$$

where $\mathbf{b}_R \equiv \mathbf{Eb}$. Equations 1.12 and 1.13 are *equivalent* in the sense that any solution vector $\mathbf{x} = \mathbf{x}^*$ that satisfies one system also satisfies the other.

Let r represent the rank of $\mathbf{A}$. Because $r < n$ (recall that $\mathbf{A}$ is singular), $\mathbf{A}_R$ contains r nonzero rows and $n - r$ zero rows. If any zero row of $\mathbf{A}_R$ is associated with a nonzero entry (say, b) in $\mathbf{b}_R$, then the system of equations is *inconsistent* or *overdetermined*, for it contains the self-contradictory "equation"

$$0x_1 + 0x_2 + \cdots + 0x_n = b \neq 0$$

If, on the other hand, every zero row of $\mathbf{A}_R$ corresponds to a zero entry in $\mathbf{b}_R$, then the equation system is *consistent*, and there is an infinity of solutions satisfying the system: $n - r$ of the unknowns may be given arbitrary values, which then determine the values of the remaining r unknowns. Under this circumstance, we say that the equation system is *underdetermined*.

Suppose now that there are *fewer* equations than unknowns—that is, $m < n$. Then r is necessarily less than n, and the equations are either overdetermined (if a zero row of $\mathbf{A}_R$ corresponds to a nonzero entry of $\mathbf{b}_R$) or underdetermined (if they are consistent). For example, consider the following system of three equations in four unknowns:

$$\begin{bmatrix} -2 & 0 & -1 & 2 \\ 4 & 0 & 1 & 0 \\ 6 & 0 & 1 & 2 \end{bmatrix} \begin{bmatrix} x_1 \\ x_2 \\ x_3 \\ x_4 \end{bmatrix} = \begin{bmatrix} 1 \\ 2 \\ 5 \end{bmatrix}$$

Adjoin the right-hand-side vector to the coefficient matrix

$$\left[\begin{array}{cccc|c} -2 & 0 & -1 & 2 & 1 \\ 4 & 0 & 1 & 0 & 2 \\ 6 & 0 & 1 & 2 & 5 \end{array} \right]$$

and reduce the coefficient matrix to row–echelon form:

1. Divide Row 1 by -2,

$$\left[\begin{array}{cccc|c} 1 & 0 & \frac{1}{2} & -1 & -\frac{1}{2} \\ 4 & 0 & 1 & 0 & 2 \\ 6 & 0 & 1 & 2 & 5 \end{array} \right]$$

2. Subtract $4 \times$ Row 1 from Row 2, and subtract $6 \times$ Row 1 from Row 3,

$$\left[\begin{array}{cccc|c} 1 & 0 & \frac{1}{2} & -1 & -\frac{1}{2} \\ 0 & 0 & -1 & 4 & 4 \\ 0 & 0 & -2 & 8 & 8 \end{array}\right]$$

3. Multiply Row 2 by -1,

$$\left[\begin{array}{cccc|c} 1 & 0 & \frac{1}{2} & -1 & -\frac{1}{2} \\ 0 & 0 & 1 & -4 & -4 \\ 0 & 0 & -2 & 8 & 8 \end{array}\right]$$

4. Subtract $\frac{1}{2} \times$ Row 2 from Row 1, and add $2 \times$ Row 2 to Row 3,

$$\left[\begin{array}{cccc|c} 1^{\swarrow} & 0 & 0 & 1 & \frac{3}{2} \\ 0 & 0 & 1^{\swarrow} & -4 & -4 \\ 0 & 0 & 0 & 0 & 0 \end{array}\right]$$

(with the leading entries marked by arrows).

Writing the result as a scalar system of equations, we get

$$x_1 + x_4 = \frac{3}{2}$$
$$x_3 - 4x_4 = -4$$
$$0x_1 + 0x_2 + 0x_3 + 0x_4 = 0$$

The third equation is uninformative (it simply states that $0 = 0$), but it does confirm that the original system of equations is consistent. The first two equations imply that the unknowns x_2 and x_4 can be given arbitrary values (say x_2^* and x_4^*), and the values of x_1 and x_3 (corresponding to the leading entries) follow:

$$x_1 = \frac{3}{2} - x_4^*$$
$$x_3 = -4 + 4x_4^*$$

and thus any vector of the form

$$\mathbf{x} = \left[\begin{array}{c} x_1 \\ x_2 \\ x_3 \\ x_4 \end{array}\right] = \left[\begin{array}{c} \frac{3}{2} - x_4^* \\ x_2^* \\ -4 + 4x_4^* \\ x_4^* \end{array}\right]$$

is a solution of the system of equations.

Now consider the system of equations

$$
\begin{bmatrix} -2 & 0 & -1 & 2 \\ 4 & 0 & 1 & 0 \\ 6 & 0 & 1 & 2 \end{bmatrix} \begin{bmatrix} x_1 \\ x_2 \\ x_3 \\ x_4 \end{bmatrix} = \begin{bmatrix} 1 \\ 2 \\ 1 \end{bmatrix}
$$

Attaching **b** to **A** and transforming the coefficient matrix to RREF yields (as the reader may wish to verify)

$$
\left[\begin{array}{cccc|c} 1 & 0 & 0 & 1 & \frac{1}{2} \\ 0 & 0 & 1 & -4 & -2 \\ 0 & 0 & 0 & 0 & 2 \end{array} \right]
$$

The last "equation,"

$$
0x_1 + 0x_2 + 0x_3 + 0x_4 = 2
$$

is contradictory, implying that the original system of equations has no solution (i.e., is overdetermined).

Suppose, finally, that there are *more* equations than unknowns: $m > n$. If **A** is of full-column rank (i.e., if $r = n$), then $\mathbf{A}_R$ consists of the order-n identity matrix followed by $m - r$ zero rows. If the equations are consistent, they therefore have a unique solution; otherwise they are overdetermined. If $r < n$, the equations are either overdetermined (if inconsistent) or underdetermined (if consistent).

To illustrate these results geometrically, consider a system of three linear equations in two unknowns:[13]

$$
\begin{aligned}
a_{11}x_1 + a_{12}x_2 &= b_1 \\
a_{21}x_1 + a_{22}x_2 &= b_2 \\
a_{31}x_1 + a_{32}x_2 &= b_3
\end{aligned}
$$

Each equation describes a line in a 2D coordinate space in which the unknowns define the axes, as illustrated schematically in Figure 1.13. If the three lines intersect at a point, as in Figure 1.13(a), then there is a *unique solution* to the equation system: Only the pair of values (x_1^*, x_2^*) simultaneously satisfies all three equations. If the three lines fail to intersect at a

---

[13]The geometric representation of linear equations by lines (or, more generally, by linear surfaces, i.e., planes in three dimensions or hyperplanes in higher dimensions) should not be confused with the geometric vector representation taken up previously in this chapter. The graphs of linear equations in two and three dimensions are reviewed in Section 3.1.2.

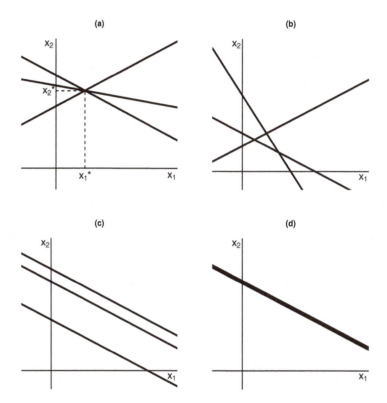

Figure 1.13   Three linear equations in two unknowns x_1 and x_2: (a) unique solution ($x_1 = x_1^*, x_2 = x_2^*$); (b) and (c) overdetermined (no solution); (d) underdetermined (three coincident lines, an infinity of solutions).

Table 1.1 Solutions of m Linear Simultaneous Equations in n Unknowns

Number of equations	$m < n$	$m = n$		$m > n$	
Rank of coefficient matrix	$r < n$	$r < n$	$r = n$	$r < n$	$r = n$
General equation system					
Consistent	Under-determined	Under-determined	Unique solution	Under-determined	Unique solution
Inconsistent	Over-determined	Over-determined	—	Over-determined	Over-determined
Homogeneous equation system					
Consistent	Nontrivial solutions	Nontrivial solutions	Trivial solution	Nontrivial solutions	Trivial solution

common point, as in Figures 1.13(b) and (c), then *no* pair of values of the unknowns simultaneously satisfies the three equations, which therefore are overdetermined. Last, if the three lines are coincident, as in Figure 1.13(d), then *any* pair of values on the common line satisfies all three equations, and the equations are underdetermined.

When the right-hand-side vector **b** in a system of linear simultaneous equations is the zero vector, the system of equations is said to be *homogeneous*:

$$\underset{(m \times n)}{\mathbf{A}} \underset{(n \times 1)}{\mathbf{x}} = \underset{(m \times 1)}{\mathbf{0}}$$

The *trivial solution* $\mathbf{x} = \mathbf{0}$ always satisfies a homogeneous system, which consequently cannot be inconsistent. From the previous work in this section, we can see that nontrivial solutions exist if rank$(\mathbf{A}) < n$—that is, when the system is underdetermined.

The results concerning the solution of linear simultaneous equations developed in this section are summarized in Table 1.1.

Linear simultaneous equations have many statistical applications, such as solving for least-squares coefficients in regression analysis (see Section 7.1).

1.4.3 Generalized Inverses

As I explained previously in this chapter, only square nonsingular matrices have inverses. All matrices, however—including singular and rectangular matrices—have *generalized inverses*, which are occasionally employed in statistical applications, such as some presentations of linear statistical models.[14]

A generalized inverse of the $(m \times n)$ matrix $\mathbf{A}$ is an $(n \times m)$ matrix $\mathbf{A}^-$ that satisfies the equation

$$\mathbf{AA^-A = A} \tag{1.14}$$

We say that $\mathbf{A}^-$ is *a* generalized inverse, not *the* generalized inverse of $\mathbf{A}$, because unless $\mathbf{A}$ is square and nonsingular (in which case $\mathbf{A}^- = \mathbf{A}^{-1}$), the generalized inverse is not unique.[15]

There are many ways to find a generalized inverse of a matrix, including by Gaussian elimination. Suppose that we begin by putting the matrix $\mathbf{A}$ in RREF by a sequence of elementary row operations; we know that we can represent this process by successive multiplication on the left by suitably configured elementary-row-operations matrices (see pages 14 and 32):

$$\mathbf{EA = E}_p \cdots \mathbf{E}_2\mathbf{E}_1\mathbf{A = A}_R \tag{1.15}$$

where $\mathbf{E} \equiv \mathbf{E}_p \cdots \mathbf{E}_2\mathbf{E}_1$ is a nonsingular $(m \times m)$ matrix. Applying an analogous series of Types II and III *elementary column operations* (pivoting is unnecessary because all of the leading entries in $\mathbf{A}_R$ are already 1), we can further reduce $\mathbf{A}_R$ to the following *canonical form*:

$$\underset{(m \times n)}{\mathbf{A}_C} \equiv \mathbf{A}_R\mathbf{E}^* = \mathbf{A}_R\mathbf{E}_1^*\mathbf{E}_2^* \cdots \mathbf{E}_q^* = \left[\begin{array}{cc} \mathbf{I}_r & \underset{(r \times n-r)}{\mathbf{0}} \\ \underset{(m-r \times r)}{\mathbf{0}} & \underset{(m-r \times n-r)}{\mathbf{0}} \end{array} \right] \tag{1.16}$$

where $\mathbf{E}^* \equiv \mathbf{E}_1^*\mathbf{E}_2^* \cdots \mathbf{E}_q^*$ is a nonsingular $(n \times n)$ matrix; the order r of the identity matrix in the upper-left corner is the rank of $\mathbf{A}$; and any or all of the zero matrices may be absent. For example, if $\mathbf{A}$ is a square nonsingular matrix of order n then $r = n$ and none of the zero matrices are required.

Putting together Equations 1.15 and 1.16, we have

$$\mathbf{A}_C = \mathbf{EAE}^* \tag{1.17}$$

---

[14]For an extensive discussion of the role of generalized inverses in statistics, See Rao and Mitra (1971).

[15]The generalized inverse can be made unique by placing additional restrictions on it beyond Equation 1.14: For example, the *Moore–Penrose generalized inverse* $\mathbf{A}^+$ satisfies four conditions: $\mathbf{AA^+A = A}$; $\mathbf{A^+AA^+ = A^+}$; $\mathbf{AA^+}$ is symmetric; and $\mathbf{A^+A}$ is symmetric. In a typical statistical application, however, one generalized inverse is as good as another.

A generalized inverse of $\mathbf{A}$ is then given by[16]

$$\mathbf{A}^- \equiv \mathbf{E}^* \mathbf{A}'_C \mathbf{E}$$

Consider, for example, the matrix

$$\mathbf{A} = \begin{bmatrix} -2 & 0 & -1 & 2 \\ 4 & 0 & 1 & 0 \\ 6 & 0 & 1 & 2 \end{bmatrix}$$

Earlier in the chapter (page 32), I transformed this matrix to RREF by a sequence of elementary row operations:

$$\mathbf{A}_R = \begin{bmatrix} 1 & 0 & 0 & 1 \\ 0 & 0 & 1 & -4 \\ 0 & 0 & 0 & 0 \end{bmatrix}$$

The reduction to canonical form is completed by exchanging Columns 2 and 3, and then sweeping out the fourth column, producing

$$\mathbf{A}_C = \begin{bmatrix} 1 & 0 & 0 & 0 \\ 0 & 1 & 0 & 0 \\ 0 & 0 & 0 & 0 \end{bmatrix}$$

Collecting the elementary row and column operations into matrices, we have (as the reader may wish to verify)

$$\mathbf{E} = \begin{bmatrix} \frac{1}{2} & \frac{1}{2} & 0 \\ -2 & -1 & 0 \\ -1 & -2 & 1 \end{bmatrix}$$

$$\mathbf{E}^* = \begin{bmatrix} 1 & 0 & 0 & -1 \\ 0 & 0 & 1 & 0 \\ 0 & 1 & 0 & 4 \\ 0 & 0 & 0 & 1 \end{bmatrix}$$

---

[16]The following proof is adapted from Healy (1986, p. 40): First, $\mathbf{A}'_C$ is a generalized inverse of $\mathbf{A}_C$ (*Reader:* Check it!); second, solving Equation 1.17 for $\mathbf{A}$ produces $\mathbf{A} = \mathbf{E}^{-1}\mathbf{A}_C\mathbf{E}^{*-1}$. Then,

$$\begin{aligned} \mathbf{A}\mathbf{A}^-\mathbf{A} &= (\mathbf{E}^{-1}\mathbf{A}_C\mathbf{E}^{*-1})(\mathbf{E}^*\mathbf{A}'_C\mathbf{E})(\mathbf{E}^{-1}\mathbf{A}_C\mathbf{E}^{*-1}) \\ &= \mathbf{E}^{-1}\mathbf{A}_C\mathbf{A}'_C\mathbf{A}_C\mathbf{E}^{*-1} \\ &= \mathbf{E}^{-1}\mathbf{A}_C\mathbf{E}^{*-1} \\ &= \mathbf{A} \end{aligned}$$

which establishes the result.

from which

$$\mathbf{A}^- = \mathbf{E}^* \mathbf{A}'_C \mathbf{E}$$

$$= \begin{bmatrix} 1 & 0 & 0 & -1 \\ 0 & 0 & 1 & 0 \\ 0 & 1 & 0 & 4 \\ 0 & 0 & 0 & 1 \end{bmatrix} \begin{bmatrix} 1 & 0 & 0 \\ 0 & 1 & 0 \\ 0 & 0 & 0 \\ 0 & 0 & 0 \end{bmatrix} \begin{bmatrix} \frac{1}{2} & \frac{1}{2} & 0 \\ -2 & -1 & 0 \\ -1 & -2 & 1 \end{bmatrix}$$

$$= \begin{bmatrix} \frac{1}{2} & \frac{1}{2} & 0 \\ 0 & 0 & 0 \\ -2 & -1 & 0 \\ 0 & 0 & 0 \end{bmatrix}$$

is a generalized inverse of $\mathbf{A}$ (as the reader can also verify).

Now consider a system of m linear simultaneous equations in n unknowns,

$$\underset{(m\times n)}{\mathbf{A}} \underset{(n\times 1)}{\mathbf{x}} = \underset{(m\times 1)}{\mathbf{b}}$$

as discussed in the preceding section, and suppose that the system of equations is consistent and underdetermined. Then

$$\mathbf{x}^* = \mathbf{A}^- \mathbf{b} \tag{1.18}$$

provides an arbitrary solution to the equations. If the equation system has a unique solution, then Equation 1.18 yields it. Finally, if the equation system is overdetermined, then the "solution" provided by Equation 1.18 will fail to satisfy the original system of equations. Thus, if the equation system is consistent, then $\mathbf{A}\mathbf{A}^-\mathbf{b} = \mathbf{b}$, and if the system is inconsistent, then $\mathbf{A}\mathbf{A}^-\mathbf{b} \neq \mathbf{b}$. The reader may wish to apply these results to the examples in the previous section.

CHAPTER 2. MATRIX DECOMPOSITIONS AND QUADRATIC FORMS

Matrix decompositions and quadratic forms are conceptually important in many statistical applications, and matrix decompositions are also central to modern statistical computation (see, e.g., the application of the QR decomposition and singular-value [SVD] decomposition to least-squares computations in Section 7.1.1). The first section of the chapter introduces eigenvalues and eigenvectors along with two closely related matrix decompositions: generalized eigenvalues and eigenvectors, and the SVD. The second section takes up the related topics of quadratic forms (and their elliptical geometry), positive-definite matrices, and the Cholesky decomposition. The third section describes the QR decomposition.

2.1 Eigenvalues and Eigenvectors

If $\mathbf{A}$ is an order-n square matrix, then the homogeneous system of linear equations

$$(\mathbf{A} - \lambda \mathbf{I}_n)\mathbf{x} = \mathbf{0} \tag{2.1}$$

or, equivalently, $\mathbf{A}\mathbf{x} = \lambda \mathbf{x}$, has nontrivial solutions only for certain values of the scalar λ. The results on the solution of linear simultaneous equations in the preceding chapter (Section 1.4.2) suggest that nontrivial solutions exist when the matrix $(\mathbf{A} - \lambda \mathbf{I}_n)$ is singular, that is, when

$$\det(\mathbf{A} - \lambda \mathbf{I}_n) = 0 \tag{2.2}$$

Equation 2.2 is called the *characteristic equation* of the matrix $\mathbf{A}$, and the values of λ for which this equation holds are called the *eigenvalues*,[1] *characteristic roots*, or *latent roots* of $\mathbf{A}$. A vector $\mathbf{x}_i$ satisfying Equation 2.1 for a particular eigenvalue λ_i is called an *eigenvector*, *characteristic vector*, or *latent vector* of $\mathbf{A}$ associated with λ_i.

---

[1] *Eigenvalue* is a partial translation of the German term *Eigenwert*, apparently introduced by the mathematician David Hilbert (1862–1943): *eigen* means "own" in German.

Because of its simplicity and straightforward extension, I will examine the (2×2) case in some detail. For this case, the characteristic equation is

$$\det \begin{bmatrix} a_{11} - \lambda & a_{12} \\ a_{21} & a_{22} - \lambda \end{bmatrix} = 0$$

$$(a_{11} - \lambda)(a_{22} - \lambda) - a_{12}a_{21} = 0$$

$$\lambda^2 - (a_{11} + a_{22})\lambda + a_{11}a_{22} - a_{12}a_{21} = 0$$

Using the quadratic formula to solve the characteristic equation produces the two roots[2]

$$\lambda_1 = \frac{1}{2}\left[a_{11} + a_{22} + \sqrt{(a_{11} + a_{22})^2 - 4(a_{11}a_{22} - a_{12}a_{21})}\right] \qquad (2.3)$$

$$\lambda_2 = \frac{1}{2}\left[a_{11} + a_{22} - \sqrt{(a_{11} + a_{22})^2 - 4(a_{11}a_{22} - a_{12}a_{21})}\right]$$

These roots are real numbers if the quantity under the radical is nonnegative. Notice, incidentally, that $\lambda_1 + \lambda_2 = a_{11} + a_{22}$ (the sum of the eigenvalues of $\mathbf{A}$ is the trace of $\mathbf{A}$), and that $\lambda_1\lambda_2 = a_{11}a_{22} - a_{12}a_{21}$ (the product of the eigenvalues is the determinant of $\mathbf{A}$). Furthermore, if $\mathbf{A}$ is singular, then at least one of λ_1 and λ_2 is zero.[3]

If $\mathbf{A}$ is symmetric (as is the case for most statistical applications of eigenvalues and eigenvectors), then $a_{12} = a_{21}$, and Equation 2.3 becomes

$$\lambda_1 = \frac{1}{2}\left[a_{11} + a_{22} + \sqrt{(a_{11} - a_{22})^2 + 4a_{12}^2}\right] \qquad (2.4)$$

$$\lambda_2 = \frac{1}{2}\left[a_{11} + a_{22} - \sqrt{(a_{11} - a_{22})^2 + 4a_{12}^2}\right]$$

The eigenvalues of a (2×2) symmetric matrix are necessarily real because the quantity under the radical in Equation 2.4 is the sum of two squares, which cannot be negative.

---

[2]Review of the *quadratic formula*: The values of x that satisfy the quadratic equation

$$ax^2 + bx + c = 0$$

where $a, b,$ and c are specific constants, are

$$x = \frac{-b \pm \sqrt{b^2 - 4ac}}{2a}$$

[3]λ_1 and λ_2 are *both* zero only if $\mathbf{A}$ is the (2×2) $\mathbf{0}$ matrix.

I will use the following (2×2) matrix as an illustration:[4]

$$\begin{bmatrix} 1 & 0.5 \\ 0.5 & 1 \end{bmatrix}$$

Here,

$$\lambda_1 = \frac{1}{2}\left[1 + 1 + \sqrt{(1-1)^2 + 4(0.5)^2}\right] = 1.5$$

$$\lambda_2 = \frac{1}{2}\left[1 + 1 - \sqrt{(1-1)^2 + 4(0.5)^2}\right] = 0.5$$

To find the eigenvectors associated with $\lambda_1 = 1.5$, solve the homogeneous system of equations

$$\begin{bmatrix} 1-1.5 & 0.5 \\ 0.5 & 1-1.5 \end{bmatrix}\begin{bmatrix} x_{11} \\ x_{21} \end{bmatrix} = \begin{bmatrix} 0 \\ 0 \end{bmatrix}$$

$$\begin{bmatrix} -0.5 & 0.5 \\ 0.5 & -0.5 \end{bmatrix}\begin{bmatrix} x_{11} \\ x_{21} \end{bmatrix} = \begin{bmatrix} 0 \\ 0 \end{bmatrix}$$

yielding

$$\mathbf{x}_1 = \begin{bmatrix} x_{11} \\ x_{21} \end{bmatrix} = \begin{bmatrix} x_{21}^* \\ x_{21}^* \end{bmatrix}$$

---

[4]This might be a correlation matrix for two variables, in which case the eigenvalues and eigenvectors of the matrix provide a *principal-components analysis* of the variables. Here is a brief sketch of principal-components analysis for two variables, each standardized to mean 0 and standard deviation 1, so that their covariance is equal to their correlation (see Section 4.2.3):

- The first principal component is the linear combination of the two variables that has maximum variance, subject to the constraint that the sum of the squared coefficients of the linear combination is 1.

- The variance of the resulting linear combination is equal to the larger of the two eigenvalues of the correlation matrix, and the coefficients of the linear combination are the elements of the corresponding eigenvector normalized to length 1 (see immediately below for the derivation of the eigenvalues and eigenvectors of the matrix in the example).

- The variance of the second principal component is given by the smaller eigenvalue and its coefficients by the corresponding normalized eigenvector.

- The two principal components are orthogonal and consequently provide an orthogonal basis for the subspace spanned by the two standardized variables, partitioning the combined variances of the two variables.

This procedure extends straightforwardly to three or more standardized variables. For the details of principal-components analysis, see, for example, Fox (2016, Section 13.1.1).

(i.e., any vector with two equal entries). Similarly, for $\lambda_2 = 0.5$, solve

$$\begin{bmatrix} 1-0.5 & 0.5 \\ 0.5 & 1-0.5 \end{bmatrix} \begin{bmatrix} x_{12} \\ x_{22} \end{bmatrix} = \begin{bmatrix} 0 \\ 0 \end{bmatrix}$$

$$\begin{bmatrix} 0.5 & 0.5 \\ 0.5 & 0.5 \end{bmatrix} \begin{bmatrix} x_{12} \\ x_{22} \end{bmatrix} = \begin{bmatrix} 0 \\ 0 \end{bmatrix}$$

which produces

$$\mathbf{x}_2 = \begin{bmatrix} x_{12} \\ x_{22} \end{bmatrix} = \begin{bmatrix} -x_{22}^* \\ x_{22}^* \end{bmatrix}$$

(i.e., any vector whose two entries are the negative of each other). The set of eigenvalues associated with each eigenvector therefore spans a 1D subspace: When one of the entries of the eigenvector is specified, the other entry follows. As well, the eigenvectors $\mathbf{x}_1$ and $\mathbf{x}_2$ are orthogonal:

$$\mathbf{x}_1 \cdot \mathbf{x}_2 = -x_{21}^* x_{22}^* + x_{21}^* x_{22}^* = 0$$

Many of the properties of eigenvalues and eigenvectors of (2×2) matrices generalize to $(n \times n)$ matrices:

- The characteristic equation, $\det(\mathbf{A} - \lambda \mathbf{I}_n) = 0$, of an $(n \times n)$ matrix is an nth-order polynomial in λ; there are, consequently, n eigenvalues, not all necessarily distinct, and some of which may be zero.[5]

- The sum of the eigenvalues of $\mathbf{A}$ is the trace of $\mathbf{A}$.

- The product of the eigenvalues of $\mathbf{A}$ is the determinant of $\mathbf{A}$.

- The number of nonzero eigenvalues of $\mathbf{A}$ is the rank of $\mathbf{A}$.

- A singular matrix, therefore, has a least one zero eigenvalue.

- If $\mathbf{A}$ is a symmetric matrix, then the eigenvalues of $\mathbf{A}$ are all real numbers.

- If the eigenvalues of $\mathbf{A}$ are distinct (i.e., all different), then the set of eigenvectors associated with a particular eigenvalue spans a 1D subspace. If, alternatively, k eigenvalues are equal, then their common set of eigenvectors spans a subspace of dimension k, and the repeated eigenvalue is said to have *multiplicity k*.

---

[5]Finding eigenvalues by solving the characteristic equation directly is not generally an attractive approach when $n > 2$, and other, more practical, methods exist for finding eigenvalues and their associated eigenvectors: For example, a method based on the QR decomposition is described later in this chapter (Section 2.3.1).

- Eigenvectors associated with distinct eigenvalues are linearly independent, and, in a symmetric matrix, are orthogonal.

Suppose that $\mathbf{A}$ is an $(n \times n)$ symmetric matrix of rank r. Let $\mathbf{\Lambda} \equiv \text{diag}(\lambda_1, \lambda_2, \ldots, \lambda_r)$ collect the nonzero eigenvalues of $\mathbf{A}$; let $\mathbf{x}_j$ represent an eigenvector corresponding to λ_j, normalized to unit length, $\|\mathbf{x}_j\| = 1$; and let $\mathbf{X} \equiv [\mathbf{x}_1, \mathbf{x}_2, \ldots, \mathbf{x}_r]$ collect these eigenvectors.[6] Then,

$$
\begin{aligned}
\mathbf{A} &= \lambda_1 \mathbf{x}_1 \mathbf{x}_1' + \lambda_2 \mathbf{x}_2 \mathbf{x}_2' + \cdots + \lambda_r \mathbf{x}_r \mathbf{x}_r' \qquad (2.5) \\
&= \mathbf{X} \mathbf{\Lambda} \mathbf{X}'
\end{aligned}
$$

Equation 2.5, called the *spectral decomposition* of the matrix $\mathbf{A}$, is the mathematical basis of such statistical techniques as principal-components analysis and factor analysis.

2.1.1   Generalized Eigenvalues and Eigenvectors

Eigenvectors and eigenvalues can be generalized in the following manner: Suppose that $\mathbf{A}$ is an $(n \times n)$ symmetric matrix, and let us replace Equation 2.1 (page 42) with

$$(\mathbf{A} - \lambda \mathbf{B})\mathbf{x} = \mathbf{0}$$

where $\mathbf{B}$ is an $(n \times n)$ symmetric, positive-definite matrix. (See Section 2.2 for the definition of positive-definiteness.) Then the values of λ that satisfy this equation are called *generalized eigenvalues of* $\mathbf{A}$ *in the metric of* $\mathbf{B}$, and the corresponding vectors $\mathbf{x}$ are *generalized eigenvectors*. It turns out that the generalized eigenvalues are the ordinary eigenvalues of $\mathbf{A}\mathbf{B}^{-1}$. Generalized eigenvalues and eigenvectors are useful in certain areas of multivariate statistics, such as for hypothesis tests in the multivariate linear model.

2.1.2   The Singular-Value Decomposition

Still another generalization of eigenvalues and eigenvectors is to rectangular matrices. Suppose, now, that $\mathbf{A}$ is an $(m \times n)$ matrix of rank r. Then $\mathbf{A}$ can be factored as

$$
\mathbf{A} = \underset{(m \times m)}{\mathbf{B}}
\begin{bmatrix}
\underset{(r \times r)}{\mathbf{\Lambda}} & \underset{(r \times n-r)}{\mathbf{0}} \\
\underset{(m-r \times r)}{\mathbf{0}} & \underset{(m-r \times n-r)}{\mathbf{0}}
\end{bmatrix}
\underset{(n \times n)}{\mathbf{C}'} \qquad (2.6)
$$

where

---

[6]If there's an eigenvalue with multiplicity greater than 1, then we can pick an arbitrary orthonormal basis for the subspace spanned by its eigenvectors to supply the corresponding columns of $\mathbf{X}$, and the eigenvalue is repeated in the diagonal of $\mathbf{\Lambda}$.

- **B** and **C** are orthogonal matrices (see page 26), and are not generally unique;

- $\mathbf{\Lambda}^2$ is a diagonal matrix containing the nonzero eigenvalues of the matrices $\mathbf{A}'\mathbf{A}$ and $\mathbf{A}\mathbf{A}'$ (which share the same eigenvalues); and

- not all of the zero matrices may be needed. (Indeed, if $r = m = n$, then Equation 2.6 reduces to the spectral decomposition in Equation 2.5.)

Equation 2.6 is termed the *singular-value decomposition* or *SVD* of the matrix **A**, and the diagonal entries of $\mathbf{\Lambda}$ are the *singular values* of **A** (which are, therefore, the square roots of the eigenvalues of $\mathbf{A}'\mathbf{A}$ and $\mathbf{A}\mathbf{A}'$).

We can make the SVD more compact by eliminating the zero submatrices from Equation 2.6,[7] producing

$$\mathbf{A} = \underset{(m \times r)(r \times r)(r \times n)}{\mathbf{B}^* \ \mathbf{\Lambda} \ \mathbf{C}^{*\prime}} \tag{2.7}$$

where $\mathbf{B}^*$ contains the first r columns of **B** and $\mathbf{C}^{*\prime}$ contains the first r rows of $\mathbf{C}'$. Both $\mathbf{B}^*$ and $\mathbf{C}^*$ are orthonormal matrices.

The SVD is useful, for example, for improving the computational efficiency and precision of least-squares calculations (see Section 7.1.1).

2.2 Quadratic Forms and Positive-Definite Matrices

The expression

$$\underset{(1 \times n)(n \times n)(n \times 1)}{\mathbf{x}' \ \mathbf{A} \ \mathbf{x}} \tag{2.8}$$

is called a *quadratic form* in **x**. In this section (as in typical statistical applications), **A** will always be a symmetric matrix. **A** is said to be *positive-definite* if the quadratic form in 2.8 is positive for all nonzero vectors **x**. **A** is *positive-semidefinite* if the quadratic form is nonnegative (i.e., positive or zero) for all nonzero vectors **x**.

If **A** is positive-definite, then the diagonal elements of **A** are all positive. Similarly, if **A** is positive-semidefinite, then all of its diagonal elements are nonnegative. (*Reader:* Can you see why?) The eigenvalues of a positive-definite matrix are all positive (and, consequently, the matrix is nonsingular);

---

[7]In statistical applications of the SVD, **A** may be a data matrix for m cases and n variables; typically, then, m would be much larger than n, and so the zero matrices in the full version of the SVD could be very large. Retaining the large zero matrices would unnecessarily burden computations.

those of a positive-semidefinite matrix are all positive or zero (and the matrix is singular if any of its eigenvalues are zero). I'll generally reserve the term *positive-semidefinite* for the case where there is at least one zero eigenvalue (and hence the matrix is singular).

Let

$$\underset{(m \times m)}{\mathbf{C}} = \underset{(m \times n)}{\mathbf{B}'} \underset{(n \times n)}{\mathbf{A}} \underset{(n \times m)}{\mathbf{B}}$$

where $\mathbf{A}$ is positive-definite and $\mathbf{B}$ is of full-column rank $m \leq n$. I will show that $\mathbf{C}$ is also positive-definite. Note, first, that $\mathbf{C}$ is symmetric:

$$\mathbf{C}' = (\mathbf{B}'\mathbf{A}\mathbf{B})' = \mathbf{B}'\mathbf{A}'\mathbf{B} = \mathbf{B}'\mathbf{A}\mathbf{B} = \mathbf{C}$$

If $\mathbf{y}$ is any $(m \times 1)$ nonzero vector, then $\underset{(n \times 1)}{\mathbf{x}} = \mathbf{B}\mathbf{y}$ is also nonzero: Because $\mathbf{B}$ is of rank m, we can select m linearly independent rows from $\mathbf{B}$, forming the nonsingular matrix $\mathbf{B}^*$. Then $\underset{(m \times 1)}{\mathbf{x}^*} = \mathbf{B}^*\mathbf{y}$, which contains a subset of the entries in $\mathbf{x}$, is nonzero because $\mathbf{y} = \mathbf{B}^{*-1}\mathbf{x}^* \neq \mathbf{0}$. Consequently,

$$\mathbf{y}'\mathbf{C}\mathbf{y} = \mathbf{y}'\mathbf{B}'\mathbf{A}\mathbf{B}\mathbf{y} = \mathbf{x}'\mathbf{A}\mathbf{x}$$

is necessarily positive, and $\mathbf{C}$ is positive-definite. By similar reasoning, if rank$(\mathbf{B}) < m$, then $\mathbf{C}$ is positive-semidefinite. The matrix $\underset{(m \times n)}{\mathbf{B}'} \underset{(n \times m)}{\mathbf{B}} = \mathbf{B}'\mathbf{I}_n\mathbf{B}$ is therefore positive-definite if $\mathbf{B}$ is of full-column rank (because $\mathbf{I}_n$ is clearly positive-definite—e.g., $\det \mathbf{I}_n = 1$), and positive-semidefinite otherwise. (Cf., the geometric discussion following Equation 1.10 on page 29.)

Positive-definite and -semidefinite matrices—such as variance–covariance matrices, correlation matrices, and matrices of sums of squares and products—play a prominent role in statistics.

2.2.1   The Elliptical Geometry of Quadratic Forms

The geometry of *ellipses* (and its generalization to higher dimensions) allows us to visualize quadratic forms in a manner that is broadly applicable to problems in statistics (see, e.g., Section 5.2.5 on the multivariate-normal distributions, and Section 7.7 on ellipses in linear least-squares regression) and that ties together some of the themes in this chapter. As in the preceding discussion of eigenvalues and eigenvectors, I'll concentrate on the 2D case, which suffices to develop almost all of the key ideas, before briefly sketching the generalization to three dimensions (*ellipsoids*) and beyond (*hyperellipsoids*).

Let us start, then, with the quadratic form

$$\mathbf{x}'\mathbf{A}\mathbf{x} = [x_1, x_2] \begin{bmatrix} a_{11} & a_{12} \\ a_{12} & a_{22} \end{bmatrix} \begin{bmatrix} x_1 \\ x_2 \end{bmatrix} \qquad (2.9)$$

where the symmetric (2×2) matrix $\mathbf{A}$ is positive-definite. Thus $a_{11} > 0$, $a_{22} > 0$, and $\det \mathbf{A} = a_{11}a_{22} - a_{12}^2 > 0$, which implies that $a_{11}a_{22} > a_{12}^2$. Thus, we can write $a_{12} = c\sqrt{a_{11}a_{22}}$, where $-1 < c < 1$. If we allow the constant $c = \pm 1$, then $\det \mathbf{A} = 0$ and $\mathbf{A}$ is positive-semidefinite.

Setting Equation 2.9 to 1 produces

$$a_{11}x_1^2 + a_{22}x_2^2 + 2a_{12}x_1x_2 = a_{11}x_1^2 + a_{22}x_2^2 + 2c\sqrt{a_{11}a_{22}}x_1x_2 = 1 \quad (2.10)$$

The locus of points in the x_1 and x_2 plane satisfying Equation 2.10 describes an ellipse centered at the origin—that is, the point $(0,0)$. Figure 2.1 shows three examples of increasing complexity:

- In Panel (a), $a_{11} = a_{22} \equiv a$ and $c = 0$ (and thus $a_{12} = 0$). In this case, the equation $ax_1^2 + ax_2^2 = 1$ describes a circle of radius $1/\sqrt{a}$. The *radius vector* shown in the graph arbitrarily points in the positive direction along the horizontal axis.

- In Panel (b), $a_{11} < a_{22}$ and $c = 0$. The equation $a_{11}x_1^2 + a_{22}x_2^2 = 1$ describes an ellipse whose *major* and *minor axes* coincide with the axes x_1 and x_2 of the coordinate space. The *major radius* of the ellipse is of length $1/\sqrt{a_{11}}$ and the *minor radius* is of length $1/\sqrt{a_{22}}$. The two radius vectors lie on the axes of the space and arbitrarily point in the positive direction along each axis.

- The general case is represented in Panel (c), drawn for $c < 0$ (and thus $a_{12} < 0$), giving the ellipse a *positive* tilt.[8] As is easily seen by setting $x_2 = 0$ and solving for x_1, the ellipse crosses the horizontal axis at $\pm 1/\sqrt{a_{11}}$; similarly, the ellipse crosses the vertical axis at $\pm 1/\sqrt{a_{22}}$.

  The axes of the ellipse (shown as broken lines) correspond to the eigenvectors of $\mathbf{A}$, with the major axis given by the *second* eigenvector and the minor axis by the *first* eigenvector. The length of the major radius is $1/\sqrt{\lambda_2}$, where λ_2 is the second eigenvalue of $\mathbf{A}$ (let's call the radius vector $\mathbf{v}_2$, with length $\|\mathbf{v}_2\| = 1/\sqrt{\lambda_2}$), and the length of the minor radius is $1/\sqrt{\lambda_1}$ (with radius vector $\mathbf{v}_1$, $\|\mathbf{v}_1\| = 1/\sqrt{\lambda_1}$).

---

[8] Although numeric scales aren't shown on the axes of the graph, to draw the ellipse in Figure 2.1 (c), I took $a_{11} = 2$, $a_{22} = 4$, and $c = -1/3$, and so $a_{12} = -2\sqrt{2}/3 \approx 0.943$.

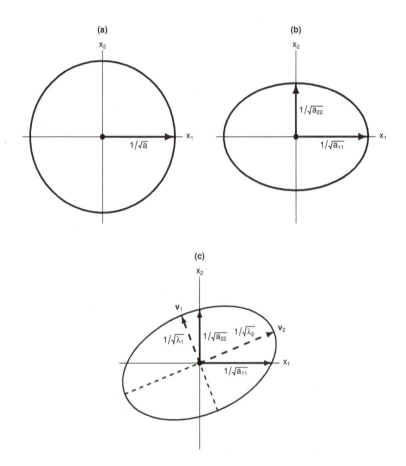

Figure 2.1   Ellipses generated by the equation $\mathbf{x}'\mathbf{A}\mathbf{x} = 1$, where $\mathbf{A}$ is a (2×2) positive-definite matrix. In (a) the off-diagonal entries of $\mathbf{A}$ are zero and the diagonal elements are both equal to $a > 0$, generating a circle of radius $1/\sqrt{a}$. In (b) the off-diagonal elements are zero, and the diagonal elements are unequal, with $a_{22} > a_{11} > 0$. In (c) the off-diagonal elements of $\mathbf{A}$ are nonzero (and negative); the axes of the ellipse no longer coincide with the axes of the coordinate space (i.e., the ellipse is tilted), and the radius vectors are the eigenvectors of $\mathbf{A}$, with the major radius $\mathbf{v}_2$ corresponding to the second eigenvector and the minor radius $\mathbf{v}_1$ corresponding to the first eigenvector.

The eigenvectors of $\mathbf{A}$ are the same as those of $\mathbf{A}^{-1}$, while the eigenvalues of $\mathbf{A}$ are the inverses of those of $\mathbf{A}^{-1}$. We could therefore also say that the major radius of the ellipse generated by $\mathbf{x}'\mathbf{A}\mathbf{x} = 1$ is the first eigenvector of $\mathbf{A}^{-1}$ normalized to length equal to the square root of its first eigenvalue, and similarly for the minor radius. Likewise, the major radius of the ellipse representing the equation $\mathbf{x}'\mathbf{A}^{-1}\mathbf{x} = 1$ has the same radii as the ellipse representing $\mathbf{x}'\mathbf{A}\mathbf{x} = 1$, but with the major and minor axes exchanged, and with the major radius of length $\sqrt{\lambda_1}$ and the minor radius of length $\sqrt{\lambda_2}$ (where, as before, the λ_js are the eigenvalues of $\mathbf{A}$). Thus, the ellipse representing $\mathbf{A}^{-1}$ is the 90° rotation and rescaling of the ellipse representing $\mathbf{A}$ (see Figure 2.2).

An interesting property of the ellipse corresponding to the inverse matrix $\mathbf{A}^{-1}$ is that its vertical "shadow" (i.e., perpendicular projection) onto the horizontal axis (or, as in Figure 2.2, a line parallel to the horizontal axis) has length equal to twice the square root of the first diagonal element of the matrix $\mathbf{A}$, $\sqrt{a_{11}}$. Similarly the horizontal shadow of the $\mathbf{A}^{-1}$ matrix onto the vertical axis has length equal to twice $\sqrt{a_{22}}$.

Recall that the off-diagonal elements of the matrix $\mathbf{A}$ can be written as $a_{12} = a_{21} = c\sqrt{a_{11}}\sqrt{a_{22}}$ for $-1 < c < 1$. Now look at the broken horizontal line in Figure 2.2, drawn through the point of vertical tangency (at the left) to the $\mathbf{A}^{-1}$ ellipse. The vertical distance between the x_1 axis and this line is $|c|\sqrt{a_{22}}$. Similarly, the distance between the x_2 axis and the line through the horizontal tangent (at the bottom) to the $\mathbf{A}^{-1}$ ellipse is $|c|\sqrt{a_{11}}$.

The area enclosed by the ellipse defined in Equation 2.10 is

$$\text{Area} = \frac{\pi}{\sqrt{\det \mathbf{A}}} = \frac{\pi}{\sqrt{a_{11}a_{22} - a_{12}^2}} \tag{2.11}$$

In the case of diagonal $\mathbf{A}$—for example, in Figure 2.1(b)—this result simplifies to Area $= \pi/\sqrt{a_{11}a_{22}}$. In the case of a circle, Figure 2.1(a), where $a_{12} = 0$ and $a_{11} = a_{22} \equiv a$, and where $1/\sqrt{a}$ is the radius of the circle, we have the familiar formula Area $= \pi/a = \pi \times \text{radius}^2$. As well, because $\det(\mathbf{A}^{-1}) = 1/\det(\mathbf{A})$ (see Section 1.1.4), the area of the ellipse generated by $\mathbf{A}$ is inversely proportional to the area of the ellipse generated by $\mathbf{A}^{-1}$. These results prove useful in statistical applications (e.g., in visualizing properties of least-squares regression: see Section 7.7).

Recall that for positive-definite $\mathbf{A}$, $a_{12}^2 < a_{11}a_{22}$. As a_{12}^2 approaches $a_{11}a_{22}$, the determinant of $\mathbf{A}$ gets smaller. If $\mathbf{A}$ is positive-semidefinite, then it is singular, $\det(\mathbf{A}) = 0$, and the "ellipse" representing $\mathbf{A}$ has infinite area; $\mathbf{A}^{-1}$ doesn't exist, but the inverse ellipse collapses to a line segment (a *degener-*

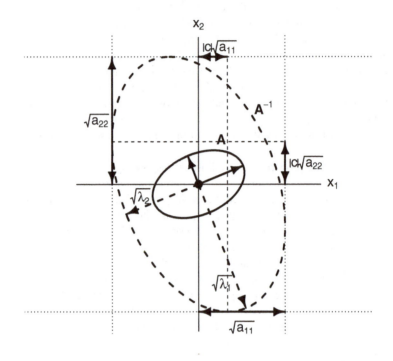

Figure 2.2   Ellipses generated by the quadratic forms $\mathbf{x}'\mathbf{A}\mathbf{x} = 1$ (labeled $\mathbf{A}$ and drawn with a solid line) and $\mathbf{x}'\mathbf{A}^{-1}\mathbf{x} = 1$ (labeled $\mathbf{A}^{-1}$ and drawn with a broken line). The major and minor radii of the ellipse generated by $\mathbf{x}'\mathbf{A}^{-1}\mathbf{x} = 1$ are, respectively, of length $\sqrt{\lambda_1}$ and $\sqrt{\lambda_2}$, where the λ_js are the eigenvalues of $\mathbf{A}$. The vertical and horizontal shadows of the ellipse corresponding to $\mathbf{A}^{-1}$ (see the dotted lines) have lengths equal to twice the square root diagonal elements of $\mathbf{A}$, respectively, $\sqrt{a_{11}}$ and $\sqrt{a_{22}}$. Broken lines are drawn parallel to each axis through the points of horizontal and vertical tangency to the $\mathbf{A}^{-1}$ ellipse (respectively to the left of and below the ellipse). The distances of these lines to the axes are $|c|\sqrt{a_{11}}$ and $|c|\sqrt{a_{22}}$, where $a_{12} = a_{21} = c\sqrt{a_{11}}\sqrt{a_{22}}$.

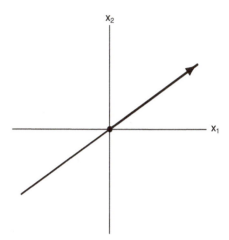

Figure 2.3   Degenerate inverse ellipse (line segment) corresponding to a positive-semidefinite matrix **A**. The arrow is a "radius" vector of the degenerate ellipse.

ate ellipse), which has zero area, as in Figure 2.3. The geometric analysis based on the eigenstructure of **A** therefore breaks down for singular **A**.[9]

The ellipses in Figures 2.1 and 2.2, and the degenerate ellipse in Figure 2.3, are centered at the origin, $(x_1 = 0, x_2 = 0)$. A simple translation of an ellipse to center $(x_1 = x_1^*, x_2 = x_2^*)$ (as in Figure 2.4) is produced by the equation

$$(\mathbf{x} - \mathbf{x}^*)'\mathbf{A}(\mathbf{x} - \mathbf{x}^*) = [x_1 - x_1^*, x_2 - x_2^*]\begin{bmatrix} a_{11} & a_{12} \\ a_{12} & a_{22} \end{bmatrix}\begin{bmatrix} x_1 - x_1^* \\ x_2 - x_2^* \end{bmatrix} = 1 \quad (2.12)$$

The geometric generalization of $\mathbf{x}'\mathbf{A}\mathbf{x} = 1$ to $p \times p$ symmetric positive-definite matrices **A** is straightforward. When $p = 3$, the equation defines an *ellipsoid* in 3D coordinate space, as illustrated in Figure 2.5. When

---

[9]It's possible to develop a more general, and substantially more complex, geometric analysis based on the singular-value decomposition of **A** that covers both symmetric positive-definite and positive-semidefinite matrices **A**; see Friendly, Monette, and Fox (2013, Appendix).

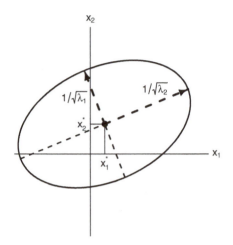

Figure 2.4 Ellipse translated from the origin to center $\mathbf{x}^* = [x_1^*, x_2^*]'$,
generated by the Equation $(\mathbf{x} - \mathbf{x}^*)'\mathbf{A}(\mathbf{x} - \mathbf{x}^*) = 1$. As before,
the lengths of the major and minor radii are given respectively
by $1/\sqrt{\lambda_2}$ and $1/\sqrt{\lambda_1}$, where the λ_js are the eigenvalues of
the matrix $\mathbf{A}$.

$p > 3$, the equation defines a *hyperellipsoid* in p-dimensional space, which
of course can't be visualized directly. As in the 2D case, the principal radii of
the (hyper)ellipsoid are the eigenvectors of $\mathbf{A}$, scaled by the inverse square
roots of the corresponding eigenvalues. In each of these cases, the volume
or hypervolume of the (hyper)ellipsoid is given by

$$V = \frac{\pi^{p/2}}{\sqrt{\det \mathbf{A}} \times \Gamma(p/2 + 1)}$$

where $\Gamma(\cdot)$ is the gamma function (see Equation 5.3 on page 129). This
equation specializes to the area of the ellipse in the 2D case (Equation 2.11).

If $\mathbf{A}$ is positive-semidefinite, then its degenerate inverse ellipsoid or hyperellipsoid is "flattened" and of dimension equal to the rank of $\mathbf{A}$. For example,
if $p = 3$ and $\text{rank}(\mathbf{A}) = 2$, then its degenerate inverse ellipsoid is a 2D elliptical "disk" in the 3D coordinate space; if $\text{rank}(\mathbf{A}) = 1$, then the inverse
ellipsoid collapses to a 1D line segment in the 3D coordinate space.

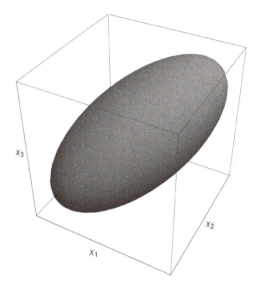

Figure 2.5 Illustrative ellipsoid generated by the equation $\mathbf{x}'\mathbf{A}\mathbf{x} = 1$ for a positive-definite matrix $\underset{(3\times3)}{\mathbf{A}}$.

2.2.2 The Cholesky Decomposition

Every $(n \times n)$ symmetric positive-definite matrix $\mathbf{A}$ can be factored uniquely as $\mathbf{A} = \mathbf{U}'\mathbf{U}$, where $\mathbf{U}$ is an upper-triangular matrix with positive diagonal elements. The matrix $\mathbf{U}$, called the *Cholesky factor* of $\mathbf{A}$, may be thought of as a kind of matrix square root (though not in the sense developed in Section 1.1.2). The Cholesky factor is named after the 19th-century French mathematician André-Louis Cholesky.

Consider, for example, the (3×3) matrix

$$\mathbf{A} = \begin{bmatrix} 1.0 & 0.5 & 0.3 \\ 0.5 & 1.0 & 0.5 \\ 0.3 & 0.5 & 1.0 \end{bmatrix}$$

and let

$$\mathbf{U} = \begin{bmatrix} u_{11} & u_{12} & u_{13} \\ 0 & u_{22} & u_{23} \\ 0 & 0 & u_{33} \end{bmatrix}$$

represent the Cholesky factor of **A**. Then,

$$\mathbf{U}'\mathbf{U} = \begin{bmatrix} u_{11}^2 & u_{11}u_{12} & u_{11}u_{13} \\ u_{12}u_{11} & u_{12}^2 + u_{22}^2 & u_{12}u_{13} + u_{22}u_{23} \\ u_{13}u_{11} & u_{13}u_{12} + u_{23}u_{22} & u_{13}^2 + u_{23}^2 + u_{33}^2 \end{bmatrix}$$

$$= \begin{bmatrix} 1.0 & 0.5 & 0.3 \\ 0.5 & 1.0 & 0.5 \\ 0.3 & 0.5 & 1.0 \end{bmatrix} = \mathbf{A}$$

from which

$$u_{11}^2 = 1.0 \Longrightarrow u_{11} = 1.0$$

$$u_{12}u_{11} = u_{12} \times 1 = 0.5 \Longrightarrow u_{12} = 0.5$$

$$u_{12}^2 + u_{22}^2 = 0.5^2 + u_{22}^2 = 1 \Longrightarrow u_{22} = \sqrt{1 - 0.5^2}$$
$$= 0.8660$$

$$u_{13}u_{11} = u_{13} \times 1 = 0.3 \Longrightarrow u_{13} = 0.3$$

$$u_{13}u_{12} + u_{23}u_{22} = 0.3 \times 0.5 + u_{23} \times 0.8660 = 0.5 \Longrightarrow$$
$$u_{23} = (0.5 - 0.3 \times 0.5)/0.8660 = 0.4041$$

$$u_{13}^2 + u_{23}^2 + u_{33}^2 = 0.3^2 + 0.4141^2 + u_{33}^2 = 1 \Longrightarrow$$
$$u_{33} = \sqrt{1 - 0.3^2 - 0.4041^2} = 0.8641$$

and thus

$$\mathbf{U} = \begin{bmatrix} 1.0 & 0.5 & 0.3 \\ 0 & 0.8660 & 0.4041 \\ 0 & 0 & 0.8641 \end{bmatrix}$$

This procedure can be extended to symmetric positive-definite matrices of any order.[10]

2.3   The QR Decomposition

Yet another matrix decomposition, the *QR decomposition*, is useful for a variety of computational problems, including finding eigenvalues and eigenvectors (see below) and for the numerically stable solution of least-squares

---

[10]It is also possible to find the Cholesky factor of a symmetric positive-semidefinite matrix, but then one or more diagonal elements of **U** will be 0, along with the other entries in the corresponding row or rows. In addition, we must take positive square roots in solving for the diagonal entries of **U**.

problems (discussed in Section 7.1.1). The QR decomposition, applicable both to square and, more generally, to rectangular matrices, expresses a target matrix $\mathbf{X}$ as the product of two matrices, $\mathbf{Q}$ and $\mathbf{R}$.

Suppose that $\mathbf{X}$ is of order $(m \times n)$ and of rank r. Then the left-hand factor $\mathbf{Q}$ is also of order $(m \times n)$, and r of its columns are orthogonal, are each of length 1, and are constructed to span the column space of $\mathbf{X}$, thus providing an orthonormal basis for this space. The remaining $n - r$ columns of $\mathbf{Q}$ (if $r < n$) consist of 0s. The right-hand factor $\mathbf{R}$ is $(n \times n)$ and upper-triangular; if $r < n$, then the $n - r$ rows of $\mathbf{R}$ corresponding to the zero columns of $\mathbf{Q}$ also consist of 0s, but the other r diagonal elements of $\mathbf{Q}$ are nonzero. Both $\mathbf{Q}$ and $\mathbf{R}$ are thus of rank r.

I'll explain how to compute the QR decomposition by *Gram–Schmidt orthogonalization*, named after the Danish mathematician Jørgen Pedersen Gram (1850–1916) and the German mathematician Erhard Schmidt (1876–1959). There are more numerically stable ways to calculate the QR decomposition, but, as will become clear, the Gram–Schmidt method has an obvious rationale.

Recall the orthogonal projection $\widehat{\mathbf{y}}$ of a vector $\mathbf{y}$ onto the subspace (i.e., the line) spanned by another vector $\mathbf{x}$, as depicted in Figure 1.9 (on page 27). The vectors $\mathbf{x}$ and $\mathbf{y} - \widehat{\mathbf{y}}$ by construction form an orthogonal basis for the space spanned by $\mathbf{x}$ and $\mathbf{y}$. We can transform the vectors $\mathbf{x}$ and $\mathbf{y} - \widehat{\mathbf{y}}$ into an orthonormal basis by dividing each by its length.

Now let's more generally consider the $(m \times n)$ matrix $\mathbf{X}$ as a collection of n column vectors, $[\mathbf{x}_1, \mathbf{x}_2, \ldots, \mathbf{x}_n]$.

- Select $\mathbf{v}_1 = \mathbf{x}_1$ as the first basis vector.[11]

- Next find the orthogonal projection of $\mathbf{x}_2$ onto $\mathbf{v}_1$,

$$\widehat{\mathbf{x}}_2 = \frac{\mathbf{v}_1 \cdot \mathbf{x}_2}{||\mathbf{v}_1||^2} \mathbf{v}_1$$

  and take $\mathbf{v}_2 = \mathbf{x}_2 - \widehat{\mathbf{x}}_2$, which is by construction orthogonal to $\mathbf{v}_1$, as the second basis vector.

- If $\mathbf{X}$ has a third column, find its orthogonal projection onto the subspace spanned by first two basis vectors; the computation is simple because the first two basis vectors are orthogonal to each other:

$$\widehat{\mathbf{x}}_3 = \frac{\mathbf{v}_1 \cdot \mathbf{x}_3}{||\mathbf{v}_1||^2} \mathbf{v}_1 + \frac{\mathbf{v}_2 \cdot \mathbf{x}_3}{||\mathbf{v}_2||^2} \mathbf{v}_2$$

---

[11]This step assumes that $\mathbf{x}_1$ is nonzero; if $\mathbf{x}_1 = \mathbf{0}$, then we'd move on to the second column of $\mathbf{X}$. The same is true of subsequent steps.

and take $\mathbf{v}_3 = \mathbf{x}_3 - \widehat{\mathbf{x}}_3$, which is orthogonal both to $\mathbf{v}_1$ and to $\mathbf{v}_2$, as the third basis vector.

- If $n > 3$, continue in this manner for $j = 4, \ldots, n$, in each case projecting $\mathbf{x}_j$ onto the preceding basis vectors, $\mathbf{v}_1, \ldots, \mathbf{v}_{j-1}$, to produce $\mathbf{v}_j = \mathbf{x}_j - \widehat{\mathbf{x}}_j$. If $r = \text{rank}(\mathbf{X}) < n$, then $n - r$ of the resulting "basis" vectors will be $\mathbf{0}$.

- Convert the nonzero basis vectors into an orthonormal basis by dividing each by its length, $\mathbf{q}_j = \mathbf{v}_j / ||\mathbf{v}_j||, j = 1, \ldots, r$. The $\mathbf{Q}$ matrix is $[\mathbf{q}_1, \ldots, \mathbf{q}_n]$, with the last $n - r$ columns equal to $\mathbf{0}$.[12]

Suppose for the moment that $\mathbf{X}$ is of full-column rank m, so that $\mathbf{Q}$ is an orthonormal matrix, $\mathbf{Q}'\mathbf{Q} = \mathbf{I}_m$. Then solving the matrix equation $\mathbf{X} = \mathbf{QR}$ produces the upper triangular matrix

$$\mathbf{R} = \mathbf{Q}^{-1}\mathbf{X} = \mathbf{Q}'\mathbf{X} \qquad (2.13)$$

$\mathbf{R} = \mathbf{Q}'\mathbf{X}$ works even when $\mathbf{X}$ is of rank $r < n$.

To illustrate, consider the matrix

$$\mathop{\mathbf{X}}_{(4\times3)} = \begin{bmatrix} 1 & 1 & 2 \\ 1 & 1 & 4 \\ 1 & 0 & 6 \\ 1 & 0 & 8 \end{bmatrix}$$

Applying the Gram–Schmidt method:

1. Set $\mathbf{v}_1 = (1, 1, 1, 1)'$.

2. Compute

$$\begin{aligned} \widehat{\mathbf{x}}_2 &= \frac{\mathbf{v}_1 \cdot \mathbf{x}_2}{||\mathbf{v}_1||^2} \mathbf{v}_1 \\ &= \frac{2}{4}(1, 1, 1, 1)' \\ &= (\tfrac{1}{2}, \tfrac{1}{2}, \tfrac{1}{2}, \tfrac{1}{2})' \\ \mathbf{v}_2 &= \mathbf{x}_2 - \widehat{\mathbf{x}}_2 \\ &= (1, 1, 0, 0)' - (\tfrac{1}{2}, \tfrac{1}{2}, \tfrac{1}{2}, \tfrac{1}{2})' \\ &= (\tfrac{1}{2}, \tfrac{1}{2}, -\tfrac{1}{2}, -\tfrac{1}{2})' \end{aligned}$$

---

[12] For notational simplicity here, I assume that the nonzero basis vectors are the first r, but this need not be the case.

3. Compute

$$
\begin{aligned}
\widehat{\mathbf{x}}_3 &= \frac{\mathbf{v}_1 \cdot \mathbf{x}_3}{||\mathbf{v}_1||^2}\mathbf{v}_1 + \frac{\mathbf{v}_2 \cdot \mathbf{x}_3}{||\mathbf{v}_2||^2}\mathbf{v}_2 \\
&= \frac{20}{4}(1,1,1,4)' + \frac{-4}{1}(\tfrac{1}{2},\tfrac{1}{2},-\tfrac{1}{2},-\tfrac{1}{2})' \\
&= (3,3,7,7)' \\
\mathbf{v}_3 &= \mathbf{x}_3 - \widehat{\mathbf{x}}_3 \\
&= (2,4,6,8)' - (3,3,7,7)' \\
&= (-1,1,-1,1)'
\end{aligned}
$$

These steps create an orthogonal basis for the column space of $\mathbf{X}$:

$$
\mathbf{V} = [\mathbf{v}_1, \mathbf{v}_2, \mathbf{v}_3] = \begin{bmatrix} 1 & \tfrac{1}{2} & -1 \\ 1 & \tfrac{1}{2} & 1 \\ 1 & -\tfrac{1}{2} & -1 \\ 1 & -\tfrac{1}{2} & 1 \end{bmatrix}
$$

To construct an orthonormal basis, we must divide each column of $\mathbf{V}$ by its length, $||\mathbf{v}_1|| = \sqrt{4} = 2$, $||\mathbf{v}_2|| = \sqrt{1} = 1$, and $||\mathbf{v}_3|| = \sqrt{4} = 2$, producing

$$
\mathbf{Q} = \begin{bmatrix} \tfrac{1}{2} & \tfrac{1}{2} & -\tfrac{1}{2} \\ \tfrac{1}{2} & \tfrac{1}{2} & \tfrac{1}{2} \\ \tfrac{1}{2} & -\tfrac{1}{2} & -\tfrac{1}{2} \\ \tfrac{1}{2} & -\tfrac{1}{2} & \tfrac{1}{2} \end{bmatrix}
$$

Finally, using Equation 2.13,

$$
\begin{aligned}
\mathbf{R} &= \mathbf{Q}'\mathbf{X} \\
&= \begin{bmatrix} \tfrac{1}{2} & \tfrac{1}{2} & -\tfrac{1}{2} \\ \tfrac{1}{2} & \tfrac{1}{2} & \tfrac{1}{2} \\ \tfrac{1}{2} & -\tfrac{1}{2} & -\tfrac{1}{2} \\ \tfrac{1}{2} & -\tfrac{1}{2} & \tfrac{1}{2} \end{bmatrix}' \begin{bmatrix} 1 & 1 & 2 \\ 1 & 1 & 4 \\ 1 & 0 & 6 \\ 1 & 0 & 8 \end{bmatrix} \\
&= \begin{bmatrix} 2 & 1 & 10 \\ 0 & 1 & -4 \\ 0 & 0 & 2 \end{bmatrix}
\end{aligned}
$$

The reader can verify that $\mathbf{X} = \mathbf{QR}$, as advertised.

2.3.1 Using the QR Decomposition to Compute Eigenvalues and Eigenvectors

One application of the QR decomposition, called the *QR algorithm* and due to Francis (1961, 1962), simultaneously computes approximate eigenvalues and eigenvectors of a square matrix of any order, including singular matrices and asymmetric square matrices with real eigenvalues. Francis's method is iterative (i.e., repetitive) and provides successively more accurate results as the iterations proceed. I'll describe a simple version of the QR algorithm; there are variations that are more computationally efficient and more general, but they are also more complicated.

1. We want to find the eigenvalues and eigenvectors of an order-n square matrix $\mathbf{A}$. To start, set the initial values $\underset{(n \times n)}{\mathbf{\Lambda}^{(0)}} = \mathbf{A}$ and $\underset{(n \times n)}{\mathbf{X}^{(0)}} = \mathbf{I}_n$. Eventually $\mathbf{\Lambda}$ will become a diagonal matrix whose diagonal elements are the eigenvalues of $\mathbf{A}$ and the successive columns of $\mathbf{X}$ will contain the corresponding normalized eigenvectors.

2. At each iteration t, compute

$$\mathbf{\Lambda}^{(t)} = \mathbf{R}^{(t-1)}\mathbf{Q}^{(t-1)}$$
$$\mathbf{X}^{(t)} = \mathbf{X}^{(t-1)}\mathbf{Q}^{(t-1)}$$

where $\mathbf{Q}^{(t-1)}$ and $\mathbf{R}^{(t-1)}$ are respectively the Q and R components of the QR decomposition of $\mathbf{\Lambda}^{(t-1)}$.

3. Repeat Step 2 until the off-diagonal elements of $\mathbf{\Lambda}^{(t)}$ are within rounding error of zero.[13]

Applied to the matrix

$$\mathbf{A} = \begin{bmatrix} 1 & 0.5 \\ 0.5 & 1 \end{bmatrix}$$

used previously in the chapter (page 44) to illustrate the computation of eigenvalues and eigenvectors, the QR algorithm produces results accurate to five decimal places in 12 iterations.

---

[13] It's not at all obvious why repeatedly multiplying its Q and R components in the reverse order should serve to diagonalize $\mathbf{\Lambda}$, producing the eigenvalues of $\mathbf{A}$, nor why $\mathbf{X}$ ends up containing the eigenvectors. The explanation isn't simple and is provided by Francis (1961, 1962).

CHAPTER 3. AN INTRODUCTION TO CALCULUS

What is now called *calculus* deals with two basic types of problems: finding the slopes of tangent lines to curves (*differential calculus*) and evaluating areas under curves (*integral calculus*). In the 17th century, the English physicist and mathematician Sir Isaac Newton (1643–1727) and the German philosopher and mathematician Gottfried Wilhelm Leibniz (1646–1716) independently demonstrated the relationship between these two kinds of problems, consolidating and extending previous work in mathematics dating to the classical period. Newton and Leibniz are generally acknowledged as the cofounders of calculus.[1] In the 19th century, the great French mathematician Augustin Louis Cauchy (1789–1857), among others, employed the concept of the limit of a function to provide a rigorous logical foundation for calculus.

After a review of some elementary mathematics—numbers, equations and graphs of lines and planes, polynomial functions, logarithms, exponentials, and basic trigonometric functions—I will briefly take up the following seminal topics in calculus in successive sections of this chapter, emphasizing basic concepts: limits of functions; the derivative of a function; the application of derivatives to optimization problems; partial derivatives of functions of several variables, constrained optimization, differential calculus in matrix form, and numerical optimization; Taylor series expansions and approximations; and the essential ideas of integral calculus.

Although a thorough and rigorous treatment is well beyond the scope of this brief book, one can get a lot of mileage out of an intuitive grounding in the fundamental ideas of calculus, along with a few essential results and basic techniques.

3.1 Review

3.1.1 Numbers

The definition of various sets of numbers is a relatively deep topic in mathematics, but the following rough distinctions will be sufficient for our purposes:

---

[1]Newton's claim that Leibniz had appropriated his work touched off one of the most famous priority disputes in the history of science.

- The *natural numbers* include zero and the positive whole numbers: $0, 1, 2, 3, \ldots$[2]

- The *integers* include all negative and positive whole numbers and zero:
$$\ldots, -3, -2, -1, 0, 1, 2, 3, \ldots$$

- The *rational numbers* consist of all numbers that can be written as ratios of two integers, $\frac{n}{m}$ with $m \neq 0$, including all of the integers and nonintegers such as $-\frac{1}{2}$ and $\frac{123}{4}$.

- The *real numbers* include all of the rational numbers along with the *irrational numbers*, such as $\sqrt{2} \approx 1.41421$ and the mathematical constants $\pi \approx 3.14159$ and $e \approx 2.71828$,[3] which cannot be written precisely as the ratio of two integers. The real numbers can be mapped into signed distances (negative to the left of zero, positive to the right) along a continuous line from $-\infty$ to $+\infty$.

- The *complex numbers* are of the form $a + bi$, where a and b are real numbers, and where $i \equiv \sqrt{-1}$. The complex numbers can be thought of as points (or vectors) in a plane: The real component a of the number gives the horizontal coordinate of the point (or tip of the vector), and the coefficient b of the "imaginary" component bi gives its vertical coordinate. The complex numbers include the real numbers (for which $b = 0$). Although complex numbers have occasional applications in statistics, I'll develop calculus in this chapter for real-valued functions of real variables.

3.1.2   Lines and Planes

A *straight line* has the equation

$$y = a + bx$$

where a and b are constants. The constant a is the *y-intercept* of the line, that is, the value of y associated with $x = 0$; and b is the *slope* of the line, that is, the change in y when x is increased by one: See Figure 3.1, which shows

---

[2] In some areas of mathematics, the natural numbers include only the positive whole numbers.

[3] The constant e is named in honor of the great 18th century Swiss mathematician Leonhard Euler, and is sometimes called *Euler's constant*.

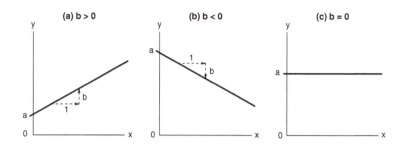

Figure 3.1   The graph in two-dimensional space of a straight line with
equation $y = a + bx$, for (a) $b > 0$, (b) $b < 0$, and (c) $b = 0$.

straight lines in the 2D coordinate space with axes x and y;[4] in each case, the
line extends infinitely to the left and right beyond the line-segment shown in
the graph. When the slope is positive, $b > 0$, the line runs from lower left to
upper right; when the slope is negative, $b < 0$, the line runs from upper left
to lower right; and when $b = 0$, the line is horizontal.

Similarly, the *linear equation*

$$y = a + b_1 x_1 + b_2 x_2$$

represents a flat *plane* in the 3D space with axes x_1, x_2, and y, as illustrated
in the 3D graph in Figure 3.2; the axes are at right angles to each other, so
think of the x_2 axis as extending directly into the page. The plane extends
infinitely in all directions beyond the lines on its surface shown in the graph.
The y-intercept of the plane, a, is the value of y when both x_1 and x_2 are zero;
b_1 represents the slope of the plane in the direction of x_1 for a fixed value
of x_2 (i.e., the change in y produced by a one-unit increase in x_1 holding x_2
constant); and b_2 represents the slope of the plane in the direction of x_2 for
a fixed value of x_1.

The equation of a straight line can be written in other forms, including

$$cx + dy = f$$

---

[4]The fundamental idea behind analytic geometry, that algebraic equations can be represented
geometrically—and that geometric figures have algebraic representations—is due to the 17th-
century French philosopher and mathematician Réne Descartes; consequently a rectilinear coordinate space is often called a *Cartesian coordinate space*.

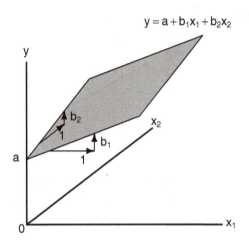

Figure 3.2   The graph in three-dimensional space of a plane with
equation $y = a + b_1x_1 + b_2x_2$. Here, the intercept a and both
slopes, b_1 and b_2, are positive.

(where $d \neq 0$), which can be transformed into slope–intercept form as

$$y = \frac{f}{d} - \frac{c}{d}x$$

Likewise, the equation

$$c_1x_1 + c_2x_2 + dy = f$$

represents a plane,

$$y = \frac{f}{d} - \frac{c_1}{d}x_1 - \frac{c_2}{d}x_2$$

3.1.3 Polynomials

Polynomials are functions of the form

$$y = a_0 + a_1x + a_2x^2 + \cdots + a_px^p$$

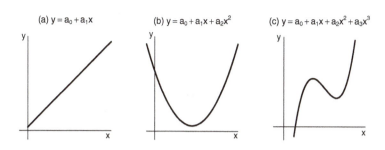

Figure 3.3 Graphs of "typical" (a) first-degree (linear), (b) second-degree (quadratic), and (c) third-degree (cubic) polynomials.

where $a_0, a_1, a_2, \ldots, a_p$ are constants, some of which (with the exception of a_p) may be zero, and the exponents, 1 (which is present implicitly in the term $a_1 x$), $2, \ldots, p$, are successive positive integers. The largest exponent, p, is called the *degree* of the polynomial. In particular, and as illustrated in Figure 3.3(a), a first-degree polynomial is a straight line,

$$y = a_0 + a_1 x$$

a second-degree polynomial is a *quadratic equation*,

$$y = a_0 + a_1 x + a_2 x^2$$

and a third-degree polynomial is a *cubic equation*,

$$y = a_0 + a_1 x + a_2 x^2 + a_3 x^3$$

A polynomial equation of degree p can have up to $p - 1$ "bends" in it, such as the single bend (change of direction) in the quadratic function in Figure 3.3(b) and the two bends in the cubic function in Figure 3.3(c).

3.1.4 Logarithms and Exponentials

Logarithms ("*logs*") are exponents: The expression

$$\log_b x = y$$

which is read as "the log of x to the base b is y," means that

$$x = b^y$$

where $x > 0$, y, and $b > 0$, $b \neq 1$ are real numbers. Thus, for example,

$$\log_{10} 10 = 1 \text{ because } 10^1 = 10$$
$$\log_{10} 100 = 2 \text{ because } 10^2 = 100$$
$$\log_{10} 1 = 0 \text{ because } 10^0 = 1$$
$$\log_{10} 0.1 = -1 \text{ because } 10^{-1} = 0.1$$

and, similarly,

$$\log_2 2 = 1 \text{ because } 2^1 = 2$$
$$\log_2 4 = 2 \text{ because } 2^2 = 4$$
$$\log_2 1 = 0 \text{ because } 2^0 = 1$$
$$\log_2 \tfrac{1}{4} = -2 \text{ because } 2^{-2} = \tfrac{1}{4}$$

Indeed, the log of 1 to any base is 0, because $b^0 = 1$ for any number $b \neq 0$. As noted, logs are defined only for positive numbers x. The most commonly used base for logarithms in mathematics is the base $e \approx 2.71828$; logs to the base e are called *natural logs*.[5] (For a justification of this terminology, see Section 3.3.4.) Other bases may be useful in data analysis because they facilitate interpretation when a variable is transformed by taking logs (e.g., to correct a positive skew or to linearize a regression). For example, increasing $\log_2 x$ by 1 is equivalent to doubling x; similarly, increasing $\log_{10} x$ by 1 increases x by an *order of magnitude* (i.e., a factor of 10).

A "typical" log function is graphed in Figure 3.4. As the graph implies, log functions have the same basic shape regardless of the base, and converting from one base, say b, to another, say a, simply involves multiplication by a constant:

$$\log_a x = \log_a b \times \log_b x = c \log_b x$$

For example,

$$\log_{10} 1000 = 3 = \log_{10} 2 \times \log_2 1000 \approx 0.301030 \times 9.965784$$

Logs inherit their properties from the properties of exponents: Because $b^{x_1} b^{x_2} = b^{x_1 + x_2}$, it follows that

$$\log(x_1 x_2) = \log x_1 + \log x_2$$

---

[5] Although I prefer always to show the base of the log function explicitly, as in $\log_{10}$ or $\log_e$ (unless the base is irrelevant, in which case log will do), many authors use unsubscripted log or ln to represent natural logs.

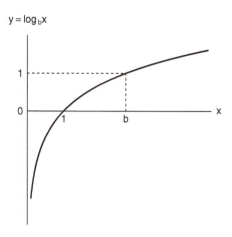

Figure 3.4 Graph of the log function $y = \log_b x$.

Similarly, because $b^{x_1}/b^{x_2} = b^{x_1 - x_2}$,

$$\log\left(\frac{x_1}{x_2}\right) = \log x_1 - \log x_2$$

and because $b^{ax} = (b^x)^a$,

$$\log(x^a) = a\log x$$

At one time, the conversion of multiplication into addition, division into subtraction, and exponentiation into multiplication simplified laborious computations. Although this motivation has faded, logs still play a prominent role in mathematics and statistics.

An *exponential function* is a function of the form

$$y = a^x$$

where $a > 0$ is a constant. The most common exponential, $y = \exp(x) = e^x$, is graphed in Figure 3.5. The log and exponential functions are inverses of each other, in the sense that $\log_a(a^x) = x$ and $a^{\log_a x} = x$.

3.1.5   Basic Trigonometric Functions

Figure 3.6 shows a *unit circle*—that is, a circle of radius 1 centered at the origin, the point $(0,0)$. The angle x produces a right triangle inscribed in

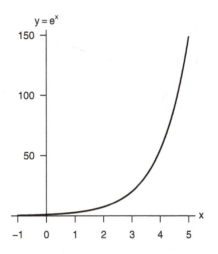

Figure 3.5   Graph of the exponential function $y = e^x$.

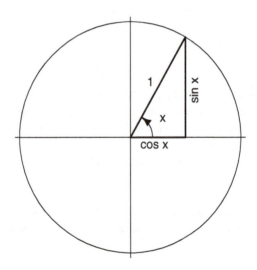

Figure 3.6   A unit circle, showing the angle x and its cosine and sine.

the circle; the angle is measured in a counterclockwise direction from the horizontal axis. The *cosine* of the angle x, denoted $\cos x$, is the signed length of the side of the triangle adjacent to the angle (i.e., "adjacent/hypotenuse," where the hypotenuse is one because it is a radius of the unit circle)[6]; the *sine* of the angle x, denoted $\sin x$, is the signed length of the side of the triangle opposite the angle (i.e., "opposite/hypotenuse"); and the *tangent* of x, $\tan x = \sin x / \cos x$, is the ratio of the signed length of the side opposite to the side adjacent to the right angle ("opposite/adjacent"). The cosine, sine, and tangent functions for angles between $-360°$ and $360°$ are shown in Figure 3.7; negative angles represent clockwise rotations. The tangent function approaches $\pm\infty$ at angles of $\pm 90°$ and $\pm 270°$. As is apparent from their graphs, the sine and cosine functions have the same shape, with $\sin x = \cos(x - 90)$.

It is sometimes mathematically convenient to measure angles in *radians* rather than in degrees, with 2π radians corresponding to 360 degrees. The circumference of the unit circle in Figure 3.6 is also 2π, and therefore, the radian measure of an angle represents the length of the arc along the unit circle subtended by the angle.

3.2 Limits

Calculus deals with *functions* of the form $y = f(x)$. I will consider the case where both the *domain* (values of the *independent variable x*) and the *range* (values of the *dependent variable y*) of the function are real numbers. The *limit* of a function concerns its behavior when x is near, but not necessarily equal to, a specific value. This is often a useful idea, especially when a function is undefined at a particular value of x, for example, because of division by zero at that x-value.

3.2.1 The "Epsilon–Delta" Definition of a Limit

A function $y = f(x)$ has a limit L at $x = x_0$ (i.e., at a particular value of x) if for any positive *tolerance ε*, no matter how small, there exists a positive number δ such that the distance between $f(x)$ and L is less than the tolerance as long as the distance between x and x_0 is smaller than δ—that is, as long

---

[6] *Signed length* takes direction into account: Points on the horizontal axis, to the right of the origin, mark off positive signed lengths (and represent positive cosines), and those to the left mark off negative signed lengths (and represent negative cosines). The same idea applies to sines, but now direction refers to the vertical axis, and thus points above the origin mark of positive lengths (positive sines) and those below mark of negative lengths (negative sines).

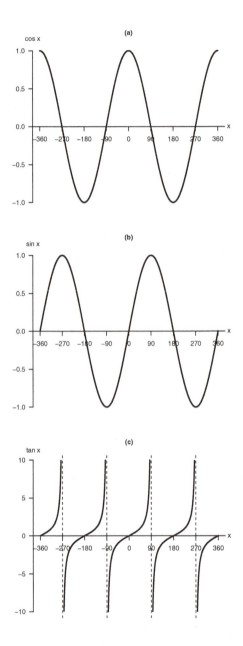

Figure 3.7 The (a) cosine, (b) sine, and (c) tangent functions for angles between $x = -360°$ and $x = 360°$. The scale on the vertical axis of the graph of the tangent function (which goes off to $-\infty$ and $+\infty$) is different from those for the sine and cosine functions (which are confined between -1 and $+1$).

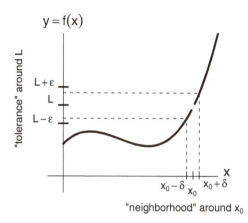

Figure 3.8 $\lim_{x \to x_0} f(x) = L$: The limit of the function $f(x)$ as x approaches x_0 is L. The gap in the curve above x_0 is meant to suggest that the function is undefined at $x = x_0$. If the function is only undefined exactly at x_0, then the gap is infinitesimally small and hence would be invisible.

as x is confined to a sufficiently small *neighborhood* of width 2δ around x_0. In symbols:

$$|f(x) - L| < \varepsilon$$

for all

$$0 < |x - x_0| < \delta$$

This possibly cryptic definition is clarified by Figure 3.8. The value of the function at x_0, that is, $f(x_0)$, need not equal L. Indeed, limits are often most useful when $f(x)$ does not exist at $x = x_0$. For L to be the limit of $f(x)$ at $x = x_0$, the function must approach this value as x approaches x_0 *both* from the left and from the right.

The following notation is used:

$$\lim_{x \to x_0} f(x) = L$$

We read this expression as, "The limit of the function $f(x)$ as x approaches x_0 is L."

3.2.2   Finding a Limit: An Example

Find the limit of

$$y = f(x) = \frac{x^2 - 1}{x - 1}$$

at $x_0 = 1$.

Notice that $f(1) = \dfrac{1^2 - 1}{1 - 1} = \dfrac{0}{0}$ is undefined. Nevertheless, as long as x is not *exactly* equal to 1, even if it is very close to it, we can divide by $x - 1$:

$$y = \frac{x^2 - 1}{x - 1} = \frac{(x+1)(x-1)}{x-1} = x + 1$$

Moreover, because $x_0 + 1 = 1 + 1 = 2$,[7]

$$
\begin{aligned}
\lim_{x \to 1} \frac{x^2 - 1}{x - 1} &= \lim_{x \to 1}(x + 1) \\
&= \lim_{x \to 1} x + \lim_{x \to 1} 1 \\
&= 1 + 1 = 2
\end{aligned}
$$

This limit is graphed in Figure 3.9.

3.2.3   Rules for Manipulating Limits

Suppose that we have two functions $f(x)$ and $g(x)$ of an independent variable x, and that each function has a limit at $x = x_0$:

$$\lim_{x \to x_0} f(x) = a$$

$$\lim_{x \to x_0} g(x) = b$$

Then the limits of functions composed from $f(x)$ and $g(x)$ by the arithmetic operations of addition, subtraction, multiplication, and division are straightforward:

$$\lim_{x \to x_0} [f(x) + g(x)] = a + b$$

$$\lim_{x \to x_0} [f(x) - g(x)] = a - b$$

$$\lim_{x \to x_0} [f(x)g(x)] = ab$$

$$\lim_{x \to x_0} [f(x)/g(x)] = a/b$$

---

[7]This result is justified by the rules for limits described immediately below.

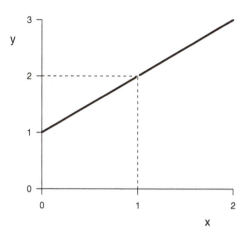

Figure 3.9 $\lim_{x \to 1} \frac{x^2-1}{x-1} = 2$, even though the function is undefined at $x = 1$.

The last result holds as long as the denominator $b \neq 0$.

Similarly, if c and n are constants and $\lim_{x \to x_0} f(x) = a$, then

$$\lim_{x \to x_0} c = c$$

$$\lim_{x \to x_0} [cf(x)] = ca$$

$$\lim_{x \to x_0} \{[f(x)]^n\} = a^n$$

Finally, it is (I hope) obvious that

$$\lim_{x \to x_0} x = x_0$$

3.3 The Derivative of a Function

Now consider a function $y = f(x)$ evaluated at two values of x:

$$\text{at } x_1: \quad y_1 = f(x_1)$$
$$\text{at } x_2: \quad y_2 = f(x_2)$$

The *difference quotient* is defined as the change in y divided by the change in x, as we move from the point (x_1, y_1) to the point (x_2, y_2):

$$\frac{y_2 - y_1}{x_2 - x_1} = \frac{\Delta y}{\Delta x} = \frac{f(x_2) - f(x_1)}{x_2 - x_1}$$

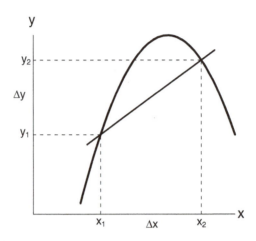

Figure 3.10   The difference quotient $\Delta y/\Delta x$ is the slope of the secant line connecting (x_1, y_1) and (x_2, y_2).

where Δ ("delta") is a shorthand denoting "change." As illustrated in Figure 3.10, the difference quotient is the slope of the *secant line* connecting the points (x_1, y_1) and (x_2, y_2).

The *derivative* of the function $f(x)$ at $x = x_1$ (so named because it is *derived* from the original function) is the limit of the difference quotient $\Delta y/\Delta x$ as x_2 approaches x_1 (i.e., as $\Delta x \to 0$):

$$\frac{dy}{dx} = \lim_{x_2 \to x_1} \frac{f(x_2) - f(x_1)}{x_2 - x_1}$$
$$= \lim_{\Delta x \to 0} \frac{f(x_1 + \Delta x) - f(x_1)}{\Delta x}$$
$$= \lim_{\Delta x \to 0} \frac{\Delta y}{\Delta x}$$

The derivative is therefore the slope of the *tangent line* to the curve $f(x)$ at $x = x_1$, as shown in Figure 3.11.

The following alternative notation is often used for the derivative:[8]

$$\frac{dy}{dx} = \frac{df(x)}{dx} = f'(x)$$

---

[8]The notation dy/dx for the derivative is due to Leibniz, while Newton introduced the "overdot" notation $\dot{y}$, which is still common in some applications in physics, particularly for derivatives with respect to time.

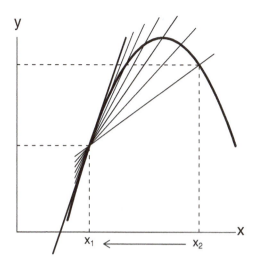

Figure 3.11   The derivative is the slope of the tangent line (the heavier solid straight line) at $f(x_1)$. As $x_2 \to x_1$, the secant line (the lighter straight lines) approaches the tangent line.

The last form, $f'(x)$, emphasizes that the derivative is itself a function of x, but the notation employing the *differentials dy* and *dx*, which may be thought of as infinitesimally small values that are nevertheless nonzero, can be productive: In many circumstances, the differentials can be manipulated as if they were numbers.[9] The operation of finding the derivative of a function is called *differentiation*.

3.3.1   The Derivative as the Limit of the Difference Quotient: An Example

Given the function $y = f(x) = x^2$, find the derivative $f'(x)$ for any value of x.

---

[9]See, for example, the "chain rule" for differentiation, introduced on page 78.

Applying the definition of the derivative as the limit of the difference quotient,

$$f'(x) = \lim_{\Delta x \to 0} \frac{f(x+\Delta x) - f(x)}{\Delta x}$$

$$= \lim_{\Delta x \to 0} \frac{(x+\Delta x)^2 - x^2}{\Delta x}$$

$$= \lim_{\Delta x \to 0} \frac{x^2 + 2x\Delta x + (\Delta x)^2 - x^2}{\Delta x}$$

$$= \lim_{\Delta x \to 0} \frac{2x\Delta x + (\Delta x)^2}{\Delta x}$$

$$= \lim_{\Delta x \to 0} (2x + \Delta x)$$

$$= \lim_{\Delta x \to 0} 2x + \lim_{\Delta x \to 0} \Delta x$$

$$= 2x + 0 = 2x$$

Division by Δx is justified here, because although Δx *approaches* zero in the limit, it never is *exactly* equal to zero. For example, the slope of the curve $y = f(x) = x^2$ at $x = 3$ is $f'(x) = 2x = 2 \times 3 = 6$.

3.3.2   Derivatives of Powers

More generally, and by similar reasoning, the derivative of

$$y = f(x) = ax^n$$

is

$$\frac{dy}{dx} = nax^{n-1}$$

For example, the derivative of the function

$$y = 3x^6$$

is

$$\frac{dy}{dx} = 6 \times 3x^{6-1} = 18x^5$$

Moreover, this rule applies as well to negative powers and to fractional powers. For example, the derivative of the function

$$y = \frac{1}{4x^3} = \tfrac{1}{4}x^{-3}$$

is

$$\frac{dy}{dx} = -3 \times \tfrac{1}{4}x^{-3-1} = -\tfrac{3}{4}x^{-4} = -\frac{3}{4x^4}$$

and the derivative of the function

$$y = \sqrt{x} = x^{\frac{1}{2}}$$

is

$$\frac{dy}{dx} = \tfrac{1}{2}x^{\frac{1}{2}-1} = \tfrac{1}{2}x^{-\frac{1}{2}} = \frac{1}{2\sqrt{x}}$$

3.3.3 Rules for Manipulating Derivatives

Suppose that a function is the sum of two other functions:

$$h(x) = f(x) + g(x)$$

The *addition rule* for derivatives follows from the addition rule for limits:

$$h'(x) = f'(x) + g'(x)$$

For example,

$$y = 2x^2 + 3x + 4$$
$$\frac{dy}{dx} = 4x + 3 + 0 = 4x + 3$$

The derivative of a constant—the constant four in the last example—is zero, because the constant can be expressed as

$$y = f(x) = 4 = 4x^0 = 4 \times 1$$

This result makes sense geometrically: A constant is represented as a horizontal line in the $\{x, y\}$ plane, and a horizontal line has a slope of zero.

The addition rule, therefore, along with the result that $\frac{d}{dx}ax^n = nax^{n-1}$, serves to differentiate any polynomial function.

Multiplication and division are more complex. The *multiplication rule* for derivatives:

$$h(x) = f(x)g(x)$$
$$h'(x) = f(x)g'(x) + f'(x)g(x)$$

The *division rule* for derivatives:

$$h(x) = f(x)/g(x)$$

$$h'(x) = \frac{g(x)f'(x) - g'(x)f(x)}{[g(x)]^2}$$

For example, the derivative of the function

$$y = (x^2 + 1)(2x^3 - 3x)$$

is

$$\frac{dy}{dx} = (x^2 + 1)(6x^2 - 3) + 2x(2x^3 - 3x)$$

and the derivative of the function

$$y = \frac{x}{x^2 - 3x + 5}$$

is

$$\frac{dy}{dx} = \frac{x^2 - 3x + 5 - (2x - 3)x}{(x^2 - 3x + 5)^2} = \frac{-x^2 + 5}{(x^2 - 3x + 5)^2}$$

The *chain rule*: If $y = f(z)$ and $z = g(x)$, then y is indirectly a function of x:

$$y = f[g(x)] = h(x)$$

The derivative of y with respect to x is

$$h'(x) = \frac{dy}{dx} = \frac{dy}{dz} \times \frac{dz}{dx}$$

as if the differential dz in the numerator and the denominator can be canceled.[10]

For example, given the function

$$y = (x^2 + 3x + 6)^5$$

find the derivative dy/dx of y with respect to x:

This problem could be solved by expanding the power—that is, by multiplying the expression in parentheses by itself five times—but that would be

---

[10]The differentials are not ordinary numbers, so thinking of the chain rule as simultaneously dividing and multiplying by the differential dz is a heuristic device, illustrating how Leibniz's notation for the derivative using differentials proves to be productive.

tedious in the extreme. It is much easier to find the derivative by using the chain rule, introducing a new variable, z, to represent the expression inside the parentheses. Let

$$z = g(x) = x^2 + 3x + 6$$

Then

$$y = f(z) = z^5$$

Differentiating y with respect to z, and z with respect to x, produces

$$\frac{dy}{dz} = 5z^4$$

$$\frac{dz}{dx} = 2x + 3$$

Applying the chain rule,

$$\frac{dy}{dx} = \frac{dy}{dz} \times \frac{dz}{dx}$$
$$= 5z^4(2x + 3)$$

Finally, substituting for z,

$$\frac{dy}{dx} = 5(x^2 + 3x + 6)^4(2x + 3)$$

The use of the chain rule in this example is typical, introducing an "artificial" variable (z) to simplify the structure of the problem.[11]

3.3.4 Derivatives of Logs and Exponentials

Logarithms and exponentials often occur in statistical applications, and so it is useful to know how to differentiate these functions.

The derivative of the log function $y = \log_e(x)$ is

$$\frac{d\log_e x}{dx} = \frac{1}{x} = x^{-1}$$

Recall that $\log_e$ is the *natural-log* function, that is, log to the base $e \approx 2.71828$. The simplicity of its derivative is one of the reasons that it is "natural" to use the base e for the natural logs.[12]

---

[11]We can often apply the chain rule informally, without literally creating a new variable, by thinking of what's inside parentheses as a variable—first differentiating the parentheses as a whole, then differentiating inside the parentheses, and finally multiplying the two derivatives.

[12]It is less common to require the derivative of the log function to another base, say b, but, reader, can you find $d\log_b x/dx$?

The derivative of the exponential function $y = e^x$ is also very simple:

$$\frac{de^x}{dx} = e^x$$

The derivative of the exponential function $y = a^x$ for any constant $a > 0$ (i.e., not necessarily e) is a bit more complicated:

$$\frac{da^x}{dx} = a^x \log_e a$$

3.3.5   Derivatives of the Basic Trigonometric Functions

The derivatives of the basic trigometric functions are as follows, with the angle x measured in radians:

$$\frac{d\cos x}{dx} = -\sin x$$

$$\frac{d\sin x}{dx} = \cos x$$

$$\frac{d\tan x}{dx} = \frac{1}{\cos^2 x} \text{ for } x \neq \pm\frac{\pi}{2}, \pm\frac{3\pi}{2}, \text{etc. (i.e., where } \cos x \neq 0)$$

Here, $\cos^2 x \equiv (\cos x)^2$.

3.3.6   Second-Order and Higher-Order Derivatives

Because derivatives are themselves functions, they can be differentiated. The *second derivative* of the function $y = f(x)$ is therefore defined as

$$f''(x) = \frac{d^2 y}{dx^2} = \frac{df'(x)}{dx}$$

Notice the alternative notation.

Likewise, the *third derivative* of the function $y = f(x)$ is the derivative of the second derivative,

$$f'''(x) = \frac{d^3 y}{dx^3} = \frac{df''(x)}{dx}$$

and so on for *higher-order derivatives*.

For example, the function

$$y = f(x) = 5x^4 + 3x^2 + 6$$

has the successive derivatives

$$f'(x) = 20x^3 + 6x$$
$$f''(x) = 60x^2 + 6$$
$$f'''(x) = 120x$$
$$f''''(x) = 120$$
$$f'''''(x) = 0$$

All derivatives beyond the fifth order are also zero.

3.4 Optimization

An important application of differential calculus, both in statistics and more generally, is to *maximization* and *minimization* problems: that is, finding maximum and minimum values of functions (e.g., *maximum*-likelihood estimation; *least*-squares regression). Such problems are collectively called *optimization*.

As illustrated in Figure 3.12, when a function is at a *relative (local) maximum* or *relative minimum* (i.e., a value higher than or lower than immediately surrounding values) or at an *absolute* or *global maximum* or *minimum* (a value at least as high or as low as all other values of the function), the tangent line to the function is flat, and hence the function has a derivative of zero at that point. A function can also have a zero derivative, however, at a point that is neither a minimum nor a maximum, such as at a *point of inflection*—that is, a point where the direction of curvature changes, as in Figure 3.13. Points at which the derivative is zero are called *stationary points*.

To distinguish among the three cases—minimum, maximum, or neither—we can appeal to the value of the second derivative (see Figure 3.14).

- At a *minimum*, the first derivative $f'(x)$ is changing from negative, through zero, to positive—that is, the first derivative is *increasing*, and therefore the second derivative $f''(x)$ is *positive*: The second derivative indicates change in the first derivative just as the first derivative indicates change in the original function.[13]

---

[13]The original application of derivatives was to the physics of motion, an application that may help illuminate the relationship between the first and second derivatives: Suppose, for example, that x represents time (e.g., in seconds) and that $y = f(x)$ represents the position of an object along a straight line at time x (e.g., in meters)—such as a car in a drag race. Then the derivative

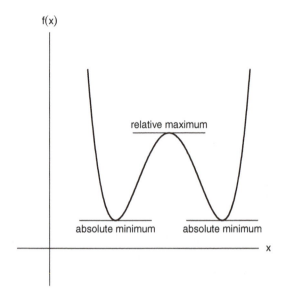

Figure 3.12   The derivative (i.e., the slope) of the function is zero where the function $f(x)$ is at a minimum or maximum.

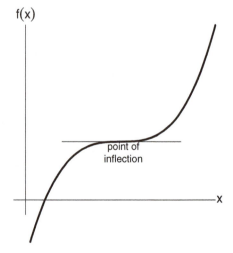

Figure 3.13   The derivative is also zero at a point of inflection in $f(x)$.

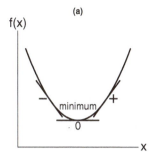
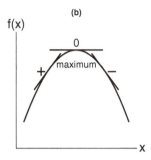

Figure 3.14   The first derivative (the slope of the function) is (a) increasing where the function $f(x)$ is at a minimum and (b) decreasing at a maximum.

- At a *maximum*, the first derivative $f'(x)$ is changing from positive, through zero, to negative—the first derivative is *decreasing*; and therefore, the second derivative $f''(x)$ is *negative*.

- At a *point of inflection*, $f''(x) = 0$.

The relationships among the original function, the first derivative, and the second derivative are illustrated in Figure 3.15: The first derivative dy/dx is zero at the two minima and at the (relative) maximum of $f(x)$; the second derivative d^2y/dx^2 is positive at the two minima, and negative at the maximum of $f(x)$.

3.4.1   Optimization: An Example

Find the *extrema* (minima and maxima) of the function

$$f(x) = 2x^3 - 9x^2 + 12x + 6$$

The function is graphed in Figure 3.16.[14]

$f'(x)$ is the *velocity* of the car (in meters per second) at time x, and the second derivative $f''(x)$ is the *acceleration* of the car, that is, the change in its velocity, at time x (in meters per second per second).

[14]Incidentally, locating stationary points and determining whether they are minima or maxima (or neither) is helpful in graphing functions.

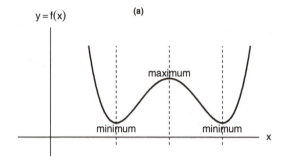

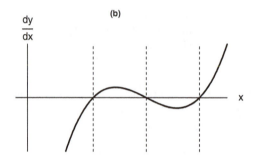

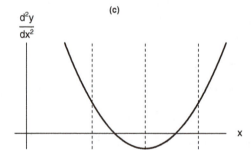

Figure 3.15   An example of (a) a function and its (b) first and (c) second derivatives.

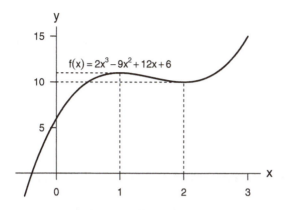

Figure 3.16   Finding the extrema of the function
$y = f(x) = 2x^3 - 9x^2 + 12x + 6$.

The first and second derivatives of the function are

$$f'(x) = 6x^2 - 18x + 12$$
$$f''(x) = 12x - 18$$

Setting the first derivative to zero and solving for the values of x that satisfy the resulting equation produces the following results:

$$6x^2 - 18x + 12 = 0$$
$$x^2 - 3x + 2 = 0$$
$$(x-2)(x-1) = 0$$

The two roots, at which $f'(x)$ is zero, are therefore $x = 2$ and $x = 1$.

- For $x = 2$,

$$f(2) = 2 \times 2^3 - 9 \times 2^2 + 12 \times 2 + 6 = 10$$
$$f'(2) = 6 \times 2^2 - 18 \times 2 + 12 = 0\checkmark$$
$$f''(2) = 12 \times 2 - 18 = 6$$

Because $f''(2)$ is *positive*, the point $(x = 2, y = 10)$ represents a (relative) *minimum*.

- Likewise, for $x = 1$,

$$f(1) = 2 \times 1^3 - 9 \times 1^2 + 12 \times 1 + 6 = 11$$
$$f'(1) = 6 \times 1^2 - 18 \times 1 + 12 = 0 \checkmark$$
$$f''(1) = 12 \times 1 - 18 = -6$$

Because $f''(1)$ is *negative*, the point $(x = 1, y = 11)$ represents a (relative) *maximum*.

3.5   Multivariable and Matrix Differential Calculus

Multivariable differential calculus—the topic of this section—finds frequent application in statistics. The essential ideas of multivariable calculus are straightforward extensions of calculus of a single independent variable, but the topic is frequently omitted from introductory treatments of calculus.

3.5.1   Partial Derivatives

Consider a function $y = f(x_1, x_2, \ldots, x_n)$ of several independent variables. The *partial derivative* of y with respect to a particular x_i is the derivative of $f(x_1, x_2, \ldots, x_n)$ treating the other xs as constants. To distinguish it from the ordinary derivative dy/dx, the standard notation for the partial derivative uses "curly ds" (actually a variation of the Greek letter delta) in place of ds: $\partial y / \partial x_i$.

For example, for the function

$$y = f(x_1, x_2) = x_1^2 + 3x_1 x_2^2 + x_2^3 + 6$$

the partial derivatives with respect to x_1 and x_2 are

$$\frac{\partial y}{\partial x_1} = 2x_1 + 3x_2^2 + 0 + 0 = 2x_1 + 3x_2^2$$

$$\frac{\partial y}{\partial x_2} = 0 + 6x_1 x_2 + 3x_2^2 + 0 = 6x_1 x_2 + 3x_2^2$$

The "trick" in partial differentiation with respect to x_i is to remember to treat all of the other xs as constants (i.e., literally to hold other xs constant). Thus, when we differentiate with respect to x_1, a term such as x_2^3 is a constant and contributes zero to the partial derivative, while both 3 and x_2^2 are treated as constants in the term $3x_1 x_2^2$.

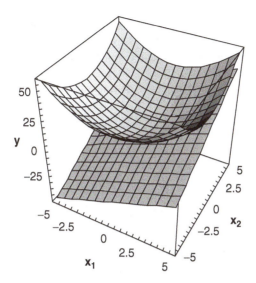

Figure 3.17   The function $y = f(x_1, x_2) = x_1^2 + x_1 x_2 + x_2^2 + 10$, showing the tangent plane at $x_1 = 1$, $x_2 = 2$. The lines drawn on the surface of the tangent plane have slopes $\partial y / \partial x_1$ in the direction of x_1 and $\partial y / \partial x_2$ in the direction of x_2.

The partial derivative $\partial f(x_1, x_2, \ldots, x_n) / \partial x_1$ gives the slope of the tangent hyperplane to the function $f(x_1, x_2, \ldots, x_n)$ in the direction of x_1.[15] For example, the tangent plane to the function

$$f(x_1, x_2) = x_1^2 + x_1 x_2 + x_2^2 + 10$$

above the pair of values $x_1 = 1$, $x_2 = 2$ is shown in Figure 3.17. The lines drawn on the surface of the tangent plane are parallel to the x_1 and x_2 axes and thus show the slopes of the original surface in the direction of each x holding the other x constant. Because the plane is flat, all of the slopes in the direction of x_1 are the same, $\partial y / \partial x_1$, as are all of the slopes in the direction of x_2, that is, $\partial y / \partial x_2$.

At a local or global minimum or maximum, the slope of the tangent hyperplane is zero in all directions. Consequently, to minimize or maximize a

---

[15] A *hyperplane* is the generalization of a linear (i.e., flat) surface to a space of more than three dimensions. The dimension of the hyperplane is one less than that of the enclosing space, just as a plane is a 2D flat surface embedded in a 3D space.

function of several variables, we can differentiate the function with respect to each variable, set the partial derivatives to zero, and solve the resulting set of simultaneous equations. I will explain later (page 92) how to distinguish maxima from minima.

Let us, for example, find the values of x_1 and x_2 that minimize the function

$$y = f(x_1, x_2) = x_1^2 + x_1 x_2 + x_2^2 + 10 \tag{3.1}$$

Differentiating,

$$\frac{\partial y}{\partial x_1} = 2x_1 + x_2 \tag{3.2}$$

$$\frac{\partial y}{\partial x_2} = x_1 + 2x_2$$

Setting these partial derivatives to zero produces the unique solution $x_1 = 0$, $x_2 = 0$. In this case, the solution is simple because the partial derivatives are linear functions of x_1 and x_2. The value of the function at its minimum is[16]

$$y = 0^2 + (0 \times 0) + 0^2 + 10 = 10$$

The slopes of the tangent plane above the pair of values $x_1 = 1$, $x_2 = 2$, illustrated in Figure 3.17, are

$$\frac{\partial y}{\partial x_1} = 2(1) + 2 = 4$$

$$\frac{\partial y}{\partial x_2} = 1 + 2(2) = 5$$

3.5.2   *Lagrange Multipliers for Constrained Optimization*

The method of Lagrange multipliers (named after the 18th-century French mathematician Joseph-Louis Lagrange) permits us to optimize a function of the form $y = f(x_1, x_2, \ldots, x_n)$ subject to a constraint of the form $g(x_1, x_2, \ldots, x_n) = 0$. The method, in effect, incorporates the constraint into the set of partial derivatives.

---

[16]Examining Equation 3.1 suggests why the function must have a minimum, and not a maximum or some other kind of stationary point, at $x_1 = x_2 = 0$: Because of the squares, any nonzero value of either x_1, x_2, or both can only increase the value of the function from the minimum value of 10.

Here is a simple example: Minimize

$$y = f(x_1, x_2) = x_1^2 + x_2^2$$

subject to the restriction that $x_1 + x_2 = 1$. (In the absence of this restriction, it is obvious that $x_1 = x_2 = 0$ minimizes the function.) Solving this constrained minimization problem with a Lagrange multiplier entails several steps:

1. Rewrite the constraint in the required form, $g(x_1, x_2, \dots, x_n) = 0$. That is, $x_1 + x_2 - 1 = 0$.

2. Construct a new function incorporating the constraint. In the general case, this function takes the form[17]

$$h(x_1, x_2, \dots, x_n, \lambda) \equiv f(x_1, x_2, \dots, x_n) - \lambda \times g(x_1, x_2, \dots, x_n)$$

The new independent variable λ is called a *Lagrange multiplier*. For the example,

$$h(x_1, x_2, \lambda) \equiv x_1^2 + x_2^2 - \lambda(x_1 + x_2 - 1)$$

3. Find the values of $x_1, x_2, \dots, x_n$ that (along with λ) optimize the function $h(x_1, x_2, \dots, x_n, \lambda)$. That is, differentiate $h(x_1, x_2, \dots, x_n, \lambda)$ with respect to each of $x_1, x_2, \dots, x_n$ and λ; set the $n+1$ partial derivatives to zero; and solve the resulting system of simultaneous equations for $x_1, x_2, \dots, x_n$ and λ. For the example,

$$\frac{\partial h(x_1, x_2, \lambda)}{\partial x_1} = 2x_1 - \lambda$$

$$\frac{\partial h(x_1, x_2, \lambda)}{\partial x_2} = 2x_2 - \lambda$$

$$\frac{\partial h(x_1, x_2, \lambda)}{\partial \lambda} = -x_1 - x_2 + 1$$

Setting the partial derivative with respect to λ to zero reproduces the constraint $x_1 + x_2 = 1$. Consequently, whatever solutions satisfy the equations produced by setting all of the partial derivatives to zero necessarily satisfy

---

[17]Some authors prefer to add, rather than subtract, the constraint,

$$h(x_1, x_2, \dots, x_n, \lambda) \equiv f(x_1, x_2, \dots, x_n) + \lambda \times g(x_1, x_2, \dots, x_n)$$

but, except for a change in the sign of λ, the two approaches are equivalent.

the constraint. In this case, there is only one solution: $x_1 = x_2 = 0.5$ (and $\lambda = 1$).

The method of Lagrange multipliers easily extends to handle several restrictions, by introducing a separate Lagrange multiplier for each restriction.

3.5.3 Differential Calculus in Matrix Form

The function $y = f(x_1, x_2, \ldots, x_n)$ of the independent variables $x_1, x_2, \ldots, x_n$ can be written as the function $y = f(\mathbf{x})$ of the vector $\mathbf{x} = [x_1, x_2, \ldots, x_n]'$. The *vector partial derivative* (or the *gradient*) of y with respect to $\mathbf{x}$ is defined as the column vector of partial derivatives of y with respect to each of the entries of $\mathbf{x}$:

$$
\frac{\partial y}{\partial \mathbf{x}} =
\begin{bmatrix}
\dfrac{\partial y}{\partial x_1} \\
\dfrac{\partial y}{\partial x_2} \\
\vdots \\
\dfrac{\partial y}{\partial x_n}
\end{bmatrix}
$$

If, therefore, y is a linear function of $\mathbf{x}$,

$$
y = \underset{(1 \times n)(n \times 1)}{\mathbf{a}' \quad \mathbf{x}} = a_1 x_1 + a_2 x_2 + \cdots + a_n x_n
$$

then $\partial y / \partial x_i = a_i$, and $\partial y / \partial \mathbf{x} = \mathbf{a}$. For example, for

$$
y = x_1 + 3x_2 - 5x_3
$$

$$
= [1, 3, -5]
\begin{bmatrix}
x_1 \\
x_2 \\
x_3
\end{bmatrix}
$$

the vector partial derivative is

$$
\frac{\partial y}{\partial \mathbf{x}} =
\begin{bmatrix}
1 \\
3 \\
-5
\end{bmatrix}
$$

Alternatively, suppose that y is a quadratic form in $\mathbf{x}$ (see Section 2.2),

$$
y = \underset{(1 \times n)(n \times n)(n \times 1)}{\mathbf{x}' \quad \mathbf{A} \quad \mathbf{x}}
$$

where the matrix $\mathbf{A}$ is symmetric. Expanding the matrix product gives us

$$
y = a_{11} x_1^2 + a_{22} x_2^2 + \cdots + a_{nn} x_n^2 + 2a_{12} x_1 x_2 + \cdots
$$
$$
+ 2a_{1n} x_1 x_n + \cdots + 2a_{n-1,n} x_{n-1} x_n
$$

and, thus,

$$\frac{\partial y}{\partial x_i} = 2(a_{i1}x_1 + a_{i2}x_2 + \cdots + a_{in}x_n) = 2\mathbf{a}'_i\mathbf{x}$$

where $\mathbf{a}'_i$ represents the ith row of $\mathbf{A}$. Placing these partial derivatives in a vector produces $\partial y/\partial \mathbf{x} = 2\mathbf{A}\mathbf{x}$.

For example, for

$$y = [x_1, x_2] \begin{bmatrix} 2 & 3 \\ 3 & 1 \end{bmatrix} \begin{bmatrix} x_1 \\ x_2 \end{bmatrix}$$
$$= 2x_1^2 + 3x_1x_2 + 3x_2x_1 + x_2^2$$
$$= 2x_1^2 + 6x_1x_2 + x_2^2$$

the partial derivatives are

$$\frac{\partial y}{\partial x_1} = 4x_1 + 6x_2$$

$$\frac{\partial y}{\partial x_2} = 6x_1 + 2x_2$$

and the vector partial derivative is

$$\frac{\partial y}{\partial \mathbf{x}} = \begin{bmatrix} 4x_1 + 6x_2 \\ 6x_1 + 2x_2 \end{bmatrix}$$
$$= 2 \begin{bmatrix} 2 & 3 \\ 3 & 1 \end{bmatrix} \begin{bmatrix} x_1 \\ x_2 \end{bmatrix} \checkmark$$

The so-called *Hessian matrix* of second-order partial derivatives of the function $y = f(\mathbf{x})$ is defined in the following manner:

$$\frac{\partial^2 y}{\partial \mathbf{x} \partial \mathbf{x}'} = \begin{bmatrix} \dfrac{\partial^2 y}{\partial x_1^2} & \dfrac{\partial^2 y}{\partial x_1 \partial x_2} & \cdots & \dfrac{\partial^2 y}{\partial x_1 \partial x_n} \\ \dfrac{\partial^2 y}{\partial x_2 \partial x_1} & \dfrac{\partial^2 y}{\partial x_2^2} & \cdots & \dfrac{\partial^2 y}{\partial x_2 \partial x_n} \\ \vdots & \vdots & \ddots & \vdots \\ \dfrac{\partial^2 y}{\partial x_n \partial x_1} & \dfrac{\partial^2 y}{\partial x_n \partial x_2} & \cdots & \dfrac{\partial^2 y}{\partial x_n^2} \end{bmatrix}$$

For instance, $\partial^2(\mathbf{x}'\mathbf{A}\mathbf{x})/\partial \mathbf{x} \partial \mathbf{x}' = 2\mathbf{A}$, for a symmetric matrix $\mathbf{A}$. The Hessian is named after the 19th-century German mathematician Ludwig Otto Hesse.

The vector partial derivatives of linear functions and quadratic forms, and the Hessian of a quadratic form, are strikingly similar to the analogous scalar derivatives of linear and quadratic functions of one variable: $d(ax)/dx = a$, $d(ax^2)/dx = 2ax$, and $d^2(ax^2)/dx^2 = 2a$.

To minimize a function $y = f(\mathbf{x})$ of several variables, we can set the vector partial derivative to $\mathbf{0}$, $\partial y/\partial \mathbf{x} = \mathbf{0}$, and solve the resulting set of simultaneous equations for $\mathbf{x}$, obtaining a solution $\mathbf{x}^*$. This solution represents a (local) minimum of the function in question if the Hessian matrix evaluated at $\mathbf{x} = \mathbf{x}^*$ is positive-definite. The solution represents a maximum if the Hessian is negative-definite.[18] Again, there is a strong parallel with the scalar results for a single x: Recall that the second derivative d^2y/dx^2 is positive at a minimum and negative at a maximum.

I showed earlier that the function

$$y = f(x_1, x_2) = x_1^2 + x_1 x_2 + x_2^2 + 10$$

has a stationary point (i.e., a point at which the partial derivatives are zero) at $x_1 = x_2 = 0$. The second-order partial derivatives of this function are

$$\frac{\partial^2 y}{\partial x_1 \partial x_2} = \frac{\partial^2 y}{\partial x_2 \partial x_1} = 1$$

$$\frac{\partial^2 y}{\partial x_1^2} = \frac{\partial^2 y}{\partial x_2^2} = 2$$

The Hessian evaluated at $x_1 = x_2 = 0$ (or, indeed, at any point), is, therefore,

$$\begin{bmatrix} \dfrac{\partial^2 y}{\partial x_1^2} & \dfrac{\partial^2 y}{\partial x_1 \partial x_2} \\ \dfrac{\partial^2 y}{\partial x_2 \partial x_1} & \dfrac{\partial^2 y}{\partial x_2^2} \end{bmatrix} = \begin{bmatrix} 2 & 1 \\ 1 & 2 \end{bmatrix}$$

This matrix is clearly positive-definite, verifying that the value $y = 10$ at $x_1 = x_2 = 0$ is a minimum of $f(x_1, x_2)$.

---

[18] The square matrix $\mathbf{H}$ (here, the Hessian) is *positive-definite* if $\mathbf{x}'\mathbf{Hx} > 0$ for any nonzero vector $\mathbf{x}$. (See Section 2.2.) A positive-definite Hessian is a sufficient but not necessary condition for a minimum. Likewise, the square matrix $\mathbf{H}$ is *negative-definite* if $\mathbf{x}'\mathbf{Hx} < 0$ for any nonzero vector $\mathbf{x}$; a negative-definite Hessian is a sufficient but not necessary condition for a maximum. The geometry of stationary points for functions of more than one independent variable is considerably more complex than for functions of a single variable, and includes phenomena such as *saddle points*, where the surface is at a minimum in one direction and a maximum in another.

3.5.4 Numerical Optimization

The preceding optimization problem is especially simple because the system of equations to be solved to minimize the *objective function* $y = f(x_1, x_2) = x_1^2 + x_1 x_2 + x_2^2 + 10$ is linear (see Equation 3.2 on page 88). More generally, the partial derivatives of an objective function may produce nonlinear equations that do not have a *closed-form* (i.e., *analytic*) *solution*. It may still be possible to solve such optimization problems, at least approximately, by using a numerical optimization method implemented on a digital computer.

The details of numerical optimization are beyond the scope of this chapter, but the general idea is reasonably straightforward. Refer again, for example, to the function $y = f(x_1, x_2) = x_1^2 + x_1 x_2 + x_2^2 + 10$, graphed in Figure 3.17 (page 87). Imagine that we know how to compute the partial derivatives of this function (Equation 3.2) but that we don't know how to solve the system of equations produced by setting the derivatives to zero.[19]

In a common analogy, numerical optimization is like searching a landscape in a thick fog for its highest point (maximization) or its lowest point (minimization): Because of the fog, we can only discern the properties of the surface close to our current location, and we hope that walking uphill will eventually take us to the top of the tallest peak or that walking downhill will take us to the bottom of the deepest valley. There is no general guarantee, however, that our route won't end at a minor peak (i.e., a local maximum) or in a superficial dip in the landscape (a local minimum), or that we won't run into some other difficulty.

In the current case, we want to minimize the objective function $f(x_1, x_2)$, which is equivalent to finding the lowest point in the "valley" formed by the function. Let's start at an arbitrary pair of values of the independent variables x_1 and x_2, $\mathbf{x}_0 = \left[x_1^{(0)}, x_2^{(0)} \right]'$, such as the point $\mathbf{x}_0 = [1, 2]'$ shown in Figure 3.17. The partial derivatives (i.e., the gradient) of the objective function at this point define the slopes in the directions of x_1 and x_2 of the tangent plane depicted in the graph.

If the gradient at $\mathbf{x}_0$ isn't the zero vector—and in our example it isn't—we aren't at the bottom of the valley. How can we get closer to the bottom? The gradient tells us which direction points uphill, and we can therefore try to take a step in the *opposite* (downhill) direction, to a new pair of values for the xs, $\mathbf{x}_1$.

---

[19]I hope that it's clear that the example is artificial, because, as noted in the previous paragraph, we *do* know how to solve the resulting set of linear simultaneous equations.

How large a step should we take? We can use the Hessian to help us decide, because the Hessian gives us information about the curvature of the function at $\mathbf{x}_0$. If the function is approximately quadratic near the current point (in the example, the function *is* quadratic), this computation should work well. Even if we don't know how to compute the Hessian, however, we can still take a step of arbitrary size in the downhill direction.

If our tentative step successfully decreases the value of y, then we can reevaluate the gradient (and, if we're using it, the Hessian) at the new point $\mathbf{x}_1$ and take another step, to $\mathbf{x}_2$. If, alternatively, the tentative step fails to decrease y, then we can try a smaller step in the same downhill direction. Eventually, after some number of successful steps, we'll find that we're unable to decrease y further, and we'll have located the minimum (or, more precisely, *a* local minimum) of the objective function, at least to a close approximation. This simple method of numerical optimization is called *gradient descent*.[20]

In describing numerical optimization, I assumed that we knew how to compute the gradient, and possibly the Hessian, of the objective function, but that may not be the case. Even so, we still may be able to proceed by approximating the gradient (and perhaps the Hessian) by taking small *finite differences*—evaluating the changes in y produced by increasing or decreasing each x in turn by a small amount from its current value, keeping the other xs at their current values.

As mentioned, if the objective function isn't "well behaved," for example, if there are multiple local minima distinct from the global minimum or if the objective function flattens out in a "ridge," then numerical optimization may run into difficulties. That's why practical methods of numerical optimization are more complex than the simple approach sketched in this section.

The method of gradient descent, and similar but more sophisticated derivative-based methods of numerical optimization, are primarily useful for optimizing functions of two or more independent variables,[21] but a one-variable example serves to demonstrate more concretely how the method works. To this end, consider the function, and its first and second derivatives, graphed in Figure 3.15 (page 84). Although not mentioned in Figure 3.15,

---

[20]If we use the Hessian, then the algorithm is called *Newton's method* (after Isaac Newton). In Newton's method, the tentative step, based on a Taylor-series approximation (see Section 3.6) to $f(\mathbf{x})$ at $\mathbf{x} = \mathbf{x}_0$, is $\mathbf{x}_1 = \mathbf{x}_0 - \mathbf{H}^{-1}(\mathbf{x}_0)\mathbf{g}(\mathbf{x}_0)$, where $\mathbf{g}(\mathbf{x}_0)$ is the gradient of $f(\mathbf{x})$ and $\mathbf{H}(\mathbf{x}_0)$ is the Hessian, both evaluated at $\mathbf{x} = \mathbf{x}_0$.

[21] 1D optimization problems can be solved more directly by searching for a minimum or maximum of $f(x)$ within a prespecified range of x-values.

the equation of the function is

$$f(x) = x^4 - 10x^3 + 35x^2 - 50x + 26$$

Its first derivative is therefore

$$f'(x) = 4x^3 - 30x^2 + 70x - 50 \tag{3.3}$$

Setting the derivative to zero and solving for x produces three roots:

$$x_1 = \tfrac{1}{2}\left(5 - \sqrt{5}\right) \approx 1.3820$$
$$x_2 = 2.5$$
$$x_3 = \tfrac{1}{2}\left(5 + \sqrt{5}\right) \approx 3.6180$$

As is apparent in Figure 3.15, $f(x_1) = f(x_3) = 1$ are absolute minima of the function, while $f(x_2) = 2.5625$ is a relative maximum.

Let's imagine, perhaps realistically, that we don't know how to solve the cubic equation produced by setting the first derivative in Equation 3.3 to zero,[22] and also, unrealistically, that we don't know how to find the second derivative. Let's further imagine that we nevertheless want to minimize $f(x)$ and thus proceed numerically by gradient descent:[23]

- I pick the arbitrary starting value $x_0 = 3$, where $f(3) = 2$. The choice is consequential, because *which* of the two minima I find will depend on the start value for x.[24] (*Reader:* Why?)

- I next compute the derivative at the start value, $f'(x_0) = f'(3) = -2$. Because the derivative is negative, I need to move to the right (i.e., in the *positive* direction) to make $f(x)$ smaller.

- I try the step $x_1 = x_0 - f'(x_0) = 3 - (-2) = 5$, but $f(5) = 26$, which is *larger* than $f(x_0) = 2$, and thus the step is too big. I then try halving

---

[22] When our mathematical knowledge fails us, we can of course try to look up the answer, or use symbolic math software, such as *Mathematica* (Wolfram, 2003).

[23] An exercise for the reader is to redo this example using Newton's method, described in Footnote 20.

[24] Moreover, were I unfortunately to pick $x_0 = 2.5$, I'd stop at the local *maximum* rather than finding a minimum of the function. Even this simple example, therefore, reveals some of the potential pitfalls of numerical optimization.

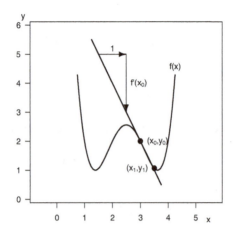

Figure 3.18 First successful step of gradient descent to minimize the function $y = f(x) = x^4 - 10x^3 + 35x^2 - 50x + 26$, moving from $(x_0 = 3, y_0 = 2)$ to $(x_1 = 3.5, y_1 = 1.0625)$; $f'(x_0) = -2$ is the first derivative evaluated at the starting value x_0.

the step, which still produces too large a value of $f(x_1)$,[25] and halving again, to arrive at $x_1 = x_0 - 0.25 f'(x_0) = 3 - (-0.5) = 3.5$, for which $f(3.5) = 1.0625 < f(x_0)$. This first successful step is shown in Figure 3.18, where we can see that it takes me quite close to the minimum of the function at $x \approx 3.6180$.

- After seven steps, each time adjusting the step size if necessary, I obtain $x_7 = 3.6180$, $f(x_7) = 1$, and $f'(x_7) = -7.0514 \times 10^{-5} \approx 0$, which is the right answer to a close approximation.

---

[25] $f[3 - 0.5(-2)] = f(4) = 2$, which is equal to $f(3)$, and thus isn't an improvement. Because $f'(x_0) = -2$ is clearly nonzero, I should be able to make $f(x)$ smaller by taking a sufficiently small step to the right of x_0, as proves to be the case.

3.6 Taylor Series

If a function $f(x)$ has infinitely many derivatives (most of which may, however, be zero) near the value $x = x_0$, then the function can be decomposed into the *Taylor series*

$$f(x) = f(x_0) + \frac{f'(x_0)}{1!}(x-x_0) + \frac{f''(x_0)}{2!}(x-x_0)^2$$
$$+ \frac{f'''(x_0)}{3!}(x-x_0)^3 + \cdots$$
$$= \sum_{n=0}^{\infty} \frac{f^{(n)}(x_0)}{n!}(x-x_0)^n \qquad (3.4)$$

where $f^{(n)}$ represents the nth-order derivative of f, and $n!$ is the *factorial* of n.[26] Taylor series are named after the 18th-century British mathematician Brook Taylor.

As long as x is sufficiently close to x_0, and as long as the function $f(\cdot)$ is sufficiently well behaved, $f(x)$ may be *approximated* by taking only the first few terms of the Taylor series. For example, if the function is nearly quadratic between x and x_0, then $f(x)$ can be approximated by the first three terms of the Taylor expansion, because the remaining derivatives will be small; similarly, if the function is nearly linear between x and x_0, then $f(x)$ can be approximated by the first two terms.

To illustrate the application of Taylor series, consider the cubic function

$$f(x) = 1 + x^2 + x^3$$

Then

$$f'(x) = 2x + 3x^2$$
$$f''(x) = 2 + 6x$$
$$f'''(x) = 6$$
$$f^{(n)}(x) = 0 \text{ for } n > 3$$

---

[26]The factorial of a nonnegative integer n is defined as $n! \equiv n(n-1)(n-2)\cdots(2)(1)$; by convention, $0!$ and $1!$ are both taken to be 1.

Let us take $x_0 = 2$; evaluating the function and its derivatives at this value of x,

$$f(2) = 1 + 2^2 + 2^3 = 13$$
$$f'(2) = 2(2) + 3(2)^2 = 16$$
$$f''(2) = 2 + 6(2) = 14$$
$$f'''(2) = 6$$

Finally, let us evaluate $f(x)$ at $x = 4$ using the Taylor-series expansion of the function around $x_0 = 2$:

$$f(4) = f(2) + \frac{f'(2)}{1!}(4-2) + \frac{f''(2)}{2!}(4-2)^2 + \frac{f'''(2)}{3!}(4-2)^3$$
$$= 13 + 16(2) + \frac{14}{2}(2^2) + \frac{6}{6}(2^3)$$
$$= 13 + 32 + 28 + 8$$
$$= 81$$

Checking by evaluating the function directly,

$$f(4) = 1 + 4^2 + 4^3 = 1 + 16 + 64 = 81\checkmark$$

In this case, using fewer than all four terms of the Taylor expansion would produce a poor approximation (because the function is cubic and the cubic term is large).

Taylor series expansions and approximations generalize to functions of several variables, most simply when the function is scalar-valued and when we can use a first- or second-order approximation. Suppose that $y = f(x_1, x_2, \ldots, x_n) = f(\mathbf{x})$, and that we want to approximate $f(\mathbf{x})$ near the value $\mathbf{x} = \mathbf{x}_0$. Then the second-order Taylor-series approximation of $f(\mathbf{x})$ is

$$f(\mathbf{x}) \approx f(\mathbf{x}_0) + [\mathbf{g}(\mathbf{x}_0)]'(\mathbf{x} - \mathbf{x}_0) + \tfrac{1}{2}(\mathbf{x} - \mathbf{x}_0)'\mathbf{H}(\mathbf{x}_0)(\mathbf{x} - \mathbf{x}_0)$$

where $\mathbf{g}(\mathbf{x}) \equiv \partial y/\partial \mathbf{x}$ and $\mathbf{H}(\mathbf{x}) \equiv \partial^2 y/\partial \mathbf{x}\,\partial \mathbf{x}'$ are, respectively, the gradient and Hessian of $f(\mathbf{x})$, both evaluated at $\mathbf{x}_0$. There is a strong analogy to the first three terms of the scalar Taylor expansion, given in Equation 3.4.

3.7 Essential Ideas of Integral Calculus

3.7.1 Areas: Definite Integrals

Consider the area A under a curve $f(x)$ between two horizontal coordinates, x_0 and x_1, as illustrated in Figure 3.19. This area can be approximated by

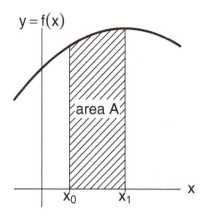

Figure 3.19 The area A under a function $f(x)$ between x_0 and x_1.

dividing the line segment between x_0 and x_1 into n small intervals, each of width Δx, and constructing a series of rectangles just touching the curve, as shown in Figure 3.20. The x-values defining the rectangles are

$$x_0, x_0 + \Delta x, x_0 + 2\Delta x, \ldots, x_1 = x_0 + n\Delta x$$

Consequently, the combined area of the rectangles is

$$\sum_{i=0}^{n-1} f(x_0 + i\Delta x)\Delta x \approx A$$

The approximation grows better as the number of rectangles n increases (and Δx grows smaller). In the limit,[27]

$$A = \lim_{\substack{\Delta x \to 0 \\ n \to \infty}} \sum_{i=0}^{n-1} f(x_0 + i\Delta x)\Delta x$$

---

[27] This approach, called *the method of exhaustion* (but not the formal notion of a limit), was known to the ancient Greeks.

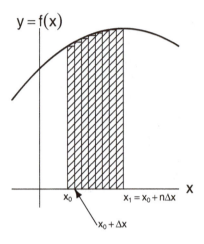

Figure 3.20   Approximating the area under a curve by summing the areas of rectangles.

The following notation is used for this limit, which is called the *definite integral* of $f(x)$ from $x = x_0$ to x_1:

$$A = \int_{x_0}^{x_1} f(x)dx$$

Here, x_0 and x_1 give the *limits of integration*, while the differential dx is the infinitesimal remnant of the width of the rectangles Δx. The symbol for the integral, $\int$, is an elongated "S," indicative of the interpretation of the definite integral as the continuous analog of a sum.

The definite integral defines a *signed area*, which may be negative if (some) values of y are less than zero, as illustrated in Figure 3.21.

3.7.2   Indefinite Integrals

Suppose that for the function $f(x)$, there exists a function $F(x)$ such that

$$\frac{dF(x)}{dx} = f(x)$$

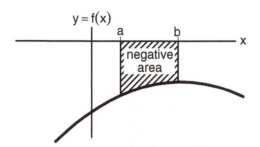

Figure 3.21 The integral $\int_a^b f(x)dx$ is negative because the y values are negative between the limits of integration a and b.

That is, $f(x)$ is the derivative of $F(x)$. Then $F(x)$ is called an *antiderivative* or *indefinite integral* of $f(x)$.

The indefinite integral of a function is not unique, for if $F(x)$ is an antiderivative of $f(x)$, then so is $G(x) = F(x) + c$, where c is a constant (i.e., not a function of x). Conversely, if $F(x)$ and $G(x)$ are both antiderivatives of $f(x)$, then for some constant c, $G(x) = F(x) + c$.

For example, the function $\frac{1}{4}x^4 + 10$ is an antiderivative of $f(x) = x^3$, as are $\frac{1}{4}x^4 - 10$ and $\frac{1}{4}x^4$. Indeed, any function of the form $F(x) = \frac{1}{4}x^4 + c$ will do.

The following notation is used for the indefinite integral: If

$$\frac{dF(x)}{dx} = f(x)$$

then we write

$$F(x) = \int f(x)dx$$

where the integral sign appears without limits of integration. That the same symbol is employed for both areas and antiderivatives (i.e., for definite and indefinite integrals), and that both of these operations are called "integration," are explained in the following section. That said, while a definite integral—an area—is a particular number, an indefinite integral is a function.

3.7.3 The Fundamental Theorem of Calculus

Newton and Leibniz figured out the connection between antiderivatives and areas under curves. The relationship that they discovered between indefinite

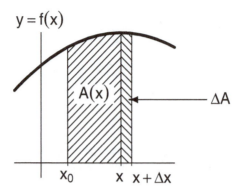

Figure 3.22   The area $A(x)$ under the curve between the fixed value x_0
and another value x; the value $x + \Delta x$ is slightly larger than x.

and definite integrals is called the *fundamental theorem of calculus*:

$$\int_{x_0}^{x_1} f(x)dx = F(x_1) - F(x_0)$$

where $F(\cdot)$ is *any* antiderivative of $f(\cdot)$.

Here is a nonrigorous proof of this theorem: Consider the area $A(x)$ under
the curve $f(x)$ between some fixed value x_0 and another (moveable) value
$x \geq x_0$, as shown in Figure 3.22. The notation $A(x)$ emphasizes that the area
is a function of x: As we move x left or right, the area $A(x)$ changes. In
Figure 3.22, $x + \Delta x$ is a value slightly to the right of x, and ΔA is the area
under the curve between x and $x + \Delta x$. A rectangular approximation to this
small area is

$$\Delta A \approx f(x)\Delta x$$

The area ΔA is also

$$\Delta A = A(x + \Delta x) - A(x)$$

Taking the derivative of A,

$$\frac{dA(x)}{dx} = \lim_{\Delta x \to 0} \frac{\Delta A}{\Delta x}$$

$$= \lim_{\Delta x \to 0} \frac{f(x)\Delta x}{\Delta x}$$

$$= f(x)$$

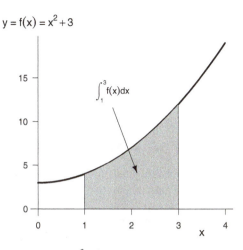

Figure 3.23 The area $A = \int_1^3 (x^2 + 3)dx$.

Consequently,

$$A(x) = \int f(x)dx$$

is a *specific*, but as yet unknown, indefinite integral of $f(x)$. Let $F(x)$ be some *other* specific, arbitrary, indefinite integral of $f(x)$. Then $A(x) = F(x) + c$, for some c (because, as we previously discovered, two indefinite integrals of the same function differ by a constant). We know that $A(x_0) = 0$, because $A(x)$ is the area under the curve between x_0 and any x, and the area under the curve between x_0 and x_0 is zero. Thus,

$$A(x_0) = F(x_0) + c = 0$$
$$c = -F(x_0)$$

and, for a particular value of $x = x_1$,

$$A(x_1) = \int_{x_0}^{x_1} f(x)dx = F(x_1) - F(x_0)$$

where (recall) $F(\cdot)$ is *an arbitrary* antiderivative of $f(\cdot)$.

For example, let us find the area (evaluate the definite integral)

$$A = \int_1^3 (x^2 + 3)dx$$

This area is graphed in Figure 3.23. It is convenient to use the antiderivative[28]

$$F(x) = \tfrac{1}{3}x^3 + 3x$$

Then

$$A = F(3) - F(1)$$
$$= \left(\tfrac{1}{3}3^3 + 3 \times 3\right) - \left(\tfrac{1}{3}1^3 + 3 \times 1\right)$$
$$= 18 - 3\tfrac{1}{3} = 14\tfrac{2}{3}$$

It can be much more challenging than in this simple example to find an antiderivative of a function. Traditional expositions of integral calculus therefore devote considerable space to techniques for integrating functions and to tables of integrals of various functions. In practical applications, it is often simplest to use a symbolic algebra program, such as *Mathematica* (Wolfram, 2003), to integrate functions (and even to differentiate complicated functions).

3.7.4   Multivariable Integral Calculus

The extension of integral calculus to functions of more than one variable is conceptually straightforward, although the details can get complicated. I'll simply sketch the basic ideas here.

Consider a function $y = f(x_1, x_2)$ of two independent variables, such as the function $y = x_1^2 + x_1 x_2 + x_2^2 + 10$ depicted in Figure 3.17 (on page 87, disregarding the tangent plane to the function shown in the graph). The function represents a 2D surface in 3D space. The definite integral

$$\int_{x_1=a}^{b} \int_{x_2=c}^{d} f(x_1, x_2) dx_1 dx_2$$

is the volume under the surface above the rectangle in the $\{x_1, x_2\}$ plane defined by $x_1 = a$ to $x_1 = b$ and $x_2 = c$ to $x_2 = d$.

Now consider a function $y = f(\mathbf{x})$ of n independent variables $\mathbf{x} = [x_1, x_2, \ldots, x_n]'$. The function represents an n-dimensional surface in $(n+1)$-dimensional space, and the definite integral

$$\int_{x_1=a}^{b} \int_{x_2=c}^{d} \cdots \int_{x_n=g}^{h} f(x_1, x_2, \ldots x_n) dx_1 dx_2 \cdots dx_n = \int_{X} f(\mathbf{x}) d^n \mathbf{x}$$

---

[28]*Reader:* Verify that $F(x) = \tfrac{1}{3}x^3 + 3x$ is an antiderivative of $f(x) = x^2 + 3$. More generally, one can find antiderivatives of polynomial functions by working the rule for differentiating powers in reverse.

is the hypervolume "under" the surface "above" the n-dimensional hyper-rectangle in the $\mathbf{x}$ hyperplane defined by $\boldsymbol{X}$. Even more generally, the region $\boldsymbol{X}$ need not be rectangular.

CHAPTER 4. ELEMENTARY PROBABILITY THEORY

The purpose of this chapter is to outline basic results in probability theory that are employed widely in applied statistics. For good reason, elementary statistics courses—particularly in the social sciences—often afford only the barest introduction to probability. To progress past a certain point, however, some background in probability theory is necessary—the background that this chapter provides: The first section of the chapter introduces basic concepts of probability theory, at least some of which are likely familiar from a first course in statistics; the second section takes up random variables and their properties; and the final section addresses transformations of random variables.

4.1 Probability Basics

In probability theory, an *experiment* is a repeatable procedure for making an observation; an *outcome* is a possible observation resulting from an experiment; and the *sample space* of the experiment is the set of all possible outcomes. Any specific *realization* of the experiment produces a particular outcome in the sample space. Sample spaces may be discrete and finite, discrete and infinite, or continuous.

If, for example, we flip a coin *twice* and record on each flip (or *trial*) whether the coin shows heads (H) or tails (T), then the sample space of the experiment is discrete and finite, consisting of the outcomes $S = \{HH, HT, TH, TT\}$. If, alternatively, we flip a coin repeatedly until a head appears, and record the number of flips required to obtain this result, then the sample space is discrete and infinite, comprising the positive integers, $S = \{1, 2, 3, \ldots\}$.[1] If we burn a light bulb until it fails, recording the burning time in hours and fractions of an hour, then the sample space of the experiment is continuous and consists of all positive real numbers (not bothering to specify an upper limit for the life of a bulb): $S = \{x \colon x > 0\}$. In this section, I will limit consideration to discrete, finite sample spaces.

An *event* is a subset of the sample space of an experiment—that is, a set of outcomes. An event is said to *occur* in a realization of the experiment

---

[1] The sample space is infinite because we may have to wait arbitrarily long to observe the first head, even though a very long wait may be highly improbable. More generally, when S is infinite but discrete, we say that it is *countably infinite*, because a one-to-one correspondence can be established between the elements of S and the natural numbers $0, 1, 2, \ldots$.

if one of its constituent outcomes occurs. For example, for $S = \{HH, HT, TH, TT\}$, the event $E \equiv \{HH, HT\}$, representing a head on the first flip of the coin, occurs if we obtain either the outcome HH or the outcome HT. The sample space S itself and the *null* or *empty event* $\emptyset \equiv \{\}$, which contains no outcomes, are both events by this definition.

4.1.1 Axioms of Probability

Let $S = \{o_1, o_2, \ldots, o_n\}$ be the sample space of an experiment; let $O_1 \equiv \{o_1\}$, $O_2 \equiv \{o_2\}, \ldots, O_n \equiv \{o_n\}$ be the *simple events*, each consisting of one of the outcomes; and let the event $E = \{o_a, o_b, \ldots, o_m\}$ be any subset of S (where subscripts $a, b, \ldots, m$ are different numbers between one and n). *Probabilities* are real numbers assigned to events in a manner consistent with the following axioms (rules)[2]:

P1: $\Pr(E) \geq 0$: The probability of an event is nonnegative.

P2: $\Pr(E) = \Pr(O_a) + \Pr(O_b) + \cdots + \Pr(O_m)$: The probability of an event is the sum of probabilities of its constituent outcomes.[3]

P3: $\Pr(S) = 1$ and $\Pr(\emptyset) = 0$: The sample space is exhaustive—some outcome must occur.

Suppose, for example, that all outcomes in the sample space $S = \{HH, HT, TH, TT\}$ are equally likely, so that

$$\Pr(HH) = \Pr(HT) = \Pr(TH) = \Pr(TT) = .25$$

Then, for $E \equiv \{HH, HT\}$, $\Pr(E) = .25 + .25 = .5$. Equally likely outcomes produce a simple example—and correspond to a "fair" coin "fairly" flipped—but any assignment of probabilities to outcomes that sum to one is consistent with the axioms.

In *classical statistics*, the perspective adopted in most applications of statistics, probabilities are interpreted as long-run proportions. Thus, if the probability of an event is .5, then the event will occur approximately half

---

[2]These axioms are similar to (and equivalent to) those proposed by the 20th-century Russian mathematician, Andrey Kolmogorov.

[3]Although there is a distinction between outcomes and simple events, each of which consists of a single outcome, it is often convenient to speak of the probability of an outcome, understanding that we mean the probability of the corresponding simple event. I will also, for example, write, as below, $\Pr(HH)$ rather than the strictly correct, but pedantic, $\Pr(\{HH\})$.

the time when the experiment is repeated many times, and the approximation is expected to improve as the number of repetitions increases. This is
sometimes termed an *objective* or *frequentist* interpretation of probability:
Probabilities are interpreted as long-run *relative frequencies*—that is, proportions.[4]

4.1.2 Relations Among Events, Conditional Probability, and Indepen-dence

A number of important relations can be defined among events. The *inter-section* of two events, E_1 and E_2, denoted $E_1 \cap E_2$, contains all outcomes
common to the two; $\Pr(E_1 \cap E_2)$ is thus the probability that *both E_1 and
E_2 occur* simultaneously. If $E_1 \cap E_2 = \emptyset$, then E_1 and E_2 are said to be *dis-joint* or *mutually exclusive*. By extension, the intersection of many events
$E_1 \cap E_2 \cap \cdots \cap E_k$ contains all outcomes that are members of each and every
event.

Consider, for example, the events $E_1 \equiv \{HH, HT\}$ (a head on the first
trial), $E_2 \equiv \{HH, TH\}$ (a head on the second trial), and $E_3 \equiv \{TH, TT\}$ (a
tail on the first trial). Then $E_1 \cap E_2 = \{HH\}, E_1 \cap E_3 = \emptyset$, and $E_2 \cap E_3 = \{TH\}$.

The *union* of two events $E_1 \cup E_2$ contains all outcomes that are in either or
both events; $\Pr(E_1 \cup E_2)$ is the probability that E_1 occurs *or* that E_2 occurs
(or that *both* occur). The union of several events $E_1 \cup E_2 \cup \cdots \cup E_k$ contains
all outcomes that are in one or more of the events. If these events are disjoint,
then

$$\Pr(E_1 \cup E_2 \cup \cdots \cup E_k) = \sum_{i=1}^{k} \Pr(E_i)$$

otherwise

$$\Pr(E_1 \cup E_2 \cup \cdots \cup E_k) < \sum_{i=1}^{k} \Pr(E_i)$$

(because some outcomes contribute more than once when the probabilities
are summed). For two events,

$$\Pr(E_1 \cup E_2) = \Pr(E_1) + \Pr(E_2) - \Pr(E_1 \cap E_2)$$

Subtracting the probability of the intersection corrects for double counting.

---

[4]Cf. the discussion of subjective probability and Bayesian statistical inference in Section 6.4.

To extend the previous example, assuming equally likely outcomes (where, recall, events E_1 and E_3 are disjoint, but E_1 and E_2 are not),

$$\begin{aligned}
\Pr(E_1 \cup E_3) &= \Pr(HH, HT, TH, TT) = 1 \\
&= \Pr(E_1) + \Pr(E_3) \\
&= .5 + .5 \checkmark \\
\Pr(E_1 \cup E_2) &= \Pr(HH, HT, TH) = .75 \\
&= \Pr(E_1) + \Pr(E_2) - \Pr(E_1 \cap E_2) \\
&= .5 + .5 - .25 \checkmark
\end{aligned}$$

The *conditional probability of E_2 given E_1* is

$$\Pr(E_2|E_1) \equiv \frac{\Pr(E_1 \cap E_2)}{\Pr(E_1)} \tag{4.1}$$

The conditional probability is interpreted as the probability that E_2 will occur if E_1 is known to have occurred. Solving Equation 4.1 for $\Pr(E_1 \cap E_2)$ produces the general *multiplication rule* for probabilities:

$$\Pr(E_1 \cap E_2) = \Pr(E_1) \Pr(E_2|E_1)$$

We can exchange the roles of E_1 and E_2 in these formulas:

$$\Pr(E_1|E_2) \equiv \frac{\Pr(E_1 \cap E_2)}{\Pr(E_2)} \tag{4.2}$$

$$\Pr(E_1 \cap E_2) = \Pr(E_2) \Pr(E_1|E_2) \tag{4.3}$$

Two events are *independent* if $\Pr(E_1 \cap E_2) = \Pr(E_1) \Pr(E_2)$ (the multiplication rule for probabilities of independent events). Independence of E_1 and E_2 implies that $\Pr(E_1) = \Pr(E_1|E_2)$ and that $\Pr(E_2) = \Pr(E_2|E_1)$: That is, the *unconditional probability* of each of two independent events is the same as the conditional probability of that event given the other. More generally, a set of events $\{E_1, E_2, \ldots, E_k\}$ is independent if, for every subset $\{E_a, E_b, \ldots, E_m\}$ containing two or more of the events,

$$\Pr(E_a \cap E_b \cap \cdots \cap E_m) = \Pr(E_a) \Pr(E_b) \cdots \Pr(E_m)$$

Appealing once more to our simple coin-flipping example, the probability of a head on the second trial (E_2) given a head on the first trial (E_1) is

$$\begin{aligned}
\Pr(E_2|E_1) &= \frac{\Pr(E_1 \cap E_2)}{\Pr(E_1)} \\
&= \frac{.25}{.5} = .5 \\
&= \Pr(E_2)
\end{aligned}$$

Likewise, $\Pr(E_1 \cap E_2) = .25 = \Pr(E_1)\Pr(E_2) = .5 \times .5$. The events E_1 and E_2 are, therefore, independent.

Independence is different from disjointness: If two events are disjoint, then they cannot occur together, and they are, therefore, *dependent*. In the preceding example, the events E_1 and E_2 are independent, not disjoint: $E_1 \cap E_2 = \{HH\} \neq \emptyset$.

The *difference* between two events $E_1 - E_2$ contains all outcomes in the first event that are not in the second. The difference $\overline{E} \equiv S - E$ is called the *complement* of the event E, and $\Pr(\overline{E}) = 1 - \Pr(E)$. From the example, where $E_1 \equiv \{HH, HT\}$ with all outcomes equally likely, $\Pr(\overline{E}_1) = \Pr(TH, TT) = .5 = 1 - .5\checkmark$.

4.1.3   Bonferroni Inequalities

Let $E \equiv E_1 \cap E_2 \cap \cdots E_k$. Then $\overline{E} = \overline{E}_1 \cup \overline{E}_2 \cup \cdots \cup \overline{E}_k$ (*Reader:* Can you see why?). Applying previous results,

$$\Pr(E_1 \cap E_2 \cap \cdots \cap E_k) = \Pr(E) = 1 - \Pr(\overline{E}) \qquad (4.4)$$

$$\geq 1 - \sum_{i=1}^{k} \Pr(\overline{E}_i)$$

Suppose that all of the events $E_1, E_2, \ldots, E_k$ have equal probabilities, say $\Pr(E_i) = 1 - b$ (so that $\Pr(\overline{E}_i) = b$). Then

$$\Pr(E_1 \cap E_2 \cap \cdots \cap E_k) \equiv 1 - a \qquad (4.5)$$

$$\geq 1 - kb$$

Equation 4.5 and the more general Equation 4.4 are called *Bonferroni inequalities*, named after Carlo Emilio Bonferroni, a 20th-century Italian mathematician.

Equation 4.5 has the following application to simultaneous statistical inference (which explains why I defined a and b as I did): Suppose that b is the Type I error rate (i.e., the "α-level") for *each* of k nonindependent statistical tests. Let a represent the combined Type I error rate for the k tests—that is, the probability of falsely rejecting *at least one* of k true null hypotheses. Then $a \leq kb$. For instance, if we test 20 true statistical hypotheses, each at an α-level of .01, then the probability of rejecting *at least one* hypothesis is at most $20 \times .01 = .20$ (i.e., no more than one chance in five)—a sober reminder that naïve "data dredging" can prove seriously misleading. Indeed, when the number of tests k is large, the Bonferroni upper bound for their combined α-level can exceed one (in which case, because it is a probability, the bound can be lowered to one).

4.2 Random Variables

A *random variable* is a function that assigns a number to each outcome of the sample space of an experiment. For the sample space $S = \{HH, HT, TH, TT\}$, introduced earlier, a random variable X that counts the number of heads in an outcome is defined as follows:

Outcome	Value x of X
HH	2
HT	1
TH	1
TT	0

If, as in this example, X is a discrete random variable,[5] then we write $p_X(x)$ for $\Pr(X = x)$, where the uppercase letter X represents the random variable, while the lowercase letter x denotes a *particular value* of the variable. Unless the identity of the random variable is ambiguous, I'll typically abbreviate $p_X(x)$ as $p(x)$.

The probabilities $p(x)$ for all values of X comprise the *probability distribution* (also called the *probability mass function*) of the random variable. If, for example, each of the four outcomes of the coin-flipping experiment has probability .25, then the probability distribution of the number of heads is

	x	p(x)
$\{TT\} \Longrightarrow$	0	.25
$\{HT, TH\} \Longrightarrow$	1	.50
$\{HH\} \Longrightarrow$	2	.25
	Sum	1.00

The table shows the events that map into each distinct value x of the random variable, and the probability of each value is therefore the probability of the corresponding event.

The *cumulative distribution function* (*CDF*) of a random variable X, written $P_X(x)$, gives the probability of observing a value of the variable that is less than or equal to a particular value:

$$P_X(x) \equiv \Pr(X \leq x) = \sum_{x' \leq x} p_X(x')$$

---

[5] A random variable X is discrete if it takes on a finite or countably infinite number of distinct values.

I'll usually abbreviate $P_X(x)$ as $P(x)$. For the example,

x	$P(x)$
0	.25
1	.75
2	1.00

Random variables defined on continuous sample spaces may themselves be continuous. We still take $P(x)$ as $\Pr(X \leq x)$, but it generally becomes meaningless to refer to the probability of observing *individual values* of X.[6] The *probability density function* $p(x)$ is, nevertheless, the continuous analog of the discrete probability distribution, defining $p(x) \equiv dP(x)/dx$.[7] Reversing this relation,[8] $P(x) = \int_{-\infty}^{x} p(x)\,dx$; and

$$\Pr(x_0 \leq X \leq x_1) = P(x_1) - P(x_0) = \int_{x_0}^{x_1} p(x)\,dx$$

Thus, as illustrated in Figure 4.1, areas under the density function represent probabilities.[9]

A particularly simple continuous probability distribution is the *rectangular* (or *uniform*) *distribution*:

$$p(x) = \begin{cases} 0 & x < a \\ \dfrac{1}{b-a} & a \leq x \leq b \\ 0 & x > b \end{cases} \qquad (4.6)$$

---

[6] As explained immediately below, probabilities correspond to *areas* under the density function $p(x)$, and the area above a *particular* value x_0 of X (i.e., a vertical line) is 0.

[7] The probability density function of a continuous random variable X is often denoted $f(x)$, and its cumulative distribution function $F(x)$, but I find $p(x)$ and $P(x)$ more natural, and prefer to reserve $f(\cdot)$ for other purposes, such as transformations of random variables (see Section 4.3).

[8] If you are unfamiliar with integral calculus, do not be too concerned (but do read Chapter 3 on calculus!): The principal point to understand is that *areas* under the density curve $p(x)$ are interpreted as probabilities, and that the *height* of the CDF $P(x)$ gives the probability of observing values of X less than or equal to the value x. The integral sign $\int$ is the continuous analog of a sum and represents the area under a curve.

[9] Because of the continuity of $p(x)$, and the associated fact that $\Pr(X = x_0) = \Pr(X = x_1) = 0$, we need not distinguish between $\Pr(x_0 \leq X \leq x_1)$ and $\Pr(x_0 < X < x_1)$. There are, however, unusual distributions that have both continuous and discrete parts, in which certain specific values of x *do* have nonzero probability. For example, some statistical models for nonnegative continuous data have $\Pr(X = 0) \neq 0$, while nonzero values of X are treated continuously. I'll not pursue this possibility here.

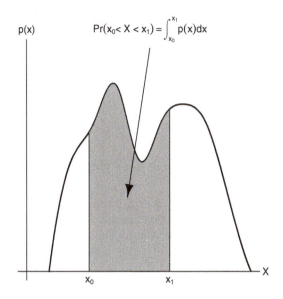

Figure 4.1   Areas under a probability density function $p(x)$ are
probabilities.

This density function is pictured in Figure 4.2(a), and the corresponding
CDF is shown in Figure 4.2(b). The total area under a density function must
be 1; here,

$$\int_{-\infty}^{\infty} p(x)dx = \int_{a}^{b} p(x)dx = \frac{1}{b-a}(b-a) = 1$$

The *support* of a random variable is the set of values for which the probability or probability density is nonzero; the support of the rectangular distribution is therefore $a \leq X \leq b$. We may abbreviate the uniform distribution
between a and b as $\text{Unif}(a,b)$.

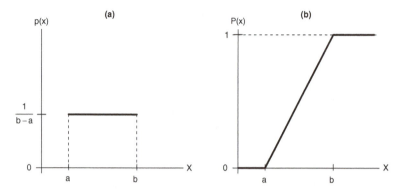

Figure 4.2   (a) The probability density function $p(x)$ and (b) the cumulative distribution function $P(x)$ for the rectangular or uniform distribution $\text{Unif}(a,b)$.

4.2.1   *Expectation and Variance*

Two fundamental properties of a random variable are its *expected value* (also called its *expectation* or *mean*) and its *variance*.[10] The expected value specifies the center of the probability distribution of the random variable (in the same sense as the mean of a set of scores specifies the center of their distribution), while the variance indicates how spread out the distribution is around its expectation. The expectation is interpretable as the mean score of the random variable that would be observed over many repetitions of the experiment, while the variance is the mean squared difference between the scores and their expectation.

In the discrete case, the expectation of a random variable X, symbolized by $E(X)$ or μ_X, is given by

$$E(X) \equiv \sum_{\text{all } x} x p(x)$$

The analogous formula for the continuous case is[11]

$$E(X) \equiv \int_{-\infty}^{\infty} x p(x)\, dx$$

---

[10]The expectation and variance are undefined for some random variables, a possibility that I will ignore here.

[11]We need only integrate over the support of X, which may not include the entire real line.

The variance of a random variable X, written $V(X)$ or σ_X^2, is defined as

$$V(X) \equiv E[(X - \mu_X)^2]$$
$$= E(X^2) - \mu_X^2$$

Thus, in the discrete case,

$$V(X) \equiv \sum_{\text{all } x} (x - \mu_X)^2 p(x)$$

while, in the continuous case,

$$V(X) \equiv \int_{-\infty}^{\infty} (x - \mu_X)^2 p(x)\,dx$$

The variance is expressed in the squared units of the random variable (e.g., "squared number of heads"), but the *standard deviation* $\sigma \equiv +\sqrt{\sigma^2}$ is measured in the same units as the variable.

For our example,

x	$p(x)$	$xp(x)$	$x - \mu$	$(x-\mu)^2 p(x)$
0	.25	0.00	-1	0.25
1	.50	0.50	0	0.00
2	.25	0.50	1	0.25
Sum	1.00	$\mu = 1.00$		$\sigma^2 = 0.50$

Thus, $E(X) = 1$, $V(X) = 0.5$, and $\sigma = \sqrt{0.5} \approx 0.707$. Similarly, for the rectangular distribution (Equation 4.6),

$$E(X) = \int_a^b x \left(\frac{1}{b-a} \right) dx = \frac{a+b}{2}$$

$$V(X) = \int_a^b \left(x - \frac{a+b}{2} \right)^2 \left(\frac{1}{b-a} \right) dx = \frac{(a-b)^2}{12}$$

4.2.2 *Joint and Conditional Probability Distributions*

The *joint probability distribution* of two discrete random variables X_1 and X_2 gives the probability of simultaneously observing any pair of values for the two variables. We write $p_{12}(x_1, x_2)$ for $\Pr(X_1 = x_1$ and $X_2 = x_2)$; it is usually unambiguous to drop the subscript on p, simply writing $p(x_1, x_2)$. The *joint probability density* $p(x_1, x_2)$ of two continuous random variables is defined analogously. Extension to the joint probability or joint probability density $p(x_1, x_2, \ldots, x_n)$ of several random variables is straightforward.

To distinguish it from the joint probability distribution, we call $p_1(x_1)$ the *marginal probability distribution* or *marginal probability density* for X_1. We can find the marginal probability distribution for one of the random variables by summing or integrating over the values of the other: $p_1(x_1) = \sum_{x_2} p(x_1, x_2)$ or $p_1(x_1) = \int_{-\infty}^{\infty} p(x_1, x_2) \, dx_2$. Once again, we can usually drop the subscript, to write $p(x_1)$.

In the fair coin-flipping experiment, for example, let X_1 count the number of heads, and let $X_2 = 1$ if both coins are the same and zero if they are different:

Outcome	Pr	x_1	x_2
HH	.25	2	1
HT	.25	1	0
TH	.25	1	0
TT	.25	0	1

The joint and marginal distributions for X_1 and X_2 are as follows:

	$p_{12}(x_1, x_2)$		
	x_2		
x_1	0	1	$p_1(x_1)$
0	0	.25	.25
1	.50	0	.50
2	0	.25	.25
$p_2(x_2)$	.50	.50	1.00

The *conditional probability distribution* or *conditional probability density* of X_1 given X_2 is

$$p_{1|2}(x_1|x_2) = \frac{p_{12}(x_1, x_2)}{p_2(x_2)}$$

It is once again usually convenient to drop the subscript, writing $p(x_1|x_2)$. For our example, the conditional distributions $p_{1|2}(x_1|x_2)$ for $x_2 = 0$ and $x_2 = 1$ are

	$p_{1|2}(x_1|x_2)$	
	x_2	
x_1	0	1
0	0	.5
1	1.0	0
2	0	.5
Sum	1.0	1.0

The *conditional expectation* of X_1 given $X_2 = x_2$—written $E_{1|2}(X_1|x_2)$ or, more compactly, $E(X_1|x_2)$—is found from the conditional distribution

$p_{1|2}(x_1|x_2)$, as is the *conditional variance* of X_1 given $X_2 = x_2$, written $V_{1|2}(X_1|x_2)$ or $V(X_1|x_2)$; for example, in the discrete case,

$$E_{1|2}(X_1|x_2) = \sum_{x_1} x_1 p_{1|2}(x_1|x_2)$$

$$V_{1|2}(X_1|x_2) = \sum_{x_1} [x_1 - E_{1|2}(X_1|x_2)]^2 p_{1|2}(x_1|x_2)$$

Using the illustrative conditional distributions $p_{1|2}(x_1|x_2)$,

$$E_{1|2}(X_1|0) = 0(0) + 1(1) + 0(2) = 1$$
$$V_{1|2}(X_1|0) = 0(0-1)^2 + 1(1-1)^2 + 0(2-1)^2 = 0$$
$$E_{1|2}(X_1|1) = .5(0) + 0(1) + .5(2) = 1$$
$$V_{1|2}(X_1|1) = .5(0-1)^2 + 0(1-1)^2 + .5(2-1)^2 = 1$$

4.2.3 Independence, Dependence, and Covariance

The random variables X_1 and X_2 are said to be *independent* if $p(x_1) = p(x_1|x_2)$ for all values of X_1 and X_2; that is, when X_1 and X_2 are independent, the marginal and conditional distributions of X_1 are identical. Equivalent conditions for independence are $p(x_2) = p(x_2|x_1)$ and $p(x_1,x_2) = p(x_1)p(x_2)$: When X_1 and X_2 are independent, their joint probability or probability density is the product of their marginal probabilities or densities. In our example, it is clear that X_1 and X_2 are *not* independent. More generally, the set of n random variables $\{X_1, X_2, \ldots, X_n\}$ is independent if for every subset $\{X_a, X_b, \ldots, X_m\}$ of size $m = 2$ or larger,

$$p(x_a, x_b, \ldots, x_m) = p(x_a)p(x_b)\cdots p(x_m)$$

The *covariance* of two random variables is a measure of their *linear* dependence:

$$C(X_1, X_2) = \sigma_{12} \equiv E[(X_1 - \mu_1)(X_2 - \mu_2)]$$
$$= E(X_1 X_2) - \mu_1 \mu_2$$

When large values of X_1 are associated with large values of X_2 (and, conversely, small values with small values), the covariance is positive; when large values of X_1 are associated with small values of X_2 (and vice versa), the covariance is negative. The covariance is zero otherwise, for instance—but not exclusively—when the random variables are independent. That is, two random variables may be *nonlinearly* related and still have covariance zero: In our previous example, X_1 and X_2 are not independent, but σ_{12} is nevertheless zero (as the reader can verify). The covariance of a variable with itself is its variance: $C(X, X) = V(X)$.

The *correlation* $\rho_{12} \equiv \sigma_{12}/(\sigma_1 \sigma_2)$ between two random variables X_1 and X_2 is a normalized version of the covariance. The smallest possible value of the correlation, $\rho = -1$, is indicative of a perfect inverse linear relationship between the random variables, while the largest value, $\rho = 1$, is indicative of a perfect direct linear relationship; $\rho = 0$ corresponds to a covariance of zero and indicates the absence of a linear relationship.

4.2.4 Vector Random Variables

It is often convenient to write a collection of random variables as a *vector random variable*: for example, $\underset{(n \times 1)}{\mathbf{x}} = [X_1, X_2, \ldots, X_n]'$. The expectation of a vector random variable is simply the vector of expectations of its elements:

$$E(\mathbf{x}) = \boldsymbol{\mu}_\mathbf{x} \equiv [E(X_1), E(X_2), \ldots, E(X_n)]'$$

The *variance–covariance matrix*[12] of a vector random variable $\mathbf{x}$ is defined in analogy to the scalar variance as

$$V(\mathbf{x}) = \underset{(n \times n)}{\boldsymbol{\Sigma}_{\mathbf{xx}}} \equiv E[(\mathbf{x} - \boldsymbol{\mu}_\mathbf{x})(\mathbf{x} - \boldsymbol{\mu}_\mathbf{x})'] = \begin{bmatrix} \sigma_1^2 & \sigma_{12} & \cdots & \sigma_{1n} \\ \sigma_{21} & \sigma_2^2 & \cdots & \sigma_{2n} \\ \vdots & \vdots & \ddots & \vdots \\ \sigma_{n1} & \sigma_{n2} & \cdots & \sigma_n^2 \end{bmatrix}$$

The diagonal entries of $V(\mathbf{x})$ are the variances of the Xs, and the off-diagonal entries are their covariances. The variance–covariance matrix $V(\mathbf{x})$ is symmetric (because $\sigma_{ij} = \sigma_{ji}$) and is either positive-definite or positive-semidefinite (see Section 2.2).

The *covariance matrix* of two vector random variables $\underset{(n \times 1)}{\mathbf{x}}$ and $\underset{(m \times 1)}{\mathbf{y}}$ is

$$C(\mathbf{x}, \mathbf{y}) = \underset{(n \times m)}{\boldsymbol{\Sigma}_{\mathbf{xy}}} \equiv E[(\mathbf{x} - \boldsymbol{\mu}_\mathbf{x})(\mathbf{y} - \boldsymbol{\mu}_\mathbf{y})'] = \begin{bmatrix} \sigma_{x_1 y_1} & \sigma_{x_1 y_2} & \cdots & \sigma_{x_1 y_m} \\ \sigma_{x_2 y_1} & \sigma_{x_2 y_2} & \cdots & \sigma_{x_2 y_m} \\ \vdots & \vdots & & \vdots \\ \sigma_{x_n y_1} & \sigma_{x_n y_2} & \cdots & \sigma_{x_n y_m} \end{bmatrix}$$

and consists of the covariances between all pairs of Xs and Ys.

---

[12]The variance–covariance matrix $V(\mathbf{x})$ may also be called the *variance matrix* or the *covariance matrix* of $\mathbf{x}$.

4.3 Transformations of Random Variables

Suppose that the random variable Y is a linear function $a + bX$ (where a and b are constants) of a discrete random variable X, which has expectation μ_X and variance σ_X^2. Then

$$E(Y) = \mu_Y = \sum_x (a + bx)p(x)$$
$$= a\sum p(x) + b\sum xp(x)$$
$$= a + b\mu_X$$

and (employing this property of the expectation operator)

$$V(Y) = E[(Y - \mu_Y)^2] = E\{[(a + bX) - (a + b\mu_X)]^2\}$$
$$= b^2 E[(X - \mu_X)^2] = b^2\sigma_X^2$$

Now, let Y be a linear function $a_1X_1 + a_2X_2$ of two discrete random variables X_1 and X_2, with expectations μ_1 and μ_2, variances σ_1^2 and σ_2^2, and covariance σ_{12}. Then

$$E(Y) = \mu_Y = \sum_{x_1}\sum_{x_2}(a_1x_1 + a_2x_2)p(x_1, x_2)$$
$$= \sum_{x_1}\sum_{x_2}a_1x_1 p(x_1, x_2) + \sum_{x_1}\sum_{x_2}a_2x_2 p(x_1, x_2)$$
$$= a_1\sum_{x_1}x_1 p(x_1) + a_2\sum_{x_2}x_2 p(x_2)$$
$$= a_1\mu_1 + a_2\mu_2$$

and

$$V(Y) = E[(Y - \mu_Y)^2]$$
$$= E\{[(a_1X_1 + a_2X_2) - (a_1\mu_1 + a_2\mu_2)]^2\}$$
$$= a_1^2 E[(X_1 - \mu_1)^2] + a_2^2 E[(X_2 - \mu_2)^2]$$
$$\quad + 2a_1a_2 E[(X_1 - \mu_1)(X_2 - \mu_2)]$$
$$= a_1^2\sigma_1^2 + a_2^2\sigma_2^2 + 2a_1a_2\sigma_{12}$$

When X_1 and X_2 are independent and, consequently, $\sigma_{12} = 0$, this expression simplifies to $V(Y) = a_1^2\sigma_1^2 + a_2^2\sigma_2^2$.

Although I have developed these rules for discrete random variables, they apply equally to the continuous case. For instance, if $Y = a + bX$ is a linear function of the continuous random variable X, then[13]

$$E(Y) = \int_{-\infty}^{\infty} (a+bx)p(x)\,dx$$
$$= a \int_{-\infty}^{\infty} p(x)\,dx + b \int_{-\infty}^{\infty} xp(x)\,dx$$
$$= a + bE(X)$$

4.3.1 Transformations of Vector Random Variables

These results generalize to vector random variables in the following manner: Let $\underset{(m\times 1)}{\mathbf{y}}$ be a linear transformation $\underset{(m\times n)}{\mathbf{A}}\ \underset{(n\times 1)}{\mathbf{x}}$ of the vector random variable $\mathbf{x}$, which has expectation $E(\mathbf{x}) = \boldsymbol{\mu}_{\mathbf{x}}$ and variance–covariance matrix $V(\mathbf{x}) = \boldsymbol{\Sigma}_{\mathbf{xx}}$. Then it can be shown (in a manner analogous to the scalar proofs given previously) that

$$E(\mathbf{y}) = \boldsymbol{\mu}_{\mathbf{y}} = \mathbf{A}\boldsymbol{\mu}_{\mathbf{x}}$$
$$V(\mathbf{y}) = \boldsymbol{\Sigma}_{\mathbf{yy}} = \mathbf{A}\boldsymbol{\Sigma}_{\mathbf{xx}}\mathbf{A}'$$

If the elements of $\mathbf{x}$ are pairwise independent, then all of the off-diagonal entries of $\boldsymbol{\Sigma}_{\mathbf{xx}}$ are zero, and the variance of each element Y_i of $\mathbf{y}$ takes an especially simple form:

$$\sigma_{Y_i}^2 = \sum_{j=1}^{n} a_{ij}^2 \sigma_{X_j}^2$$

At times, when $\mathbf{y} = f(\mathbf{x})$, we need to know not only $E(\mathbf{y})$ and $V(\mathbf{y})$, but also the probability distribution of $\mathbf{y}$. Indeed, the transformation $f(\cdot)$ may be nonlinear. Suppose that there is the same number of elements n in $\mathbf{y}$ and $\mathbf{x}$; that the function $f(\cdot)$ is differentiable; and that $f(\cdot)$ is one to one over the domain of $\mathbf{x}$-values under consideration (i.e., there is a unique pairing of $\mathbf{x}$-values and $\mathbf{y}$-values). This last property implies that we can write the inverse transformation $\mathbf{x} = f^{-1}(\mathbf{y})$. The probability density for $\mathbf{y}$ is given by

$$p(\mathbf{y}) = p(\mathbf{x})\left|\det\left(\frac{\partial\mathbf{x}}{\partial\mathbf{y}}\right)\right| = p(\mathbf{x})\left|\det\left(\frac{\partial\mathbf{y}}{\partial\mathbf{x}}\right)\right|^{-1}$$

---

[13]The integral $\int$ is the continuous analog of the sum Σ, as explained in Chapter 3 on calculus (see Section 3.7.1).

where $|\det(\partial\mathbf{x}/\partial\mathbf{y})|$, called the *Jacobian* of the transformation, is the absolute value of the $(n \times n)$ determinant

$$\det \begin{bmatrix} \dfrac{\partial X_1}{\partial Y_1} & \cdots & \dfrac{\partial X_n}{\partial Y_1} \\ \vdots & \ddots & \vdots \\ \dfrac{\partial X_1}{\partial Y_n} & \cdots & \dfrac{\partial X_n}{\partial Y_n} \end{bmatrix}$$

and $|\det(\partial\mathbf{y}/\partial\mathbf{x})|$ is similarly defined.[14]

---

[14]The Jacobian is named after the 19th-century German mathematician Carl Gustav Jacob Jacobi.

CHAPTER 5. COMMON PROBABILITY DISTRIBUTIONS

Many of the distributions discussed in this chapter—such as the binomial distributions, the normal distributions, the t-distributions, the F-distributions, and the chi-square distributions—are likely old friends (or at least nodding acquaintances) from a course in basic statistics. In the first and second sections of the chapter, I describe families of discrete and continuous distributions that are prominent in statistics. The third section is devoted to exponential families of distributions, a synthesis that includes most of the distributional families described earlier in the chapter and that plays an important role in modern statistical modeling.

5.1 Some Discrete Probability Distributions

In this section, I define several important families of discrete probability distributions: the binomial and Bernoulli distributions; the multinomial distributions; the Poisson distributions, which can be construed as an approximation to the binomial; and the negative binomial distributions. It is sometimes convenient to refer to a family of probability distributions in the singular—for example, the "binomial *distribution*" rather than the "binomial *distributions*."

5.1.1 The Binomial and Bernoulli Distributions

The coin-flipping experiment described in the preceding chapter (see in particular Section 4.2) gives rise to a binomial random variable that counts the number of heads in two independent flips of a fair coin. To extend this example, let the random variable X count the number of heads in n independent flips of a coin. Let ϕ denote the probability (not necessarily .5) of obtaining a head on any given flip; then $1 - \phi$ is the probability of obtaining a tail. The probability of observing exactly x heads and $n - x$ tails [i.e., $\Pr(X = x)$] is given by the *binomial distribution*

$$p(x) = \binom{n}{x} \phi^x (1 - \phi)^{n-x} \qquad (5.1)$$

where x is any integer between 0 and n, inclusive; the factor $\phi^x (1 - \phi)^{n-x}$ is the probability of observing x heads and $n - x$ tails in a *particular* arrange-

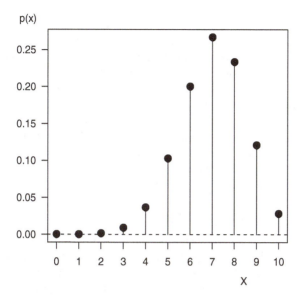

Figure 5.1 The binomial distribution for $n = 10$ and $\phi = .7$.

ment[1]; and $\binom{n}{x} \equiv n!/[x!(n-x)!]$, called the *binomial coefficient*, is the number of *different* arrangements of x heads and $n-x$ tails.[2] Figure 5.1 shows the binomial distribution for $n = 10$ and $\phi = .7$.

The expectation of the binomial random variable X is $E(X) = n\phi$, and its variance is $V(X) = n\phi(1-\phi)$. If the products $n\phi$ and $n(1-\phi)$ are sufficiently large (say, both at least equal to 10), then the discrete binomial

---

[1] For example, suppose that the x heads precede the $n-x$ tails. Then the probability of observing that arrangement is $\underbrace{\phi \times \cdots \times \phi}_{x \text{ of these}} \times \underbrace{(1-\phi) \times \cdots \times (1-\phi)}_{n-x \text{ of these}} = \phi^x(1-\phi)^{n-x}$. Because the product is the same regardless of the arrangement of the ϕs and $(1-\phi)$s, this is the probability of *any* specific sequence of x heads and $n-x$ tails.

[2] Recall that the exclamation point is the *factorial* operator:

$$n! \equiv n \times (n-1) \times \cdots \times 2 \times 1 \text{ for integer } n > 1$$
$$\equiv 1 \text{ for } n = 0 \text{ or } 1$$

distribution can be accurately approximated by the continuous normal distribution with the same mean and standard deviation.[3]

A binomial random variable is to be distinguished from a *Bernoulli random variable*, which takes on the values 1 and 0 with probabilities ϕ and $1 - \phi$, respectively. The mean and variance of a Bernoulli random variable X are $E(X) = \phi$ and $V(X) = \phi(1 - \phi)$. A Bernoulli random variable could be used to model a *single* flip of a coin, for example, assigning $X = 1$ to a head and $X = 0$ to a tail. The *sum* of n independent, identically distributed Bernoulli random variables is therefore binomially distributed, and the Bernoulli distribution is a limiting case of the binomial distribution when the number of trials $n = 1$. The Bernoulli distribution is named after the 17th-century Swiss mathematician Jacob Bernoulli.

5.1.2   The Multinomial Distributions

Imagine n repeated, independent trials of a process that on each trial can give rise to one of k different categories of outcomes. Let the random variable X_i count the number of outcomes in category i. Let ϕ_i denote the probability of obtaining an outcome in category i on any given trial. Then $\sum_{i=1}^{k} \phi_i = 1$ and $\sum_{i=1}^{k} X_i = n$.

Suppose, for instance, that we toss a die n times, letting X_1 count the number of ones, X_2 the number of twos, ..., X_6 the number of sixes. Then $k = 6$, and ϕ_1 is the probability of obtaining a 1 on any toss, ϕ_2 is the probability of obtaining a 2, and so on. If the die is "fair," then $\phi_1 = \phi_2 = \cdots = \phi_6 = 1/6$.

Returning to the general case, the vector random variable $\mathbf{x} \equiv [X_1, X_2, \ldots, X_k]'$ follows the *multinomial distribution*,

$$p(\mathbf{x}) = p(x_1, x_2, \ldots, x_k) = \frac{n!}{x_1! x_2! \cdots x_k!} \phi_1^{x_1} \phi_2^{x_2} \cdots \phi_k^{x_k}$$

The rationale for this formula is similar to that of the binomial distribution: $\phi_1^{x_1} \phi_2^{x_2} \cdots \phi_k^{x_k}$ gives the probability of obtaining x_1 outcomes in Category 1, x_2 in Category 2, and so on, in a *particular* arrangement; and $n!/(x_1! x_2! \cdots x_k!)$ counts the number of *different* arrangements. If $k = 2$, then $x_2 = n - x_1$, and the multinomial distribution reduces to the binomial distribution of Equation 5.1 (on page 122).

The expectations of the elements of $\mathbf{x}$ are $E(X_i) = n\phi_i$; their variances are $V(X_i) = n\phi_i(1 - \phi_i)$; and their covariances are $C(X_i, X_j) = -n\phi_i\phi_j$. Because of the constraint that $\sum_{i=1}^{k} X_i = n$, the variance–covariance matrix of $\mathbf{x}$ is

---

[3]The normal distributions are discussed below in Section 5.2.1.

necessarily singular, but it is typically positive-definite if we remove one of the X_is.

5.1.3 *The Poisson Distributions*

The 19th-century French mathematician Siméon-Denis Poisson introduced the distribution that bears his name as an approximation to the binomial. The approximation is accurate when n is large and ϕ is small, and when the product of the two, $\lambda \equiv n\phi$, is neither large nor small. The *Poisson distribution* is

$$p(x) = \frac{\lambda^x e^{-\lambda}}{x!} \quad \text{for } x = 0, 1, 2, 3, \ldots \text{ and } \lambda > 0$$

where $e \approx 2.71828$ is the mathematical constant. Although the domain of X is all nonnegative integers, the approximation works because $p(x) \approx 0$ when x is sufficiently large.

The Poisson distribution arises naturally in several other contexts. Suppose, for example, that we observe a process that randomly produces events of a particular kind (e.g., births or auto accidents), counting the number of events X that occur in a fixed time interval. This count follows a Poisson distribution if the following conditions hold:

- Although the particular time points at which the events occur are random, the probabilistic *rate* of occurrence is fixed during the interval of observation.

- If we focus attention on a sufficiently small subinterval of length s, then the probability of observing one event in that subinterval is proportional to its length, λs, and the probability of observing more than one event is negligible. In this context, it is natural to think of the parameter λ of the Poisson distribution as the *rate of occurrence* of the event.

- The occurrence of events in nonoverlapping subintervals is independent.

The expectation of a Poisson random variable is $E(X) = \lambda$, and its variance is also $V(X) = \lambda$. Figure 5.2 illustrates the Poisson distribution with rate parameter $\lambda = 5$ (implying that, on average, five events occur during the fixed period of observation—i.e., a unit interval of time, such as a month).

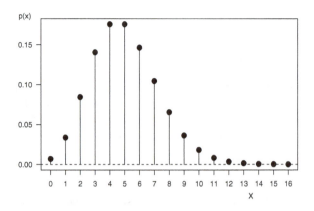

Figure 5.2   The Poisson distribution with rate parameter $\lambda = 5$.

5.1.4   The Negative Binomial Distributions

Imagine an experiment in which a coin is flipped independently until a fixed "target" number of *s heads* is achieved, and let the random variable X count the number of *tails* that are observed before the target is reached. Then X follows a *negative binomial distribution*, with probability distribution

$$p(x) = \binom{s+x-1}{x} \phi^s (1-\phi)^x \text{ for } x = 0, 1, 2, \ldots$$

where ϕ is the probability of a head on an individual flip of the coin. The expectation of the negative binomial random variable is $E(X) = s(1-\phi)/\phi$, and its variance is $V(X) = s(1-\phi)/\phi^2$. Figure 5.3 shows the negative binomial distribution for $s = 4$ and $\phi = .5$.

5.2   Some Continuous Distributions

In this section, I describe several important families of continuous distributions: the normal, chi-square, t-, F-, multivariate-normal, exponential, inverse Gaussian, gamma, beta, and Wishart distributions.

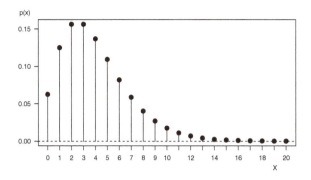

Figure 5.3 Negative binomial distribution for $s = 4$ and $\phi = .5$.

5.2.1 The Normal Distributions

A *normally distributed* (or *Gaussian*) random variable X has probability density function

$$p(x) = \frac{1}{\sigma\sqrt{2\pi}} \exp\left[-\frac{(x-\mu)^2}{2\sigma^2}\right] \text{ for } -\infty < x < \infty \qquad (5.2)$$

where the parameters of the distribution μ and σ^2 are, respectively, the mean and variance of X. There is, therefore, a different normal distribution for each choice of μ and σ^2; several examples are shown in Figure 5.4. The common abbreviated notation $X \sim N(\mu, \sigma^2)$ means that X is normally distributed with expectation μ and variance σ^2.[4] The Gaussian distributions are named after the great German mathematician Carl Friedrich Gauss (1777–1855), although they were first introduced in 1734 by the French mathematician Abraham de Moivre as an approximation to the binomial distribution.

Of particular importance is the *unit-normal* (or *standard-normal*) random variable $Z \sim N(0, 1)$, with density function

$$\phi(z) = \frac{1}{\sqrt{2\pi}} \exp(-z^2/2) \text{ for } -\infty < z < \infty$$

---

[4]Some authors use the alternative notation $N(\mu, \sigma)$, giving the mean and *standard deviation* $\sigma = +\sqrt{\sigma^2}$ of the normally distributed variable rather than its mean and *variance*. Still another convention is to express a normal distribution as $X \sim N(\mu, 1/\sigma^2)$, where $1/\sigma^2$ (the inverse of the variance) is the *precision* of X.

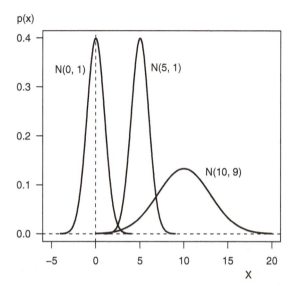

Figure 5.4 Normal density functions: $N(0,1)$, $N(5,1)$, and $N(10,9)$.

The CDF of the unit-normal distribution, $\Phi(z)$, is shown in Figure 5.5. Any normally distributed random variable $X \sim N(\mu, \sigma^2)$ can be transformed to the unit-normal distribution by *standardization*[5]:

$$Z \equiv \frac{X - \mu}{\sigma}$$

5.2.2   *The Chi-Square (χ^2) Distributions*

If $Z_1, Z_2, \ldots, Z_n$ are independently distributed unit-normal random variables, then

$$X^2 \equiv Z_1^2 + Z_2^2 + \cdots + Z_n^2$$

---

[5]*Any* random variable with finite mean and variance can be standardized to mean zero and variance one, but standardization leaves the *shape* of the distribution unchanged—in particular, it does not magically transform a nonnormal variable to normality.

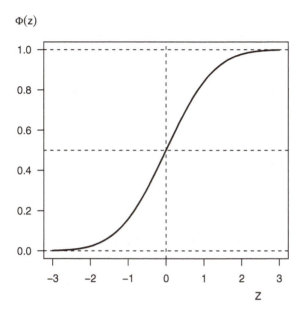

$\Phi(z)$

Figure 5.5 The cumulative distribution function $\Phi(z)$ of the unit-normal distribution.

follows a *chi-square distribution* with *n degrees of freedom*, abbreviated χ_n^2. The probability density function of the chi-square variable is

$$P(x^2) = \frac{1}{2^{n/2}\Gamma(\frac{n}{2})}(x^2)^{(n-2)/2}\exp(-x^2/2) \text{ for } x^2 \geq 0$$

where $\Gamma(\cdot)$ is the *gamma function*

$$\Gamma(v) \equiv \int_0^\infty e^{-v}z^{v-1}dz \tag{5.3}$$

(for the generic argument $v > 0$), which is a kind of continuous generalization of the factorial function; in particular, when v is a nonnegative integer, $v! = \Gamma(v+1)$. In the current case,

$$\Gamma\left(\frac{n}{2}\right) = \begin{cases} \left(\frac{n}{2}-1\right)! & \text{for } n \text{ even} \\ \left(\frac{n}{2}-1\right)\left(\frac{n}{2}-2\right)\cdots\left(\frac{3}{2}\right)\left(\frac{1}{2}\right)\sqrt{\pi} & \text{for } n \text{ odd} \end{cases}$$

The expectation and variance of a chi-square random variable are $E(X^2) = n$ and $V(X^2) = 2n$, respectively. Several chi-square distributions are graphed

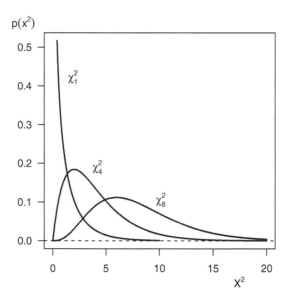

Figure 5.6   Chi-square density functions: χ_1^2, χ_4^2, and χ_8^2.

in Figure 5.6. As is suggested by the graph, the chi-square distributions are positively skewed but grow more symmetric (and approach normality) as degrees of freedom increase.

If $X_1^2, X_2^2, \ldots, X_k^2$ are independent chi-square random variables with n_1, $n_2, \ldots, n_k$ degrees of freedom, consecutively, then $X \equiv X_1^2 + X_2^2 + \cdots + X_n^2$ is chi-square distributed with $n = n_1 + n_2 + \cdots + n_k$ degrees of freedom.

5.2.3   Student's t-Distributions

If Z follows a unit-normal distribution, and X^2 independently follows a chi-square distribution with n degrees of freedom, then

$$t \equiv \frac{Z}{\sqrt{\frac{X^2}{n}}}$$

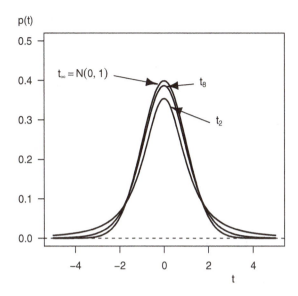

Figure 5.7 t density functions: t_2, t_8, and $t_\infty = N(0, 1)$.

is a *Student's t* random variable with n degrees of freedom, abbreviated t_n.[6] The probability density function of t is

$$p(t) = \frac{\Gamma\left(\frac{n+1}{2}\right)}{\sqrt{\pi n}\,\Gamma\left(\frac{n}{2}\right)} \times \frac{1}{\left(1 + \frac{t^2}{n}\right)^{(n+1)/2}} \quad \text{for } -\infty < t < \infty \qquad (5.4)$$

From the symmetry of this formula around $t = 0$, it is clear that $E(t) = 0$.[7] It can be shown that $V(t) = n/(n-2)$, for $n > 2$; thus, the variance of t is large for small degrees of freedom, and approaches one as n increases.

Several t-distributions are shown in Figure 5.7. As degrees of freedom grow, the t-distribution approaches the unit-normal distribution, and in the

---

[6]I write a lowercase t rather than T for the random variable in deference to nearly universal usage.

[7]When $n = 1$, the expectation $E(t)$ does not exist, but the *median* of t (the t-value with half the density below it and half above) and its *mode* (the t-value with the highest density) are still zero; t_1 is called the *Cauchy distribution*, named after the 19th-century French mathematician Augustin Louis Cauchy.

limit, $t_\infty = N(0, 1)$. The normal approximation to the t-distribution is quite close for n as small as 30.

Student's t-distribution is named after William Sealy Gossett, an early 20th-century English statistician employed by the Guiness brewery in Dublin, who wrote under the pen name "Student." Student's t-distribution played an important role in the development of small-sample statistical inference.

5.2.4 The F-Distributions

Let X_1^2 and X_2^2 be independently distributed chi-square variables with n_1 and n_2 degrees of freedom, respectively. Then

$$F \equiv \frac{X_1^2/n_1}{X_2^2/n_2}$$

follows an *F-distribution* with n_1 numerator degrees of freedom and n_2 denominator degrees of freedom, abbreviated F_{n_1,n_2}. The F-distribution was named in honor of its discoverer, the great British statistician Sir R. A. Fisher, by the 20th-century American statistician George W. Snedecor.

The probability density for F is

$$p(f) = \frac{\Gamma\left(\frac{n_1+n_2}{2}\right)}{\Gamma\left(\frac{n_1}{2}\right)\Gamma\left(\frac{n_2}{2}\right)} \left(\frac{n_1}{n_2}\right)^{n_1/2} f^{(n_1-2)/2} \left(1 + \frac{n_1}{n_2}f\right)^{-(n_1+n_2)/2} \quad \text{for } f \geq 0$$

(5.5)

Comparing Equations 5.4 and 5.5, it can be shown that $t_n^2 = F_{1,n}$. Moreover, as n_2 grows larger, F_{n_1,n_2} approaches $\chi_{n_1}^2/n_1$ and, in the limit, $F_{n,\infty} = \chi_n^2/n$.

For $n_2 > 2$, the expectation of F is $E(F) = n_2/(n_2 - 2)$, which is approximately one for large values of n_2. For $n_2 > 4$,

$$V(F) = \frac{2n_2^2(n_1+n_2-2)}{n_1(n_2-2)^2(n_2-4)}$$

Figure 5.8 shows several F probability density functions. The F-distributions are positively skewed.

5.2.5 The Multivariate-Normal Distributions

The joint probability density for a *multivariate-normal* vector random variable $\mathbf{x} = [X_1, X_2, \ldots, X_n]'$ with mean vector $\boldsymbol{\mu}$ and positive-definite variance–covariance matrix $\boldsymbol{\Sigma}$ is given by

$$p(\mathbf{x}) = \frac{1}{(2\pi)^{n/2}\sqrt{\det \boldsymbol{\Sigma}}} \exp\left[-\frac{1}{2}(\mathbf{x}-\boldsymbol{\mu})'\boldsymbol{\Sigma}^{-1}(\mathbf{x}-\boldsymbol{\mu})\right] \qquad (5.6)$$

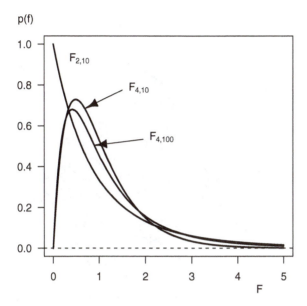

Figure 5.8 F density functions: $F_{2,10}$, $F_{4,10}$, and $F_{4,100}$.

which is abbreviated as $\mathbf{x} \sim N_n(\boldsymbol{\mu}, \boldsymbol{\Sigma})$.

If $\mathbf{x}$ is multivariately normally distributed, then the marginal distribution of each of its components is univariate normal, $X_i \sim N(\mu_i, \sigma_i^2)$;[8] and the conditional distribution of any subset of variables given the others, $p(\mathbf{x}_1 | \mathbf{x}_2)$, where $\mathbf{x} = \{\mathbf{x}_1, \mathbf{x}_2\}$, is also normal. Furthermore, if $\mathbf{x} \sim N_n(\boldsymbol{\mu}, \boldsymbol{\Sigma})$, and

$$\underset{(m \times 1)}{\mathbf{y}} = \underset{(m \times n)(n \times 1)}{\mathbf{A} \quad \mathbf{x}}$$

is a linear transformation of $\mathbf{x}$ with $\text{rank}(\mathbf{A}) = m \leq n$, then $\mathbf{y} \sim N_m(\mathbf{A}\boldsymbol{\mu}, \mathbf{A}\boldsymbol{\Sigma}\mathbf{A}')$. We say that a vector random variable $\mathbf{x}$ follows a *singular normal distribution* if the covariance matrix $\boldsymbol{\Sigma}$ of $\mathbf{x}$ is singular, but if a maximal linearly independent subset of $\mathbf{x}$ is multivariately normally distributed.

A *bivariate-normal* density function for $\mu_1 = 5$, $\mu_2 = 6$, $\sigma_1 = 1.5$, $\sigma_2 = 3$, and $\rho_{12} = .5$—that is, $\sigma_{12} = (.5)(1.5)(3) = 2.25$—is depicted in Figure 5.9.

The exponent in the formula for the multivariate-normal distribution (Equation 5.6) includes a quadratic form in the inverse of the covariance matrix,

---

[8]The converse is *not* true: Each X_i can be *univariately* normally distributed without $\mathbf{x}$ being *multivariate* normal.

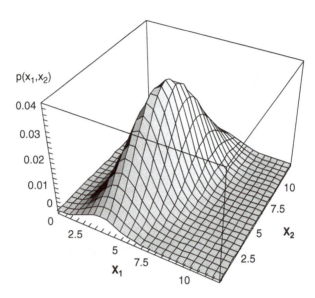

Figure 5.9   The bivariate-normal density function for $\mu_1 = 5$, $\mu_2 = 6$, $\sigma_1 = 1.5$, $\sigma_2 = 3$, and $\sigma_{12} = 2.25$. The slices of the density surface shown by the lines drawn on the surface, representing the conditional distributions of each variable given specific values of the other, are normal both in the direction of X_1 and in the direction of X_2.

$(\mathbf{x} - \boldsymbol{\mu})'\boldsymbol{\Sigma}^{-1}(\mathbf{x} - \boldsymbol{\mu})$, and consequently (using the results on ellipses and ellipsoids developed in Section 2.2.1) the *density contours* (i.e., levels of constant density) of the distribution are ellipsoidal in the general case and ellipses when $n = 2$.

Figure 5.10 graphs two density contours for the bivariate-normal distribution shown in Figure 5.9:

- Both ellipses are centered at the point of means $(\mu_1 = 5, \mu_2 = 6)$.

- The larger (solid-line) ellipse is drawn by setting the quadratic form in the exponent of the bivariate-normal distribution to $\chi^2_{2,.95}$, the .95 *quantile* (or 95th *percentile*) of the chi-square distribution (the value

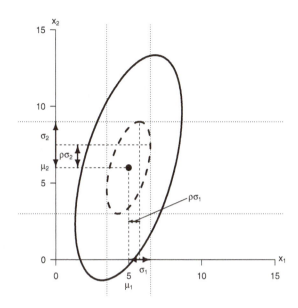

Figure 5.10   Elliptical density contours for the bivariate-normal
distribution with $\mu_1 = 5$, $\mu_2 = 6$, $\sigma_1 = 1.5$, $\sigma_2 = 3$, and
$\sigma_{12} = \rho\sigma_1\sigma_2 = 2.25$. The larger (solid-line) ellipse encloses
a probability of .95, while the smaller (broken-line) ellipse is
the standard concentration ellipse.

of χ_2^2 with probability .95 below it),[9] thus enclosing a probability of
.95: If we repeatedly sample from this bivariate-normal distribution,
then in the long run 95% of observations will fall within the .95 concentration ellipse.

- The smaller (broken-line) ellipse is the *standard concentration ellipse*,
  drawn by setting the quadratic form to one. The quantities shown in
  the graph follow from the properties of the elliptical representation of
  quadratic forms, discussed in Section 2.2.1. In particular, the shadows
  of the standard ellipse on the horizontal and vertical axes are, respectively, twice the standard deviations of the variables, $\sigma_1 = 1.5$ and

---

[9]Recall from Section 5.2.2 that a chi-square random variable with 2 degrees of freedom is the
sum of two squared standard-normal random variables. The quadratic form $(\mathbf{x} - \boldsymbol{\mu})'\boldsymbol{\Sigma}^{-1}(\mathbf{x} - \boldsymbol{\mu})$
is in effect a 2D (more generally, a multidimensional) standardization.

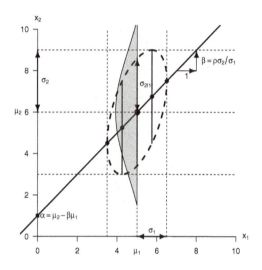

Figure 5.11   The standard data ellipse for the bivariate-normal
distribution, showing conditional distributions of $X_2|X_1$ and
the population regression line $E(X_2) = \alpha + \beta X_1$ of X_2 on X_1.
The conditional distribution $(X_2|X_1 = \mu_1) \sim N(\mu_2, \sigma^2_{2|1})$
appears at the center of the graph, and two other conditional
distributions are shown as vertical slices of the ellipse.

$\sigma_2 = 3$; and the lines drawn from the vertical and horizontal points
of tangency to the lines through the point of means give the product
of the absolute value of the correlation and each standard deviation,
$\rho\sigma_1 = .5 \times 1.5 = 0.75$ and $\rho\sigma_2 = .5 \times 3 = 1.5$.[10]

As depicted in Figure 5.11, vertical slices of the standard bivariate-normal
concentration ellipse represent the conditional distributions of $X_2|X_1$,
which are each univariate-normal. One such distribution, $(X_2|X_1 = \mu_1)$

---

[10]Here the correlation ρ between X_1 and X_2 is positive. More generally, the distances between
lines through the point of means and through the points of tangency are the *absolute value* of
the correlation times the standard deviations of the two variables, $|\rho|\sigma_1$ and $|\rho|\sigma_2$.

$\sim N(\mu_2, \sigma_{2|1}^2)$ is depicted on the graph; at $X_1 = \mu_1$, the conditional variance of X_2 is $\sigma_{2|1}^2 = \sigma_2^2(1 - \rho^2)$.

The length of each vertical slice is twice the conditional standard deviation of X_2 when X_1 is fixed to a particular value. The centers of the slices represent the conditional means of X_2 given X_1, thus constituting the *population regression* of X_2 on X_1. The regression is linear, with $E(X_2|X_1) = \alpha + \beta X_1$, where $\beta = \sigma_{12}/\sigma_1^2 = \rho\sigma_2/\sigma_1$ and $\alpha = \mu_2 - \beta\mu_1$. This property generalizes to higher dimensions: The population regression of any subset of multivariately normal random variables on any other subset is linear.

As is apparent from the graph, the population regression line goes through the point of means (μ_1, μ_2), and as X_1 gets closer to $\mu_1 - \sigma_1$ or to $\mu_1 + \sigma_1$, the conditional expectation of X_2 gets closer to the corresponding point of vertical tangency to the ellipse. The population regression line, therefore, goes through the points of vertical tangency and is *not* the major axis of the ellipse. A corollary is that the line for the regression X_1 on X_2 (not shown in the graph) goes through the points of *horizontal* tangency to the ellipse and is consequently distinct from the regression of X_2 on X_1.

5.2.6 *The Exponential Distributions*

The exponential distributions are a continuous family indexed by the *rate parameter* λ, with density function

$$p(x) = \lambda e^{-\lambda x} \text{ for } x \geq 0$$

The expectation and variance of X are $E(X) = 1/\lambda$ and $V(X) = 1/\lambda^2$, respectively. Several exponential distributions for different values of the rate parameter appear in Figure 5.12. The exponential distributions, which are highly positively skewed, are frequently used to model time-to-event data when the "hazard" of occurrence of an event is constant during the period of observation. The rate parameter is then interpretable as the average number of events that occur in a unit interval of time (e.g., births per year).

5.2.7 *The Inverse-Gaussian Distributions*

The inverse-Gaussian distributions are a continuous family indexed by two parameters, μ and λ, with density function

$$p(x) = \sqrt{\frac{\lambda}{2\pi x^3}} \exp\left[-\frac{\lambda(x-\mu)^2}{2x\mu^2}\right] \text{ for } x > 0$$

The expectation and variance of X are $E(X) = \mu$ and $V(X) = \mu^3/\lambda$, respectively. Figure 5.13 shows several inverse-Gaussian distributions. The vari-

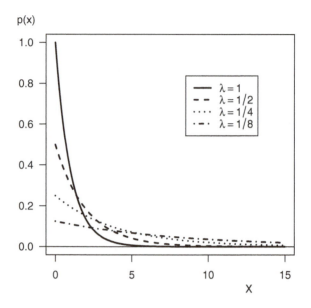

Figure 5.12 Exponential distributions for several values of the rate
parameter λ.

ance of the inverse-Gaussian distribution increases with its mean; skewness
also increases with the value of μ and decreases with λ.

The inverse-Gaussian distributions and the gamma distributions (immediately below) are often useful for modeling nonnegative continuous data.

5.2.8 The Gamma Distributions

The gamma distributions are a family of continuous distributions with probability density function indexed by the *scale parameter* $\omega > 0$ and *shape
parameter* $\psi > 0$:

$$p(x) = \left(\frac{x}{\omega}\right)^{\psi-1} \frac{\exp\left(\frac{-x}{\omega}\right)}{\omega\Gamma(\psi)} \text{ for } x > 0$$

where $\Gamma(\cdot)$ is the gamma function (Equation 5.3 on page 129). The expec-
tation and variance of the gamma distribution are $E(X) = \omega\psi$ and $V(X) = \omega^2\psi$, respectively. Figure 5.14 shows gamma distributions for scale $\omega = 1$
and several values of the shape ψ. (Altering the scale parameter would
change only the labeling of the horizontal axis in the graph.) As the shape
parameter gets larger, the distribution grows more symmetric.

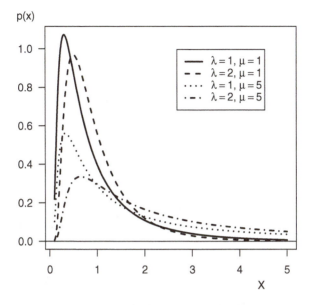

Figure 5.13 Inverse-Gaussian distributions for several combinations of values of the parameters μ and λ.

If $X_1, X_2, \ldots, X_k$ are independent gamma random variables with common scale ω and shape parameters $\psi_1, \psi_2, \ldots, \psi_k$, consecutively, then $X \equiv X_1 + X_2 + \cdots + X_k$ is gamma distributed with scale ω and shape $\psi = \psi_1 + \psi_2 + \cdots + \psi_k$.

The chi-square distribution with n degrees of freedom is equal to the gamma distribution with scale parameter $\omega = 2$ and shape $\psi = n/2$. The exponential distribution with rate parameter λ is equal to the gamma distribution with shape $\psi = 1$ and scale $\omega = 1/\lambda$.

5.2.9 The Beta Distributions

The beta distributions are a family of continuous distributions with two *shape parameters* $\alpha > 0$ and $\beta > 0$, and with density function

$$p(x) = \frac{x^{\alpha-1}(1-x)^{\beta-1}}{B(\alpha,\beta)} \text{ for } 0 \leq x \leq 1 \qquad (5.7)$$

where

$$B(\alpha,\beta) \equiv \frac{\Gamma(\alpha)\Gamma(\beta)}{\Gamma(\alpha+\beta)}$$

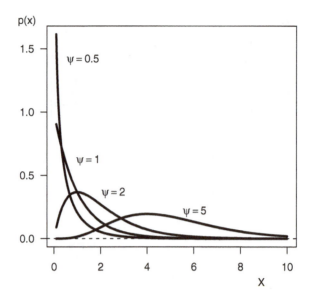

Figure 5.14   Several gamma distributions for scale $\omega = 1$ and various values of the shape parameter ψ.

is the *beta function*. The expectation and variance of the beta distribution are, respectively, $E(X) = \alpha/(\alpha+\beta)$ and

$$V(X) = \frac{\alpha\beta}{(\alpha+\beta)^2(\alpha+\beta+1)}$$

The expectation, therefore, depends on the relative size of the parameters, with $E(X) = 0.5$ when $\alpha = \beta$. The skewness of the beta distribution also depends on the relative sizes of the parameters, and the distribution is symmetric when $\alpha = \beta$. The variance declines as α and β grow. Figure 5.15 shows several beta distributions. As is apparent from these graphs, the shape of the beta distribution is very flexible.[11] The beta distribution with parameters α and β is abbreviated Beta(α, β).

---

[11]For an application of the beta distribution that takes advantage of its flexibility, see the discussion of Bayesian inference for a proportion in Section 6.4.

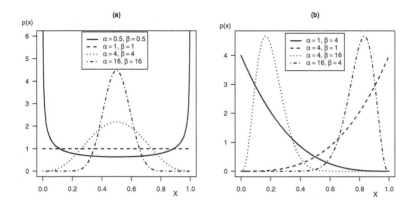

Figure 5.15 Beta distributions for several combinations of values of the shape parameters α and β. As is apparent in Panel (a), the beta distribution reduces to the rectangular distribution when $\alpha = \beta = 1$. Symmetric beta distributions, for which $\alpha = \beta$, are shown in Panel (a) and asymmetric distributions in Panel (b).

5.2.10   *The Wishart Distributions*

Suppose that the rows $i = 1, \ldots, n$ of the $(n \times p)$ matrix $\mathbf{X}$, $n > p$, are independently sampled from the multivariate-normal distribution $\mathbf{x}'_i \sim N_p(\boldsymbol{\mu}, \boldsymbol{\Sigma})$ (Section 5.2.5), where the population covariance matrix $\boldsymbol{\Sigma}$ is positive-definite. The matrix

$$\mathbf{V} = \mathbf{X}'\mathbf{X} - n\boldsymbol{\mu}\boldsymbol{\mu}'$$

follows an order-p *Wishart distribution* with covariance matrix $\boldsymbol{\Sigma}$ and n degrees of freedom, abbreviated $W_{p,n}(\boldsymbol{\Sigma})$.[12]

The density function for the Wishart distribution is rather complicated:

$$p(\mathbf{V}^*) = \frac{1}{2^{np/2}\,(\det\boldsymbol{\Sigma})^{n/2}\,\Gamma_p\left(\frac{n}{2}\right)}\,(\det\mathbf{V}^*)^{(n-p-1)/2}\exp\left[-\tfrac{1}{2}\operatorname{trace}\left(\boldsymbol{\Sigma}^{-1}\mathbf{V}^*\right)\right]$$

---

[12]The Wishart distributions are named after their discoverer, the 20th-century Scottish statistician John Wishart.

where $\mathbf{V}^*$ is a particular value of $\mathbf{V}$,[13] and where $\Gamma_p(\cdot)$ is a multivariate generalization of the gamma function $\Gamma(\cdot)$ (given in Equation 5.3 on page 129):

$$\Gamma_p(n) = \pi^{p(p-1)/4} \prod_{j=1}^{p} \Gamma\left(n + \frac{1-j}{2}\right)$$

The expectation of $\mathbf{V}$ is $E(\mathbf{V}) = n\mathbf{\Sigma}$, and the variances of its elements are $V(V_{jj'}) = n(\sigma_{jj'}^2 + \sigma_j^2 \sigma_{j'}^2)$, where the $\sigma_{jj'}$s and σ_j^2s are, respectively, the covariances and variances in $\mathbf{\Sigma}$.

Except for using the population means $\boldsymbol{\mu}$ rather than $\overline{\mathbf{x}}$ (i.e., the sample column means of $\mathbf{X}$), and omitting the divisor $n-1$, the mean-deviation sum of squares and products matrix $\mathbf{V}$ is similar to the sample covariance matrix of $\mathbf{X}$:

$$\mathbf{S} = \frac{1}{n-1}\left(\mathbf{X}'\mathbf{X} - n\overline{\mathbf{x}}\,\overline{\mathbf{x}}'\right)$$

Indeed, $(n-1)\mathbf{S}$ is Wishart distributed with $n-1$ degrees of freedom: $(n-1)\mathbf{S} \sim W_{p,n-1}(\mathbf{\Sigma})$. Because it is the sampling distribution of (a multiple of) the estimated covariance matrix of a normal population, the Wishart distribution has applications in multivariate statistics and Bayesian statistical inference.

The chi-square distributions (Section 5.2.2) are a special case of the Wishart distributions, with $p = 1$ and $\underset{(1\times 1)}{\mathbf{\Sigma}} = \sigma^2 = 1$; that is, $\chi_n^2 = W_{1,n}(1)$. Slightly more generally, the Wishart distribution for $p = 1$ and $\underset{(1\times 1)}{\mathbf{\Sigma}} = \sigma^2$ is the gamma distribution with scale parameter $\omega = 2\sigma^2$ and shape parameter $\psi = n/2$ (see Section 5.2.8).

5.3   Exponential Families of Distributions

In the two preceding sections, I separately introduced various families of discrete and continuous distributions commonly used in statistics, occasionally pointing out relationships between them, but it's remarkably possible to express all but two of these distributional families[14]—and others not discussed in this chapter—within a unifying framework called *exponential families of*

---

[13] An unobvious point is that $\mathbf{V}^*$ cannot be just *any* $p \times p$ matrix. Because the sample was drawn from a population with a positive-definite covariance matrix, and because $n > p$, $\mathbf{V}^*$ is constrained to be symmetric positive-definite.

[14] The exceptions taken up in this chapter are the families of t- and F-distributions, which are not exponential families.

distributions (not to be confused with the unfortunately similarly named exponential distributions described previously in Section 5.2.6). Because the advantages of casting a set of distributions as an exponential family are primarily technical, and because the subject quickly becomes complicated, I'll simply sketch the general idea here, illustrating it with a few examples. Exponential distributional families play a prominent role, for example, in the theory and application of *generalized linear models*.[15]

Suppose that we have a vector random variable $\mathbf{x} = [X_1, X_2, \ldots, X_k]'$ whose distribution depends on a vector of parameters $\boldsymbol{\alpha} = [\alpha_1, \alpha_2, \ldots, \alpha_p]'$. In a particular application, either $\mathbf{x}$ or $\boldsymbol{\alpha}$, or both, may be scalars. As well, $\mathbf{x}$ may be discrete or continuous. The distribution of $\mathbf{x}$ is a member of an exponential family if its probability or probability density $p(\mathbf{x})$ can be written in the following general form:

$$p(\mathbf{x}) = h(\mathbf{x})\exp[\boldsymbol{\eta}'(\boldsymbol{\alpha})T(\mathbf{x}) - A(\boldsymbol{\alpha})] \tag{5.8}$$

where

- $h(\mathbf{x})$ is a scalar function of $\mathbf{x}$;

- $\boldsymbol{\eta}(\boldsymbol{\alpha})$ transforms $\boldsymbol{\alpha}$ into a vector of r independent *canonical parameters*; if the parameters in $\boldsymbol{\alpha}$ are independent (in the sense that none are a function of others), then $r = p$, and otherwise, if there are dependencies among the elements of $\boldsymbol{\alpha}$, then $r < p$;

- $T(\mathbf{x})$ is an $(r \times 1)$ vector of minimal sufficient statistics for the parameters[16]; and

- $A(\boldsymbol{\alpha})$ is a scalar function of $\boldsymbol{\alpha}$.

To demonstrate how Equation 5.8 works, I'll apply it to the binomial distributions (a univariate discrete family with a single parameter), the normal distributions (a univariate continuous family with two parameters), and the multinomial distributions (a multivariate discrete family with several parameters).[17]

---

[15] Introduced in an influential paper by Nelder and Wedderburn (1972), generalized linear models (GLMs) include many commonly used regression models, such as linear, logit, and Poisson-regression models, among others.

[16] See Section 6.2.4 for an explanation of sufficiency, which means, roughly, that the statistics in $T(\mathbf{x})$ exhaust the information in $\mathbf{x}$ about the parameters $\boldsymbol{\alpha}$.

[17] A nontrivial exercise for the reader is to show that the results here are equivalent to the formulas for the binomial, normal, and multinomial distributions given earlier in the chapter.

5.3.1 The Binomial Family

There is a scalar random variable X for the binomial family, counting the number of "successes" in n independent trials (e.g., the number of heads in n independent flips of a coin; see Section 5.1.1). The single parameter of the distribution is $\alpha = \phi$, the probability of success on an individual trial, and the canonical parameter is $\eta(\phi) = \log_e[\phi/(1-\phi)]$, the log-odds (or logit) of success. A sufficient statistic for the parameter is x itself—that is, $T(x) = x$—and $h(x) = \binom{n}{x}$, the binomial coefficient. Finally, $A(\phi) = -n\log_e(1-\phi)$.

5.3.2 The Normal Family

The value of the scalar random variable X for the normal family depends on two independent parameters, the mean μ and variance σ^2 (see Section 5.2.1), and so $\boldsymbol{\alpha} = [\mu, \sigma^2]'$. The canonical parameter vector is $\eta(\mu, \sigma^2) = [\mu/\sigma^2, -1/(2\sigma^2)]'$. A vector of sufficient statistics is $T(\mathbf{x}) = [x, x^2]'$; $h(\mathbf{x}) = 1/\sqrt{2\pi}$ (and hence turns out not to depend on $\mathbf{x}$); and $A(\mu, \sigma^2) = \mu^2/(2\sigma^2) + \log_e \sigma$.

5.3.3 The Multinomial Family

For the multinomial family (Section 5.1.2), the vector random variable $\mathbf{x} = [X_1, X_2, \ldots, X_k]'$ counts the number of values in n independent trials falling into each of k categories. The parameters of the distribution are the probabilities $\boldsymbol{\alpha} = [\phi_1, \phi_2, \ldots, \phi_k]'$ that a single trial falls into each category. These probabilities are subject to the constraint $\sum_{i=1}^{k} \phi_i = 1$, and so only $k-1$ of them are independent; for example, $\phi_k = 1 - \sum_{i=1}^{k-1} \phi_i$. There are, therefore, only $r = k-1$ canonical parameters, and these are

$$\eta(\phi_1, \phi_2, \ldots, \phi_k) = \left[\log_e \frac{\phi_1}{1 - \sum_{i=1}^{k-1} \phi_i}, \ldots, \log_e \frac{\phi_{k-1}}{1 - \sum_{i=1}^{k-1} \phi_i}\right]'$$

that is, the logits comparing each of the first $k-1$ categories to the last.[18]

A vector of minimal sufficient statistics is $T(\mathbf{x}) = [x_1, x_2, \ldots, x_{k-1}]$ because the category counts in $\mathbf{x}$ are subject to the constraint $\sum X_i = n$, and so the count in the last category is $x_k = n - \sum_{i=1}^{k-1} x_i$. The function $h(\mathbf{x}) = n!/(x_1! \times x_2! \times \cdots \times x_k!)$, and

$$A(\phi_1, \phi_2, \ldots, \phi_k) = -n\log_e\left(1 - \sum_{i=1}^{k-1} \phi_i\right) = -n\log_e \phi_k$$

---

[18] Singling out the last category for this role is a notational convenience: We could equally well form logits comparing all other categories to *any* specific category.

CHAPTER 6. AN INTRODUCTION TO STATISTICAL THEORY

Just as probability theory is rarely prominent in elementary statistics courses for students in the social sciences, such courses rarely venture beyond the basics of statistical inference. Instead, the focus is (understandably) on the big ideas, such as point estimation, sampling distributions, confidence intervals, hypothesis tests, and, perhaps (but not commonly), simple Bayesian inference. This chapter introduces fundamental ideas of mathematical statistics, beyond those covered in the two preceding chapters on probability theory and statistical distributions.

The first section of the chapter outlines asymptotic distribution theory, which is often required to determine properties of statistical estimators, a subject that is taken up in the second section. The third section develops the broadly applicable and centrally important method of maximum-likelihood estimation and closely associated procedures of statistical inference—likelihood-ratio, Wald, and score tests and confidence intervals. The final section of the chapter introduces Bayesian estimation, including Markov-chain Monte Carlo (MCMC) methods for approximating otherwise intractable probability distributions.

6.1 Asymptotic Distribution Theory

Partly because it may be difficult to determine the small-sample properties of statistical estimators, it is of interest to investigate how an estimator behaves as the sample size grows. *Asymptotic distribution theory* provides tools for this investigation. I will merely outline the theory here: More complete accounts are available in many sources, including some of the references in the Preface (see page xx).

6.1.1 Probability Limits

Although asymptotic distribution theory applies to sequences of random variables, it is necessary first to consider the *nonstochastic infinite sequence* $\{a_1, a_2, \ldots, a_n, \ldots\}$. By "nonstochastic" I mean that each a_n is a fixed number rather than a random variable. As the reader may be aware, this sequence has a *limit* a when, given any positive number ε, no matter how small, there is a positive integer $n(\varepsilon)$ such that $|a_n - a| < \varepsilon$ for all $n > n(\varepsilon)$. In words: a_n can be made arbitrarily close to a by picking n sufficiently large. The

145

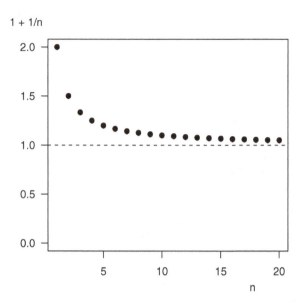

Figure 6.1   The first 20 values of the sequence $a_n = 1 + 1/n$, which has the limit $a = 1$.

notation $n(\varepsilon)$ stresses that the required value of n depends on the selected criterion ε—a smaller, more stringent, value of ε typically requires a larger $n(\varepsilon)$.[1] To describe this state of affairs compactly, we write $\lim_{n \to \infty} a_n = a$. If, for example, $a_n = 1 + 1/n$, then $\lim_{n \to \infty} a_n = 1$; this sequence and its limit are graphed in Figure 6.1.

Consider now a *sequence of random variables* $\{X_1, X_2, \ldots, X_n, \ldots\}$. In a typical statistical application, X is some estimator and n is the size of the sample from which the estimator is calculated. Let $p_n \equiv \Pr(|X_n - a| < \delta)$, where a is a constant and δ is a small positive number. Think of p_n as the probability that X_n is *close* to a. Suppose that the *nonstochastic* sequence of probabilities $\{p_1, p_2, \ldots, p_n, \ldots\}$ approaches a limit of one,[2] that is, $\lim_{n \to \infty} \Pr(|X_n - a| < \delta) = 1$. Then, as n grows, the random variable X_n concentrates more and more of its probability in a small region around a,

---

[1] Cf. the definition of the limit of a *function*, discussed in Section 3.2.

[2] To say that $\{p_1, p_2, \ldots, p_n, \ldots\}$ is a *nonstochastic*; sequence is only apparently contradictory: Although these probabilities are based on random variables, the probabilities themselves are each specific numbers—such as .6, .9, and so forth.

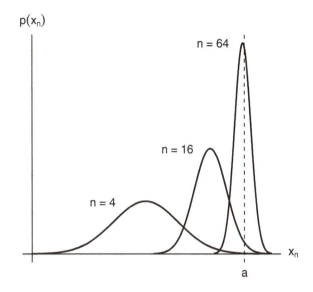

Figure 6.2　　plim $X_n = a$: As n grows, the distribution of X_n concentrates more and more of its probability in a small region around a.

a situation that is illustrated in Figure 6.2. If this result holds regardless of how small δ is, then we say that a is the *probability limit* of X_n, denoted plim $X_n = a$. It is common to drop the subscript n to write the even more compact expression, plim $X = a$.

Probability limits have the following very useful properties: If plim $X = a$, and if $Y = f(X)$ is some continuous function of X, then plim $Y = f(a)$. Likewise, if plim $X = a$, plim $Y = b$, and $Z = f(X, Y)$ is a continuous function of X and Y, then plim $Z = f(a, b)$.

6.1.2 *Asymptotic Expectation and Variance*

We return to the sequence of random variables $\{X_1, X_2, \ldots, X_n, \ldots\}$. Let μ_n denote the expectation of X_n. Then $\{\mu_1, \mu_2, \ldots, \mu_n, \ldots\}$ is a nonstochastic sequence. If this sequence approaches a limit μ, then we call μ the *asymptotic expectation* of X, also written $\mathscr{E}(X)$.

Although it seems natural to define an asymptotic variance analogously as the limit of the sequence of variances, this definition is not useful because (as the following example illustrates) $\lim_{n \to \infty} V(X_n)$ is zero in most interesting cases. Suppose that we calculate the mean $\overline{X}_n$ for a sample of size n drawn from a population with mean μ and variance σ^2. We know, from elementary statistics, that $E(\overline{X}_n) = \mu$ and that

$$V(\overline{X}_n) = E[(\overline{X}_n - \mu)^2] = \frac{\sigma^2}{n}$$

Consequently, $\lim_{n\to\infty} V(\overline{X}_n) = 0$. Inserting the factor $\sqrt{n}$ within the square, however, produces the expectation $E\{[\sqrt{n}(\overline{X}_n - \mu)]^2\} = \sigma^2$. Then dividing by n and taking the limit yields the answer that we want, defining the *asymptotic variance* of the sample mean:

$$\begin{aligned}
\mathcal{V}(\overline{X}) &\equiv \lim_{n\to\infty} \frac{1}{n} E\{[\sqrt{n}(\overline{X}_n - \mu)]^2\} \\
&= \frac{1}{n} \mathcal{E}\{[\sqrt{n}(\overline{X}_n - \mu)]^2\} \\
&= \frac{\sigma^2}{n}
\end{aligned}$$

This result is uninteresting for the present illustration because $\mathcal{V}(\overline{X}) = V(\overline{X})$; indeed, it is this equivalence that motivated the definition of the asymptotic variance in the first place. In certain applications, however, it is possible to find the asymptotic variance of a statistic when the finite-sample variance is intractable. Then we can apply the asymptotic result as an approximation in large-enough samples.[3]

In the general case, where X_n has expectation μ_n, the asymptotic variance of X is defined to be[4]

$$\mathcal{V}(X) \equiv \frac{1}{n} \mathcal{E}\{[\sqrt{n}(X_n - \mu_n)]^2\} \tag{6.1}$$

---

[3]This, of course, begs the question of how large is "large enough." Unfortunately, the answer depends on context and isn't necessarily captured by a simple rule. In the central limit theorem example immediately below, asymptotic properties assert themselves for n as small as 25, while in an example of asymptotic likelihood–based inference in Section 6.3.3, we get very poor results for a small sample with $n = 10$. In many simple applications, asymptotic properties are sufficiently accurate for, say, n of about 100, and, as a general matter, as the number of parameters to be estimated grows, we require more observations for asymptotic approximations to be adequate.

[4]It is generally preferable to define asymptotic expectation and variance in terms of the asymptotic distribution (see the next section), because the sequences used for this purpose in the current section do not exist in all cases (see Theil, 1971, pp. 375–376; also see McCallum, 1973). My use of the symbols $\mathcal{E}(\cdot)$ and $\mathcal{V}(\cdot)$ for asymptotic expectation and variance is convenient but not standard: The reader should be aware that these symbols are sometimes used in place of $E(\cdot)$ and $V(\cdot)$ to denote *ordinary* expectation and variance.

6.1.3 Asymptotic Distribution

Let $\{P_1, P_2, \ldots, P_n, \ldots\}$ represent the CDFs of a sequence of random variables $\{X_1, X_2, \ldots, X_n, \ldots\}$. The CDF of X converges to the *asymptotic distribution* P if, given any positive number ε, however small, we can find a sufficiently large $n(\varepsilon)$ such that $|P_n(x) - P(x)| < \varepsilon$ for all $n > n(\varepsilon)$ and for all values x of the random variable. In words, $P_n(x)$ can be made arbitrarily close to $P(x)$ by picking a big enough n.

A familiar illustration is provided by the *central-limit theorem*, which (in one of its versions) states that the mean of a set of independent and identically distributed random variables with finite expectations and variances follows an approximate normal distribution, the approximation improving as the number of random variables increases. Consider, for example, the mean of a sample of size n from the highly skewed exponential distribution with rate parameter $\lambda = 1$, for which the mean μ and variance σ^2 are both equal to 1. The exponential distribution is a special case of the gamma distribution, with shape parameter $\psi = 1$ and scale $\omega = 1/\lambda$; therefore, the sample sum $\sum_{i=1}^{n} X_i$ (and hence $n\overline{X}$) is gamma distributed with scale $\omega = 1$ and shape $\psi = n$.[5] Figure 6.3 shows how the density function for the sampling distribution of the sample mean from this exponential population changes as the sample size grows, in each case comparing the true gamma sampling distribution of $\overline{X}$ with the normal approximation $N(1, 1/n)$: The normal approximation increases in accuracy (and the variance of the sampling distribution of $\overline{X}$ decreases) as the sample size gets larger.

6.1.4 Vector and Matrix Random Variables

The results of this section extend straightforwardly to vectors and matrices: We say that $\text{plim} \underset{(m \times 1)}{\mathbf{x}} = \underset{(m \times 1)}{\mathbf{a}}$ when $\text{plim} X_i = a_i$ for $i = 1, 2, \ldots, m$. Likewise, $\text{plim} \underset{(m \times p)}{\mathbf{X}} = \underset{(m \times p)}{\mathbf{A}}$ means that $\text{plim} X_{ij} = a_{ij}$ for all i and j. The asymptotic expectation of the vector random variable $\underset{(m \times 1)}{\mathbf{x}}$ is defined as the vector of asymptotic expectations of its elements, $\boldsymbol{\mu} = \mathscr{E}(\mathbf{x}) \equiv [\mathscr{E}(X_1), \mathscr{E}(X_2), \ldots, \mathscr{E}(X_m)]'$. The asymptotic variance–covariance matrix of $\mathbf{x}$ is given by

$$\mathscr{V}(\mathbf{x}) \equiv \frac{1}{n} \mathscr{E}\{[\sqrt{n}(\mathbf{x}_n - \boldsymbol{\mu}_n)][\sqrt{n}(\mathbf{x}_n - \mu_n)]'\}$$

---

[5]The exponential and gamma distributions are described, respectively, in Sections 5.2.6 and 5.2.8.

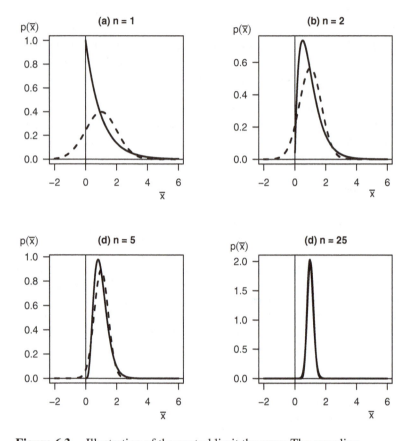

Figure 6.3   Illustration of the central limit theorem: The sampling distribution of the sample mean $\overline{X}$ for samples from an exponential population with rate parameter $\lambda = 1$, for various sample sizes n. Panel (a), for $n = 1$, corresponds to the population distribution of X. In each panel, the solid line gives the density function of the true (gamma) sampling distribution of $\overline{X}$, while the broken line gives the density function for the normal approximation $N(1, 1/n)$. In Panel (d), where $n = 25$, the normal approximation is virtually indistinguishable from the true sampling distribution.

6.2 Properties of Estimators

Most of the material in this and the following section can be traced to a remarkable seminal paper on estimation by Fisher (1922)—arguably the most important statistical paper of the 20th century (see Aldrich, 1997).

An *estimator* is a sample statistic (i.e., a function of the observations of a sample) used to estimate an unknown population parameter. Because its value varies from one sample to the next, an estimator is a random variable. An *estimate* is the value of an estimator for a particular sample. The probability distribution of an estimator is called its *sampling distribution*, and the variance of this distribution is called the *sampling variance* of the estimator.

6.2.1 Bias and Unbias

An estimator A of the parameter α is *unbiased* if $E(A) = \alpha$. The difference $E(A) - \alpha$ (which is zero for an unbiased estimator) is the *bias* of A.

Suppose, for example, that we draw n independent observations X_i from a population with mean μ and variance σ^2. Then the sample mean $\overline{X} \equiv \sum X_i/n$ is an unbiased estimator of μ, while

$$S_*^2 \equiv \frac{\sum (X_i - \overline{X})^2}{n} \tag{6.2}$$

is a biased estimator of σ^2, because $E(S_*^2) = [(n-1)/n]\sigma^2$; the bias of S_*^2 is, therefore, $-\sigma^2/n$. Sampling distributions of unbiased and biased estimators are illustrated in Figure 6.4.

Asymptotic Bias and Unbias

The *asymptotic bias* of an estimator A of α is $\mathscr{E}(A) - \alpha$, and the estimator is *asymptotically unbiased* if $\mathscr{E}(A) = \alpha$. Thus, S_*^2 is asymptotically unbiased, because its bias $-\sigma^2/n \to 0$ as $n \to \infty$.

6.2.2 Mean-Squared Error and Efficiency

To say that an estimator is unbiased means that its average value over repeated samples is equal to the parameter being estimated. This is clearly a desirable property for an estimator to possess, but it is cold comfort if the estimator does not provide estimates that are close to the parameter: In forming the expectation, large negative estimation errors for some samples could offset large positive errors for others.

The *mean-squared error (MSE)* of an estimator A of the parameter α is literally the average squared difference between the estimator and the parameter: $\text{MSE}(A) \equiv E[(A - \alpha)^2]$. Squaring prevents negative and positive

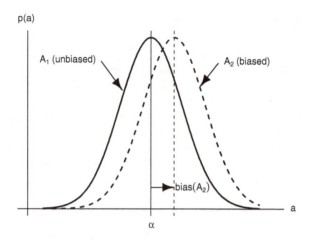

Figure 6.4   The estimator A_1 (whose sampling distribution is given by the solid curve) is an unbiased estimator of α because $E(A_1) = \alpha$; the estimator A_2 (the broken curve) has a positive bias, because $E(A_2) > \alpha$.

errors from cancelling each other. The *efficiency* of an estimator is inversely proportional to its mean-squared error. We generally prefer a more efficient estimator to a less efficient one.

The mean-squared error of an unbiased estimator is simply its sampling variance, because $E(A) = \alpha$. For a biased estimator,

$$
\begin{aligned}
\mathrm{MSE}(A) &= E[(A - \alpha)^2] \\
&= E\{[A - E(A) + E(A) - \alpha]^2\} \\
&= E\{[A - E(A)]^2\} + [E(A) - \alpha]^2 + 2[E(A) - E(A)][E(A) - \alpha] \\
&= V(A) + [\mathrm{bias}(A)]^2 + 0
\end{aligned}
$$

The efficiency of an estimator increases, therefore, as its sampling variance and bias decline. In comparing two estimators, an advantage in sampling variance can more than offset a disadvantage due to bias, as illustrated in Figure 6.5.

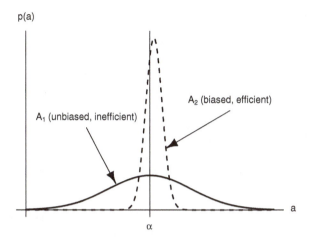

Figure 6.5   Relative efficiency of estimators: Even though it is biased, A_2
(broken curve) is a more efficient estimator of α than the
unbiased estimator A_1 (solid curve), because the smaller
variance of A_2 more than compensates for its small bias.

Asymptotic Efficiency

Asymptotic efficiency is inversely proportional to *asymptotic mean-squared
error (AMSE)*, which, in turn, is the sum of asymptotic variance and squared
asymptotic bias.

6.2.3   Consistency

An estimator A of the parameter α is *consistent* if $\operatorname{plim} A = \alpha$. A sufficient
(but not necessary[6]) condition for consistency is that an estimator is asymptotically unbiased and that the sampling variance of the estimator approaches
zero as n increases; this condition implies that the mean-squared error of the
estimator approaches a limit of zero. Figure 6.2 (page 147) illustrates consistency, if we construe X as an estimator of a. The estimator S_*^2 given in
Equation 6.2 (on page 151) is a consistent estimator of the population variance σ^2 even though it is biased in finite samples.

---

[6]There are cases in which $\operatorname{plim} A = \alpha$, but the variance and asymptotic expectation of A do not
exist. See Johnston (1972, p. 272) for an example.

6.2.4   Sufficiency

Sufficiency is a more abstract property than unbias, efficiency, or consistency (although sufficiency and efficiency are closely related): A statistic S based on a sample of observations is *sufficient* for the parameter α if the statistic exhausts all of the information about α that is present in the sample. More formally, suppose that the observations $X_1, X_2, \ldots, X_n$ are drawn from a probability distribution with parameter α, and let the statistic $S \equiv f(X_1, X_2, \ldots, X_n)$. Then S is a sufficient statistic for α if the probability distribution of the observations *conditional* on the value of S, that is, $p(x_1, x_2, \ldots, x_n | S = s)$, does not depend on α. The sufficient statistic S *need not* be an estimator of α.

To illustrate the idea of sufficiency, suppose that n observations are independently sampled, and that each observation X_i takes on the value 1 with probability ϕ and the value 0 with probability $1 - \phi$. That is, the X_i are independent, identically distributed Bernoulli random variables (see Section 5.1.1). I will demonstrate that the sample sum $S \equiv \sum_{i=1}^{n} X_i$ is a sufficient statistic for ϕ: If we know the value s of S, then there are $\binom{n}{s}$ different possible arrangements of the s 1s and $n - s$ 0s, each with probability $1/\binom{n}{s}$.[7] Because this probability does not depend on the parameter ϕ, the statistic S is sufficient for ϕ. By a similar argument, the sample proportion $P \equiv S/n$ is also a sufficient statistic. The proportion P—but not the sum S—is an estimator of ϕ.

The concept of sufficiency can be extended to sets of parameters and statistics: Given a sample of (possibly multivariate) observations $\mathbf{x}_1, \mathbf{x}_2, \ldots, \mathbf{x}_n$, a vector of statistics $\mathbf{s} = [S_1, S_2, \ldots, S_p]' \equiv f(\mathbf{x}_1, \mathbf{x}_2, \ldots, \mathbf{x}_n)$ is *jointly sufficient* for the parameters $\boldsymbol{\alpha} = [\alpha_1, \alpha_2, \ldots, \alpha_k]'$ if the conditional distribution of the observations given $\mathbf{s}$ does not depend on $\boldsymbol{\alpha}$. It can be shown, for example, that the mean $\overline{X}$ and variance S^2 calculated from an independent random sample are jointly sufficient statistics for the parameters μ and σ^2 of a normal distribution (as are the sample sum $\sum X_i$ and sum of squares $\sum X_i^2$, which jointly contain the same information as $\overline{X}$ and S^2). A set of sufficient statistics is called *minimally sufficient* if there is no smaller sufficient set.

6.2.5   Robustness

An estimator is said to be *robust* when its efficiency (and its efficiency relative to other estimators) does not strongly depend on the distribution of the data.

---

[7]The random variable S has a binomial distribution; see Section 5.1.1.

There is also another sense of robustness, termed *robustness of validity*, which is to be distinguished from *robustness of efficiency*: A procedure for statistical inference is said to be robust if its validity does not strongly depend on the distribution of the data. Thus the *p*-value for a robust hypothesis test is approximately correct even when the distributional assumptions (e.g., an assumption of normality) on which the test is based are violated. Similarly, the validity of a confidence interval is robust if the confidence interval has approximately the stated level of coverage—for example, a 95% confidence interval covers the parameter in roughly 95% of samples—even when distributional assumptions are violated. Robustness of validity can be cold comfort when a test or confidence interval is based on an inefficient estimator: The test may have low power and the confidence interval may be very wide.

To make robustness of efficiency more concrete, let us focus on a simple setting: estimating the center (or *location*) μ of a symmetric distribution based on an independent random sample of observations drawn from the distribution.[8] As long as X has finite variance σ^2, the variance of the sample mean $\overline{X}$ is $V(\overline{X}) = \sigma^2/n$, where n is the size of the sample (a familiar result from basic statistics). The variance of the sample median, however, depends on the distribution of X:

$$V(\text{median}) \approx \frac{1}{4n[p(x_{.5})]^2} \qquad (6.3)$$

where $p(x_{.5})$ is the density at the population median of X (i.e., its .5 quantile).

Applied to a normal population, $X \sim N(\mu, \sigma^2)$, the variance of the median is $V(\text{median}) = \pi\sigma^2/2n$,[9] and therefore the sample median is a less efficient estimator of μ than the sample mean is:

$$\frac{V(\text{median})}{V(\overline{X})} = \frac{\pi\sigma^2/2n}{\sigma^2/n} = \frac{\pi}{2} \approx 1.57$$

We would need a sample more than one-and-a-half times as large to estimate μ with a specified degree of precision using the sample median rather than the mean.

---

[8] In the *absence* of symmetry, what we mean by the center of the distribution becomes ambiguous.

[9] This result follows from Equation 6.3 and the formula for the normal density function (Equation 5.2 on page 127).

In contrast, suppose now that X is t-distributed with 3 degrees of freedom, a distribution with heavier tails than the normal distribution. Then (using the properties of the t-distribution given in Section 5.2.3), $\sigma^2 = 3/(3-2) = 3$, $p(x_{.5}) = p(0) = 0.3675$, and, consequently,

$$V(\overline{X}) = \frac{3}{n}$$

$$V(\text{median}) = \frac{1}{4n(0.3675^2)} = \frac{1.851}{n}$$

In this case, therefore, the mean is only $1.851/3 = 0.617$ (i.e., 62%) as efficient as the median.

Robustness is closely related to *resistance* to unusual data: A resistant estimator is little affected by a small fraction of outlying data. The mean has low resistance to outliers, as is simply demonstrated: I drew a sample of six observations from the standard-normal distribution, obtaining

$$\begin{array}{lll} X_1 = -0.068 & X_2 = -1.282 & X_3 = 0.013 \\ X_4 = 0.141 & X_5 = -0.980 & X_6 = 1.263 \end{array} \tag{6.4}$$

The mean of these six values is $\overline{X} = -0.152$. Now imagine adding a seventh observation, X_7, allowing it to take on all possible values from -10 to $+10$ (or, with greater imagination, from $-\infty$ to $+\infty$). The result, called the *influence function* of the mean, is graphed in Figure 6.6(a). It is apparent from this figure that as the discrepant seventh observation grows more extreme, the sample mean chases it.

A related concept in assessing resistance is the *breakdown point* of an estimator: The breakdown point is the fraction of "bad" data that the estimator can tolerate without being affected to an arbitrarily large extent. The mean has a breakdown point of zero, because, as we have just seen, a *single* bad observation can change the mean by an arbitrary amount. The median, in contrast, has a breakdown point of 50%, because fully half the data can be bad without causing the median to become completely unstuck.

M-Estimation

The mean minimizes the *least-squares (LS) objective function*

$$\sum_{i=1}^{n} \rho_{LS}(X_i - \widehat{\mu}) \equiv \sum_{i=1}^{n} (X_i - \widehat{\mu})^2$$

That is, ρ_{LS} is smaller for $\widehat{\mu} = \overline{x}$ than for any other value of $\widehat{\mu}$. The shape of the influence function for the mean follows from the derivative of the

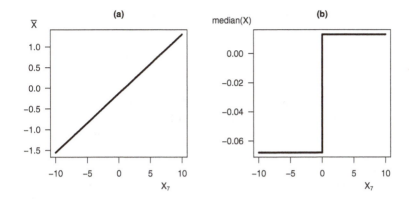

Figure 6.6   The influence functions for (a) the mean and (b) the median, adding the value X_7 to the sample $X_1 = -0.068$, $X_2 = -1.282$, $X_3 = 0.013$, $X_4 = 0.141$, $X_5 = -0.980$, $X_6 = 1.263$. The influence function for the median is bounded, while that for the mean is not. The vertical axes for the two graphs have very different scales.

objective function with respect to the *residual* $E \equiv X - \widehat{\mu}$:

$$\psi_{LS}(E) \equiv \rho'_{LS}(E) = 2E$$

Influence, therefore, is proportional to E. It is convenient to redefine the least-squares objective function as $\rho_{LS}(E) \equiv \frac{1}{2}E^2$, so that $\psi_{LS}(E) = E$.

Now consider the sample median as an estimator of μ. The median minimizes the *least-absolute-values (LAV) objective function*:

$$\sum_{i=1}^{n} \rho_{LAV}(E_i) = \sum_{i=1}^{n} \rho_{LAV}(X_i - \widehat{\mu}) \equiv \sum_{i=1}^{n} |X_i - \widehat{\mu}|$$

As a result, the median is much more resistant than the mean to outliers. The influence function of the median for the illustrative sample is shown in Figure 6.6(b). In contrast to the mean, the influence of a discrepant observation on the median is *bounded*. Once again, the derivative of the objective function gives the shape of the influence function[10]

$$\psi_{\text{LAV}}(E) \equiv \rho'_{\text{LAV}}(E) = \begin{cases} 1 & \text{for } E > 0 \\ 0 & \text{for } E = 0 \\ -1 & \text{for } E < 0 \end{cases}$$

Although the median is more resistant than the mean to outliers, we have seen that it is less efficient than the mean if the distribution of X is normal. Other estimators combine resistance to outliers with greater robustness of efficiency. Estimators that can be expressed as minimizing an objective function of the form $\sum_{i=1}^{n} \rho(E_i)$ are called *M-estimators*.[11]

Two common M-estimators are the *Huber* and the *biweight* (or *bisquare*). The Huber estimator is named after the Swiss statistician Peter J. Huber, who introduced M-estimation; the biweight is due to the 20th-century American statistician John W. Tukey, who made many important contributions to statistics, including to robust estimation.

- The Huber objective function is a compromise between least squares and LAV, behaving like least squares near the center of the data and like LAV in the tails:

$$\rho_H(E) \equiv \begin{cases} \frac{1}{2}E^2 & \text{for } |E| \leq k \\ k|E| - \frac{1}{2}k^2 & \text{for } |E| > k \end{cases}$$

The Huber objective function ρ_H and its derivative, the influence function ψ_H, are graphed in Figure 6.7:[12]

$$\psi_H(E) = \begin{cases} k & \text{for } E > k \\ E & \text{for } |E| \leq k \\ -k & \text{for } E < -k \end{cases}$$

The value k, which demarcates the central part of the data from the tails, is called a *tuning constant*.

---

[10]Strictly speaking, the derivative of ρ_{LAV} is undefined at $E = 0$, where the function abruptly changes direction, but setting $\psi_{\text{LAV}}(0) \equiv 0$ is convenient.

[11]Estimators that can be written in this form can be thought of as generalizations of maximum-likelihood estimators (discussed in Section 6.3), hence the term *M-estimator*. The maximum-likelihood estimator is produced by taking $\rho_{\text{ML}}(x - \mu) \equiv -\log_e p(x - \mu)$ for an appropriate probability or probability density function $p(\cdot)$.

[12]My terminology here is loose, but convenient: Strictly speaking, the ψ-function is not the influence function, but it has the same shape as the influence function.

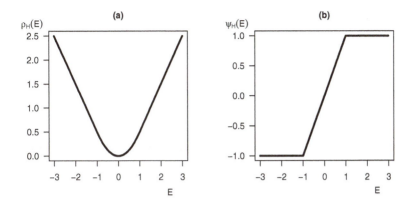

Figure 6.7 Huber (a) objective function ρ_H and (b) "influence function" ψ_H. To calibrate these graphs, the tuning constant is set to $k = 1$. (See the text for a discussion of the tuning constant.)

It is most natural to express the tuning constant as a multiple of the *scale* (i.e., the spread) of the variable X, that is, to take $k = cS$, where S is a measure of scale. The sample standard deviation is a poor measure of scale in this context, because it is even more affected than the mean by outliers. A common robust measure of scale is the *median absolute deviation (MAD)*:

$$MAD \equiv \text{median}\left|X_i - \widehat{\mu}\right|$$

The estimate $\widehat{\mu}$ can be taken, at least initially, as the median value of X. We can then define $S \equiv MAD/0.6745$, which ensures that S estimates the standard deviation σ when the population is normal. Using $k = 1.345S$ (i.e., $1.345/0.6745 \approx 2$ MADs) produces 95% efficiency relative to the sample mean when the population is normal, along with considerable resistance to outliers when it is not. A smaller tuning constant can be employed for more resistance.

- The biweight objective function levels off at very large residuals:[13]

$$\rho_{BW}(E) \equiv \begin{cases} \frac{k^2}{6}\left\{1 - \left[1 - \left(\frac{E}{k}\right)^2\right]^3\right\} & \text{for } |E| \leq k \\ \frac{k^2}{6} & \text{for } |E| > k \end{cases}$$

The influence function for the biweight estimator, therefore, "re-descends" to zero, *completely discounting* observations that are sufficiently outlying:

$$\psi_{BW}(E) = \begin{cases} E\left[1 - \left(\frac{E}{k}\right)^2\right]^2 & \text{for } |E| \leq k \\ 0 & \text{for } |E| > k \end{cases}$$

The functions ρ_{BW} and ψ_{BW} are graphed in Figure 6.8. Using $k = 4.685S$ (i.e., $4.685/0.6745 \approx 7$ MADs) produces 95% efficiency when sampling from a normal population.

Both the Huber and the biweight estimators achieve a breakdown point of 50% when the MAD is used to estimate scale.

Calculation of M-estimators usually requires an *iterative* (i.e., repetitive) procedure (although iteration is not necessary for the mean and median, which, as we have seen, fit into the M-estimation framework). An estimating equation for $\widehat{\mu}$ is obtained by setting the derivative of the objective function (with respect to $\widehat{\mu}$) to zero, obtaining

$$\sum_{i=1}^{n} \psi(X_i - \widehat{\mu}) = 0 \tag{6.5}$$

There are several general approaches to solving Equation 6.5; probably the most straightforward, and the simplest to implement computationally, is to reweight the mean iteratively:

1. Define the *weight function* $w(E) \equiv \psi(E)/E$. Then the estimating equation becomes

$$\sum_{i=1}^{n} (X_i - \widehat{\mu})w_i = 0 \tag{6.6}$$

---

[13]The term *bisquare* applies literally to the ψ-function and to the weight function (hence "biweight") to be introduced presently—not to the objective function.

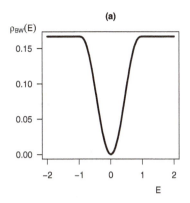
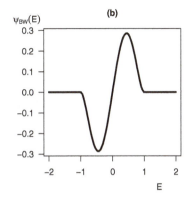

Figure 6.8 Biweight (a) objective function ρ_{BW} and (b) "influence function" ψ_{BW}. To calibrate these graphs, the tuning constant is set to $k = 1$. The influence function "re-descends" to zero when $|E|$ is large.

where

$$w_i \equiv w\left(X_i - \widehat{\mu}\right)$$

The solution of Equation 6.6 is the weighted mean,

$$\widehat{\mu} = \frac{\sum w_i X_i}{\sum w_i}$$

The weight functions corresponding to the least-squares, LAV, Huber, and bisquare objective functions are shown in Table 6.1 and graphed in Figure 6.9. The least-squares weight function accords equal weight to each observation, while the bisquare gives zero weight to observations that are sufficiently outlying; the LAV and Huber weight functions descend toward zero but never quite reach it.

2. Select an initial estimate $\widehat{\mu}^{(0)}$, such as the median of the X-values.[14] Using $\widehat{\mu}^{(0)}$, calculate an initial estimate of scale $S^{(0)}$ and initial weights $w_i^{(0)} = w(X_i - \widehat{\mu}^{(0)})$. Set the iteration counter $t = 0$. The scale is required to calculate the tuning constant $k = cS$ (for prespecified c).

---

[14]Because the estimating equation for a re-descending M-estimator, such as the bisquare, can have more than one root, the selection of an initial estimate might be consequential.

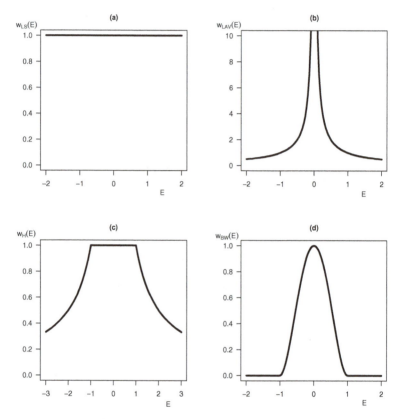

Figure 6.9   Weight functions $w(E)$ for the (a) least-squares, (b) least-absolute-values, (c) Huber, and (d) biweight estimators. The tuning constants for the Huber and biweight estimators are taken as $k = 1$. The vertical axis in the graph for the LAV estimator and the horizontal axis in the graph for the Huber estimator are different from the others.

Table 6.1 Weight Functions $w(E) = \psi(E)/E$ for Several M-Estimators

Objective Function $\rho(E)$	Weight Function $w(E)$
Least squares	1
Least absolute values	$1/\|E\|$ (for $E \neq 0$)
Huber	1 for $\|E\| \leq k$
	$k/\|E\|$ for $\|E\| > k$
Bisquare (biweight)	$\left[1 - \left(\frac{E}{k} \right)^2 \right]^2$ for $\|E\| \leq k$
	0 for $\|E\| > k$

3. At each iteration t, calculate $\widehat{\mu}^{(t)} = \sum w_i^{(t-1)} X_i / \sum w_i^{(t-1)}$. Stop when the change in $\widehat{\mu}^{(t)}$ is negligible from one iteration to the next.

To illustrate the application of these estimators, recall our sample of six observations from the standard normal distribution $N(0, 1)$ (given in Equation 6.4 on page 156); let us contaminate the sample with the outlying value $X_7 = 10$. Using $c = 1.345$ for the Huber estimator and $c = 4.685$ for the biweight,

$$\overline{X} = 1.298, \text{median}(X) = 0.013, \widehat{\mu}_H = 0.201, \text{ and } \widehat{\mu}_{BW} = -0.161$$

It is clear that the sample mean $\overline{X}$ is seriously affected by the outlier but that the other estimators are not.

6.3 Maximum-Likelihood Estimation

The *method of maximum likelihood* produces estimators that have both a reasonable intuitive basis and many desirable statistical properties. The method is very broadly applicable and is typically simple to apply. Moreover, once a maximum-likelihood estimator is derived, the general theory of maximum-likelihood estimation provides standard errors, statistical tests, and other results useful for statistical inference. A disadvantage of the method, however, is that it frequently requires strong assumptions about the structure of the data. The method of maximum likelihood was codified early in the 20th century by R. A. Fisher, but it was used much earlier by mathematicians such as Carl Friedrich Gauss.

The likelihood function, on which the method of maximum likelihood is based, plays a central role in classical statistical inference, but it is also important in Bayesian inference (discussed in Section 6.4).

6.3.1   Preliminary Example

Let us first consider a simple example: Suppose that we want to estimate the probability ϕ of getting a head on flipping a particular coin. We flip the coin independently 10 times (i.e., we sample $n = 10$ flips), with the following result: *HHTHHHHTTHH*. The probability of obtaining this sequence—*in advance of* collecting the data—is a function of the unknown parameter ϕ:

$$
\begin{aligned}
\Pr(\text{data}|\text{parameter}) &= \Pr(HHTHHHHTTHH|\phi) \\
&= \phi\phi(1-\phi)\phi\phi\phi(1-\phi)(1-\phi)\phi\phi \\
&= \phi^7(1-\phi)^3
\end{aligned}
$$

This is simply the product of probabilities for 10 independent Bernoulli random variables (taking $X_i = 1$ for a head and $X_i = 0$ for a tail, $i = 1, \ldots, 10$; see Section 5.1.1).

The data for our particular sample are *fixed*, however: We have already collected them. The parameter ϕ also has a fixed value, but this value is unknown, and so we can let it vary in our imagination between 0 and 1, treating the probability of the observed data as a function of ϕ. This function is called the *likelihood function*:

$$
\begin{aligned}
L(\text{parameter}|\text{data}) &= L(\phi|HHTHHHHTTHH) \\
&= \phi^7(1-\phi)^3
\end{aligned}
$$

The values of the probability function and the likelihood function are therefore the same, but the probability function is a function of the data with the parameter fixed, while the likelihood function is a function of the parameter with the data fixed.

Here are some representative likelihoods for different values of ϕ:[15]

ϕ	$L(\phi \vert \text{data}) = \phi^7(1-\phi)^3$
.0	0.0
.1	.0000000729
.2	.00000655
.3	.0000750
.4	.000354
.5	.000977
.6	.00179
.7	.00222
.8	.00168
.9	.000478
1.0	0.0

The full likelihood function is graphed in Figure 6.10. Although each value of $L(\phi \vert \text{data})$ is a notional probability, the function $L(\phi \vert \text{data})$ is *not* a probability distribution or a density function: It does not integrate to 1, for example.

In the present instance, the probability of obtaining the sample of data that we have in hand, *HHTHHHTTHH*, is small regardless of the true value of ϕ. This is usually the case: Unless the sample is very small, *any specific sample result*—including the one that is realized—will have low probability in advance of collecting data.

Nevertheless, the likelihood contains useful information about the unknown parameter ϕ. For example, ϕ *cannot* be 0 or 1, because if it were either of these values, then the observed data (which includes both heads and tails) could not have been obtained. Reversing this reasoning, the value of ϕ that is most supported by the data is the one for which the likelihood is largest. This value is the *maximum-likelihood estimate (MLE)* of ϕ, denoted $\widehat{\phi}$. Here, $\widehat{\phi} = .7$, which is just the sample proportion of heads, 7/10.

Generalization of the Example

More generally, for n independent flips of the coin, producing a particular sequence that includes x heads and $n - x$ tails,

$$L(\phi \vert \text{data}) = \Pr(\text{data} \vert \phi) = \phi^x(1 - \phi)^{n-x}$$

---

[15]The likelihood is a *continuous* function of ϕ for values of ϕ between 0 and 1. This contrasts, in the present case, with the probability function, because there is a *finite* number $(2^{10} = 1,024)$ of possible samples.

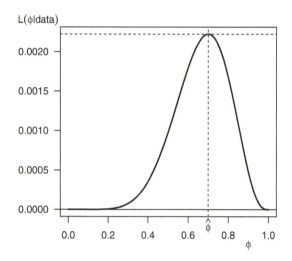

Figure 6.10   The likelihood function
$$L(\phi|HHTHHHTTHH) = \phi^7(1-\phi)^3.$$

We want the value of ϕ that maximizes $L(\phi|\text{data})$, which we often abbreviate $L(\phi)$. As is typically the case, it is simpler—and equivalent—to find the value of ϕ that maximizes the *log of the likelihood*,[16] here

$$\log_e L(\phi) = x\log_e \phi + (n-x)\log_e(1-\phi) \tag{6.7}$$

Differentiating $\log_e L(\phi)$ with respect to ϕ,

$$\begin{aligned}
\frac{d\log_e L(\phi)}{d\phi} &= \frac{x}{\phi} + (n-x)\frac{1}{1-\phi}(-1) \\
&= \frac{x}{\phi} - \frac{n-x}{1-\phi}
\end{aligned}$$

---

[16]The log function (see Section 3.1.4) is a *positive monotone* (i.e., strictly increasing) *function*: If $x_1 > x_2$, then $\log(x_1) > \log(x_2)$ (and vice versa). Consequently, the value of ϕ that maximizes $\log_e L(\phi|\text{data})$ must also maximize $L(\phi|\text{data})$.

The derivative of the log likelihood with respect to the parameter is called the *score* (or *score function*), $S(\phi) \equiv d \log_e L(\phi) / d\phi$. Setting the score to zero and solving for ϕ produces the MLE, which, as before, is the sample proportion x/n (as the reader may wish to verify). The maximum-likelihood *estimator* is $\widehat{\phi} = X/n$. To avoid this slightly awkward substitution of estimator for estimate in the last step, we can replace x by X in the log likelihood function (Equation 6.7).

6.3.2 Properties of Maximum-Likelihood Estimators

Under very broad conditions, maximum-likelihood estimators have the following general properties:

- Maximum-likelihood estimators are consistent.

- They are asymptotically unbiased, although they may be biased in finite samples.

- They are asymptotically efficient—no asymptotically unbiased estimator has a smaller asymptotic variance.

- They are asymptotically normally distributed.

- If there is a sufficient statistic for a parameter, then the maximum-likelihood estimator of the parameter is a function of a sufficient statistic.

- If $\widehat{\alpha}$ is the MLE of α, and if $\beta = f(\alpha)$ is a function of α, then $\widehat{\beta} = f(\widehat{\alpha})$ is the MLE of β.

- The asymptotic sampling variance of the MLE $\widehat{\alpha}$ of a parameter α can be obtained from the second derivative of the log likelihood:

$$\mathcal{V}(\widehat{\alpha}) = \frac{1}{-E\left[\dfrac{d^2 \log_e L(\alpha)}{d\alpha^2}\right]} \tag{6.8}$$

The denominator of $\mathcal{V}(\widehat{\alpha})$ is called the *expected or Fisher information* (named after R. A. Fisher),[17]

$$\mathcal{I}(\alpha) \equiv -E\left[\frac{d^2 \log_e L(\alpha)}{d\alpha^2}\right]$$

In practice, we substitute the MLE $\widehat{\alpha}$ into Equation 6.8 to obtain an *estimate* of the asymptotic sampling variance, $\widehat{\mathcal{V}}(\widehat{\alpha})$.[18]

- $L(\widehat{\alpha})$ is the value of the likelihood function at the MLE $\widehat{\alpha}$, while $L(\alpha)$ is the likelihood for the true (but generally unknown) parameter α. The *log-likelihood-ratio statistic*

$$G^2 \equiv 2\log_e \frac{L(\widehat{\alpha})}{L(\alpha)} = 2[\log_e L(\widehat{\alpha}) - \log_e L(\alpha)]$$

  follows an asymptotic chi-square distribution with 1 degree of free-dom. Because, by definition, the MLE maximizes the likelihood for our *particular* sample, the value of the likelihood at the true parame-ter value α is generally *smaller* than at the MLE $\widehat{\alpha}$ (unless, by good fortune, $\widehat{\alpha}$ and α happen to coincide).

Establishing these results is well beyond the scope of this chapter,[19] but the results do make some intuitive sense. For example, if the log likelihood has a sharp peak, then the MLE is clearly differentiated from nearby val-ues. Under these circumstances, the second derivative of the log likelihood is a large negative number; there is a lot of "information" in the data con-cerning the value of the parameter; and the sampling variance of the MLE

---

[17] Strictly speaking, the Fisher information is the variance of the score evaluated at the parameter value α:

$$\mathcal{I}(\alpha) = E\left[\left(\frac{d\log_e L(\alpha)}{d\alpha}\right)^2 \bigg|_\alpha\right]$$

In most instances, however, this is equivalent to the generally more convenient formula given in the text. The variance of the score is simply the expectation of its square, because the expected score is zero at α.

[18] It is also possible, and sometimes computationally advantageous, to base an estimate of the variance of the MLE $\widehat{\alpha}$ on the *observed information*,

$$\mathcal{I}_O(\widehat{\alpha}) \equiv -\frac{d^2 \log_e L(\widehat{\alpha})}{d\widehat{\alpha}^2}$$

[19] See the references on mathematical statistics given in the Preface, page xx.

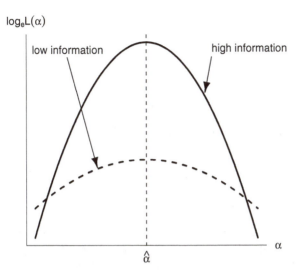

Figure 6.11   Two imagined log likelihoods: one strongly peaked (shown as a solid curve), providing high information about the parameter α, and the other flat (broken curve), providing low information about α.

is small. If, in contrast, the log likelihood is relatively flat at its maximum, then alternative estimates quite different from the MLE are nearly as good as the MLE; there is little information in the data concerning the value of the parameter; and the sampling variance of the MLE is large (see Figure 6.11).

6.3.3   Statistical Inference: Wald, Likelihood-Ratio, and Score Tests

The properties of maximum-likelihood estimators described in the previous section lead directly to three common and general procedures—called the *Wald test*, the *likelihood-ratio test*, and the *score test*—for testing the statistical hypothesis H_0: $\alpha = \alpha_0$. The score test is sometimes called the *Lagrange-multiplier test*.[20] The Wald and likelihood-ratio tests can be "turned around" to produce confidence intervals for α.

Wald test. Relying on the asymptotic normality of the MLE $\widehat{\alpha}$, we calculate the Wald test statistic (named after the Austrian American mathemati-

---

[20]Lagrange multipliers for constrained optimization are described in Section 3.5.2.

cian Abraham Wald, 1902–1950)

$$Z_0 \equiv \frac{\widehat{\alpha} - \alpha_0}{\sqrt{\widehat{\mathscr{V}}(\widehat{\alpha})}}$$

which is asymptotically distributed as $N(0, 1)$ under H_0.

Likelihood-ratio test. Employing the log-likelihood ratio, the test statistic

$$G_0^2 \equiv 2\log_e \frac{L(\widehat{\alpha})}{L(\alpha_0)} = 2[\log_e L(\widehat{\alpha}) - \log_e L(\alpha_0)]$$

is asymptotically distributed as χ_1^2 under H_0.

Score test. Recall that the score $S(\alpha) \equiv d\log_e L(\alpha)/d\alpha$ is the slope of the log likelihood at a particular value of α. At the MLE, the score is zero: $S(\widehat{\alpha}) = 0$. It can be shown that the *score statistic*

$$S_0 \equiv \frac{S(\alpha_0)}{\sqrt{\mathscr{I}(\alpha_0)}}$$

is asymptotically distributed as $N(0, 1)$ under H_0.

Unless the log likelihood is quadratic, the three test statistics can produce somewhat different results in specific samples, although the tests are asymptotically equivalent. In certain contexts, the score test has the practical advantage of not requiring the computation of the MLE $\widehat{\alpha}$ (because S_0 depends only on the null value α_0, which is specified in H_0). In most instances, however, the likelihood-ratio test is more reliable than the Wald and score tests in smaller samples.

Figure 6.12 shows the relationship among the three test statistics, and clarifies the intuitive rationale of each: The Wald test measures the distance between $\widehat{\alpha}$ and α_0, using the standard error to calibrate this distance. If $\widehat{\alpha}$ is far from α_0, for example, then doubt is cast on H_0. The likelihood-ratio test measures the distance between $\log_e L(\widehat{\alpha})$ and $\log_e L(\alpha_0)$; if $\log_e L(\widehat{\alpha})$ is much larger than $\log_e L(\alpha_0)$, then H_0 is probably wrong. Finally, the score test statistic measures the slope of the log likelihood at α_0; if this slope is very steep, then we are probably far from the peak of the likelihood function, also casting doubt on H_0.

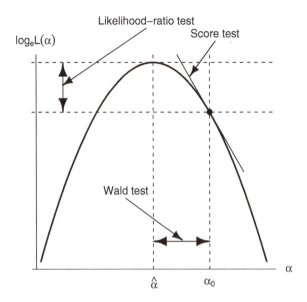

Figure 6.12 Tests of the hypothesis H_0: $\alpha = \alpha_0$: The likelihood-ratio test compares $\log_e L(\widehat{\alpha})$ to $\log_e L(\alpha_0)$; the Wald test compares $\widehat{\alpha}$ to α_0; and the score test examines the slope of $\log_e L(\alpha)$ at $\alpha = \alpha_0$.

An Illustration

It is instructive to apply these results to our previous example, in which we sought to estimate the probability ϕ of obtaining a head from a coin based on a sample of n independent flips of the coin. Recall that the MLE of ϕ is the sample proportion $\widehat{\phi} = X/n$, where X counts the number of heads in the sample. The second derivative of the log likelihood (Equation 6.7 on page 166) is

$$\frac{d^2 \log_e L(\phi)}{d\phi^2} = -\frac{X}{\phi^2} - \left[-\frac{n-X}{(1-\phi)^2}(-1) \right]$$

$$= \frac{-X + 2\phi X - n\phi^2}{\phi^2(1-\phi)^2}$$

Noting that $E(X) = n\phi$, the expected information is

$$\mathscr{I}(\phi) = -\frac{-n\phi + 2n\phi^2 - n\phi^2}{\phi^2(1-\phi^2)} = \frac{n}{\phi(1-\phi)}$$

and the asymptotic variance of $\widehat{\phi}$ is $\mathcal{V}(\widehat{\phi}) = [\mathcal{I}(\phi)]^{-1} = \phi(1-\phi)/n$, a familiar result: In this case, the asymptotic variance coincides with the exact, finite-sample variance of $\widehat{\phi}$. The *estimated* asymptotic sampling variance is $\widehat{\mathcal{V}}(\widehat{\phi}) = \widehat{\phi}(1-\widehat{\phi})/n$.

For our sample of $n = 10$ flips with $X = 7$ heads, $\widehat{\mathcal{V}}(\widehat{\phi}) = (.7 \times .3)/10 = 0.0210$, and a 95% asymptotic confidence interval for ϕ based on the Wald statistic is

$$\phi = .7 \pm 1.96 \times \sqrt{0.0210} = .7 \pm .284$$

where 1.96 is the familiar .975 quantile of the standard-normal distribution. Alternatively, to test the hypothesis that the coin is fair, H_0: $\phi = .5$, we can calculate the Wald test statistic

$$Z_0 = \frac{.7 - .5}{\sqrt{0.0210}} = 1.38$$

which corresponds to a two-tail p-value [from $N(0, 1)$] of .168.

The log likelihood, recall, is

$$\begin{aligned}\log_e L(\phi) &= X \log_e \phi + (n - X) \log_e (1 - \phi) \\ &= 7 \log_e \phi + 3 \log_e (1 - \phi)\end{aligned}$$

Using this equation,

$$\begin{aligned}\log_e L(\widehat{\phi}) &= \log_e L(.7) = 7 \log_e .7 + 3 \log_e .3 = -6.1086 \\ \log_e L(\phi_0) &= \log_e L(.5) = 7 \log_e .5 + 3 \log_e .5 = -6.9315\end{aligned}$$

The likelihood-ratio test statistic for H_0 is, therefore,

$$G_0^2 = 2[-6.1086 - (-6.9315)] = 1.646$$

which corresponds to a p-value (from χ_1^2) of .199.

Finally, for the score test,

$$S(\phi) = \frac{d \log_e L(\phi)}{d\phi} = \frac{X}{\phi} - \frac{n - X}{1 - \phi}$$

from which

$$S(\phi_0) = \frac{7}{.5} - \frac{3}{.5} = 8$$

Evaluating the expected information at ϕ_0 produces

$$\mathcal{I}(\phi_0) = \mathcal{I}(.5) = \frac{10}{.5 \times .5} = 40$$

The score statistic is, therefore,

$$S_0 = \frac{S(\phi_0)}{\sqrt{\mathscr{I}(\phi_0)}} = \frac{8}{\sqrt{40}} = 1.265$$

for which the two-tail p-value [from $N(0, 1)$] is .206.

The three tests are in reasonable agreement, but all are quite inaccurate! An exact test, using the null binomial distribution of X (the number of heads: see Section 5.1.1),

$$p(x) = \binom{10}{x}.5^x.5^{10-x} = \binom{10}{x}.5^{10}$$

yields a two-tail p-value of .3438 [corresponding to $\Pr(X \leq 3$ or $X \geq 7)$]. The lesson to be drawn from this example is that we must be careful in applying asymptotic results to small samples.[21]

6.3.4 Several Parameters

The maximum-likelihood method can be generalized straightforwardly to simultaneous estimation of several parameters. Let $p\left(\underset{(n \times m)}{\mathbf{X}} \mid \underset{(k \times 1)}{\boldsymbol{\alpha}}\right)$ represent the probability or probability density for n possibly multivariate observations $\mathbf{X}$ ($m \geq 1$), which depend on k independent parameters $\boldsymbol{\alpha}$.[22] The likelihood is $L(\boldsymbol{\alpha}) \equiv L(\boldsymbol{\alpha}|\mathbf{X})$ is a function of the parameters $\boldsymbol{\alpha}$, and we seek the values $\widehat{\boldsymbol{\alpha}}$ that maximize this function. As before, it is generally more convenient to work with $\log_e L(\boldsymbol{\alpha})$ in place of $L(\boldsymbol{\alpha})$. To maximize the likelihood, we find the vector partial derivative $\partial \log_e L(\boldsymbol{\alpha})/\partial \boldsymbol{\alpha}$, set this derivative to $\mathbf{0}$, and solve the resulting matrix equation for $\widehat{\boldsymbol{\alpha}}$. If there is more than one root, then we choose the solution that produces the largest likelihood.[23]

As in the case of a single parameter, the maximum-likelihood estimator is consistent, asymptotically unbiased, asymptotically efficient, asymptotically normal (but now *multivariate* normal), and based on sufficient statistics. The

---

[21] So-called *higher-order asymptotics* can provide greater accuracy in small samples, but they are seldom used; see, for example, Barndorf-Nielsen and Cox (1994).

[22] To say that the parameters are *independent* means that the value of none of the parameters can be obtained from the values of the others. If there is a dependency among the parameters, then the redundant parameter can simply be replaced by a function of other parameters.

[23] When the equations produced by setting the partial derivatives to zero are nonlinear, we may not know how to solve them analytically. See the discussion of numerical methods for optimization in Section 3.5.4.

asymptotic variance–covariance matrix of the MLE is

$$\underset{(k\times k)}{\mathscr{V}(\widehat{\boldsymbol{\alpha}})} = \left\{ -E\left[\frac{\partial^2 \log_e L(\boldsymbol{\alpha})}{\partial \boldsymbol{\alpha}\, \partial \boldsymbol{\alpha}'} \right] \right\}^{-1} \tag{6.9}$$

The matrix in braces in Equation 6.9 (the negative expectation of the Hessian of the log likelihood) is called the *expected* or *Fisher information matrix*, $\mathscr{I}(\boldsymbol{\alpha})$ (not to be confused with the identity matrix **I**).[24] Moreover, if $\beta = f(\boldsymbol{\alpha})$, then the MLE of β is $\widehat{\beta} = f(\widehat{\boldsymbol{\alpha}})$. The formulas for several parameters therefore closely parallel those for one parameter.

Generalizations of the score and Wald tests follow directly. The Wald statistic for H_0: $\boldsymbol{\alpha} = \boldsymbol{\alpha}_0$ is

$$Z_0^2 \equiv (\widehat{\boldsymbol{\alpha}} - \boldsymbol{\alpha}_0)' \widehat{\mathscr{V}}(\widehat{\boldsymbol{\alpha}})^{-1} (\widehat{\boldsymbol{\alpha}} - \boldsymbol{\alpha}_0)$$

The score vector is $S(\boldsymbol{\alpha}) \equiv \partial \log_e L(\boldsymbol{\alpha})/\partial \boldsymbol{\alpha}$; and the score statistic is

$$S_0^2 \equiv S(\boldsymbol{\alpha}_0)' \mathscr{I}(\boldsymbol{\alpha}_0)^{-1} S(\boldsymbol{\alpha}_0)$$

The likelihood-ratio test also generalizes straightforwardly:

$$G_0^2 \equiv 2 \log_e \left[\frac{L(\widehat{\boldsymbol{\alpha}})}{L(\boldsymbol{\alpha}_0)} \right]$$

All three test statistics are asymptotically distributed as χ_k^2 under H_0.

Each of these tests can be adapted to more complex hypotheses. Suppose, for example, that we wish to test the hypothesis H_0 that p of the k elements of $\boldsymbol{\alpha}$ are equal to particular values. Let $L(\widehat{\boldsymbol{\alpha}}_0)$ represent the maximized likelihood under the constraint represented by the hypothesis (i.e., setting the p parameters equal to their hypothesized values, but leaving the other parameters free to be estimated); $L(\widehat{\boldsymbol{\alpha}})$ represents the globally maximized likelihood when the constraint is relaxed. Then, under the hypothesis H_0,

$$G_0^2 \equiv 2 \log_e \left[\frac{L(\widehat{\boldsymbol{\alpha}})}{L(\widehat{\boldsymbol{\alpha}}_0)} \right]$$

---

[24] As in the case of a single parameter, a slightly more general definition of the Fisher information is

$$\mathscr{I}(\boldsymbol{\alpha}) = E\left[\left(\frac{\partial \log_e L(\boldsymbol{\alpha})}{\partial \boldsymbol{\alpha}} \right) \left(\frac{\partial \log_e L(\boldsymbol{\alpha})}{\partial \boldsymbol{\alpha}} \right)' \bigg|\, \boldsymbol{\alpha} \right]$$

Similarly, it is also possible to work with the *observed* information at the MLE $\widehat{\boldsymbol{\alpha}}$.

has an asymptotic chi-square distribution with p degrees of freedom.

The following example (adapted from Theil, 1971, pp. 389–390) illustrates these results: A sample of n independent observations X_i is drawn from a normally distributed population with unknown mean μ and variance σ^2. We want to estimate μ and σ^2. The likelihood function is

$$L(\mu, \sigma^2) = \prod_{i=1}^{n} \frac{1}{\sigma\sqrt{2\pi}} \exp\left[-\frac{(X_i - \mu)^2}{2\sigma^2}\right]$$

$$= (2\pi\sigma^2)^{-n/2} \exp\left[-\frac{1}{2\sigma^2} \sum_{i=1}^{n} (X_i - \mu)^2\right]$$

and the log likelihood is

$$\log_e L(\mu, \sigma^2) = -\frac{n}{2} \log_e 2\pi - \frac{n}{2} \log \sigma^2 - \frac{1}{2\sigma^2} \sum (X_i - \mu)^2$$

with partial derivatives

$$\frac{\partial \log_e L(\mu, \sigma^2)}{\partial \mu} = \frac{1}{\sigma^2} \sum (X_i - \mu)$$

$$\frac{\log_e L(\mu, \sigma^2)}{\partial \sigma^2} = -\frac{n}{2\sigma^2} + \frac{1}{2\sigma^4} \sum (X_i - \mu)^2$$

Setting the partial derivatives to zero and solving simultaneously for the maximum-likelihood estimators of μ and σ^2 produces

$$\widehat{\mu} = \frac{\sum X_i}{n} = \overline{X}$$

$$\widehat{\sigma}^2 = \frac{\sum (X_i - \overline{X})^2}{n}$$

The matrix of second partial derivatives of the log likelihood is

$$\begin{bmatrix} \dfrac{\partial^2 \log_e L}{\partial \mu^2} & \dfrac{\partial^2 \log_e L}{\partial \mu \partial \sigma^2} \\ \dfrac{\partial^2 \log_e L}{\partial \sigma^2 \partial \mu} & \dfrac{\partial^2 \log_e L}{\partial (\sigma^2)^2} \end{bmatrix} = \begin{bmatrix} -\dfrac{n}{\sigma^2} & -\dfrac{1}{\sigma^4} \sum (X_i - \mu) \\ -\dfrac{1}{\sigma^4} \sum (X_i - \mu) & \dfrac{n}{2\sigma^4} - \dfrac{1}{\sigma^6} \sum (X_i - \mu)^2 \end{bmatrix}$$

Taking expectations, and noting that $E(X_i - \mu) = 0$ and that $E[(X_i - \mu)^2] = \sigma^2$, produces the negative of the expected information matrix:

$$-\mathcal{I}(\mu, \sigma^2) = \begin{bmatrix} -\dfrac{n}{\sigma^2} & 0 \\ 0 & -\dfrac{n}{2\sigma^4} \end{bmatrix}$$

The asymptotic variance–covariance matrix of the maximum-likelihood estimators is, as usual, the inverse of the information matrix:

$$\mathscr{V}(\widehat{\mu}, \widehat{\sigma}^2) = [\mathscr{I}(\mu, \sigma^2)]^{-1} = \begin{bmatrix} \frac{\sigma^2}{n} & 0 \\ 0 & \frac{2\sigma^4}{n} \end{bmatrix}$$

The result for the sampling variance of $\widehat{\mu} = \overline{X}$ is the usual one (σ^2/n). The MLE of σ^2 is biased but consistent (and is the estimator S_*^2 given previously in Equation 6.2 on page 151).

In many applications, including the examples in this chapter, the data comprise an independent random sample of n identically distributed observations. The likelihood for the data is then the product of likelihood components for the observations, $L_i(\boldsymbol{\alpha})$, and the log likelihood is the sum of the logs of these components:

$$L(\boldsymbol{\alpha}) = \prod_{i=1}^{n} L_i(\boldsymbol{\alpha})$$

$$\log_e L(\boldsymbol{\alpha}) = \sum_{i=1}^{n} \log_e L_i(\boldsymbol{\alpha})$$

The score function consequently is also a sum of casewise terms:

$$S(\boldsymbol{\alpha}) = \sum_{i=1}^{n} S_i(\boldsymbol{\alpha}) = \sum_{i=1}^{n} \frac{\partial \log_e L_i(\boldsymbol{\alpha})}{\partial \boldsymbol{\alpha}}$$

Finally, the information for the sample is n times the information in an individual observation (denoted $\mathscr{I}_1$):

$$\mathscr{I}(\boldsymbol{\alpha}) = n\mathscr{I}_1(\boldsymbol{\alpha}) = nE\left[\frac{\partial^2 \log_e L_i(\boldsymbol{\alpha})}{\partial \boldsymbol{\alpha} \, \partial \boldsymbol{\alpha}'}\right]$$

This last result holds because the expectation of the second partial derivative of the likelihood is identical for all n observations.

6.3.5   The Delta Method

As I have explained, if $\beta = f(\alpha)$, and if $\widehat{\alpha}$ is the maximum-likelihood estimator of α, then $\widehat{\beta} = f(\widehat{\alpha})$ is the maximum-likelihood estimator of β. This result implies that $\widehat{\beta}$ is asymptotically normally distributed with asymptotic expectation β, even when the function $f(\cdot)$ is nonlinear.

The *delta method* produces an estimate of the asymptotic variance of $\widehat{\beta}$ based on a first-order Taylor-series approximation (see Section 3.6) to $f(\widehat{\alpha})$ around the true value of the parameter α:

$$\widehat{\beta} = f(\widehat{\alpha}) \approx f(\alpha) + f'(\alpha)(\widehat{\alpha} - \alpha) \tag{6.10}$$

Here, $f'(\alpha) = df(\alpha)/d\alpha$ is the derivative of $f(\alpha)$ with respect to α.

The first term on the right-hand side of Equation 6.10, $f(\alpha)$, is a constant (because the parameter α has a fixed value), and the second term is linear in $\widehat{\alpha}$ (again because α, and hence $f'(\alpha)$, are constants); thus

$$\mathcal{V}(\widehat{\beta}) \approx [f'(\alpha)]^2 \, \mathcal{V}(\widehat{\alpha})$$

where $\mathcal{V}(\widehat{\alpha})$ is the asymptotic variance of $\widehat{\alpha}$. In practice, we substitute the MLE $\widehat{\alpha}$ for α to obtain the *estimated* asymptotic variance of $\widehat{\beta}$:

$$\widehat{\mathcal{V}}(\widehat{\beta}) = [f'(\widehat{\alpha})]^2 \, \mathcal{V}(\widehat{\alpha})$$

To illustrate the application of the delta method, recall that the sample proportion $\widehat{\phi}$ is the maximum-likelihood estimator of the population proportion ϕ, with asymptotic (and, indeed, finite-sample) variance $\mathcal{V}(\widehat{\phi}) = \phi(1-\phi)/n$, where n is the sample size. The *log-odds*, or *logit*, is defined as

$$\Lambda = f(\phi) \equiv \log_e \frac{\phi}{1-\phi}$$

The MLE of Λ is therefore $\widehat{\Lambda} = \log_e[\widehat{\phi}/(1-\widehat{\phi})]$, and the approximate asymptotic sampling variance of the sample logit is

$$\begin{aligned}
\mathcal{V}(\widehat{\Lambda}) &\approx [f'(\phi)]^2 \, \mathcal{V}(\widehat{\phi}) \\
&= \left[\frac{1}{\phi(1-\phi)}\right]^2 \frac{\phi(1-\phi)}{n} \\
&= \frac{1}{n\phi(1-\phi)}
\end{aligned}$$

Finally, the estimated asymptotic sampling variance of the logit is $\widehat{\mathcal{V}}(\widehat{\Lambda}) = 1/[n\widehat{\phi}(1-\widehat{\phi})]$.

The delta method extends readily to functions of several parameters: Suppose that $\beta \equiv f(\alpha_1, \alpha_2, \ldots, \alpha_k) = f(\boldsymbol{\alpha})$, and that $\widehat{\boldsymbol{\alpha}}$ is the MLE of $\boldsymbol{\alpha}$, with asymptotic covariance matrix $\mathcal{V}(\widehat{\boldsymbol{\alpha}})$. Then the approximate asymptotic variance of $\widehat{\beta} = f(\widehat{\boldsymbol{\alpha}})$ is

$$\mathcal{V}(\widehat{\beta}) \approx [\mathbf{g}(\boldsymbol{\alpha})]' \, \mathcal{V}(\widehat{\boldsymbol{\alpha}}) \mathbf{g}(\boldsymbol{\alpha}) = \sum_{i=1}^{k} \sum_{j=1}^{k} v_{ij} \times \frac{\partial \widehat{\beta}}{\partial \alpha_i} \times \frac{\partial \widehat{\beta}}{\partial \alpha_j}$$

where $\mathbf{g}(\boldsymbol{\alpha}) \equiv \partial\widehat{\beta}/\partial\boldsymbol{\alpha}$ and v_{ij} is the i,jth entry of $\mathscr{V}(\widehat{\boldsymbol{\alpha}})$. The estimated asymptotic variance of $\widehat{\beta}$ is thus

$$\widehat{\mathscr{V}}(\widehat{\beta}) = \left[\mathbf{g}(\widehat{\boldsymbol{\alpha}})\right]' \mathscr{V}(\widehat{\boldsymbol{\alpha}})\mathbf{g}(\widehat{\boldsymbol{\alpha}})$$

The delta method is not only applicable to functions of maximum-likelihood estimators, but more generally to functions of estimators that are asymptotically normally distributed.

6.4   Introduction to Bayesian Inference

This section introduces Bayesian statistics, an alternative approach to statistical inference. The treatment here is very brief, presenting and illustrating the principal ideas of Bayesian inference but not developing the topic in any detail. The section also includes an introduction to Markov-chain Monte Carlo (MCMC) methods for approximating probability distributions, a topic of great importance to practical applications of Bayesian inference.

6.4.1   *Bayes's Theorem*

Recall (from page 109) the definition of *conditional probability*: The probability of an event A given that another event B is known to have occurred is

$$\Pr(A|B) = \frac{\Pr(A \cap B)}{\Pr(B)} \tag{6.11}$$

Likewise, the conditional probability of B given A is

$$\Pr(B|A) = \frac{\Pr(A \cap B)}{\Pr(A)} \tag{6.12}$$

Solving Equation 6.12 for the *joint probability* of A and B produces

$$\Pr(A \cap B) = \Pr(B|A)\Pr(A)$$

and substituting this result into Equation 6.11 yields *Bayes's theorem*:

$$\Pr(A|B) = \frac{\Pr(B|A)\Pr(A)}{\Pr(B)} \tag{6.13}$$

Bayes's theorem is named after its discoverer, the Reverend Thomas Bayes, an 18th-century English mathematician.

Bayesian statistical inference is based on the following interpretation of Equation 6.13: Let A represent some uncertain proposition whose truth or falsity we wish to establish—for example, the proposition that a parameter is equal to a particular value. Let B represent observed data that are relevant to the truth of the proposition. We interpret the unconditional probability $\Pr(A)$, called the *prior probability* of A, as our strength of belief in the truth of A prior to collecting data, and $\Pr(B|A)$ as the probability of obtaining the observed data assuming the truth of A—that is, the *likelihood* of the data given A (in the sense of the preceding section). The *unconditional* probability of the data B is[25]

$$\Pr(B) = \Pr(B|A)\Pr(A) + \Pr(B|\overline{A})\Pr(\overline{A})$$

Then $\Pr(A|B)$, given by Equation 6.13 and called the *posterior probability* of A, represents our revised strength of belief in A in light of the data B.

Bayesian inference is therefore a rational procedure for updating one's beliefs on the basis of evidence. This *subjectivist* interpretation of probabilities contrasts with the *frequentist* interpretation of probabilities as long-run proportions (see page 108). Bayes's theorem follows from elementary probability theory *whether or not* one accepts its subjectivist interpretation, but it is the latter that gives rise to common procedures of Bayesian statistical inference.[26]

I'll conclude this section with a simple application of Bayes's theorem that I present as an exercise for the reader, an example that nicely reinforces the point that Bayes's theorem is just a consequence of basic probability theory. The application is well-known, but most people find the result surprising (and it is topical as I write this in 2020):

- Suppose that 10% of the population of a country have been infected by a disease-causing virus and have developed antibodies to it that convey immunity to the disease. Let A represent the event that a person selected at random from the population has *antibodies* to the virus, so $\Pr(A) = .1$ and $\Pr(\overline{A}) = .9$.

---

[25]This is an application of the *law of total probability*: Given an event B and a set of k disjoint events $A_1, \ldots, A_k$ for which $\sum_{i=1}^{k} \Pr(A_i) = 1$ (i.e., the events A_i partition the sample space S),

$$\Pr(B) = \sum_{i=1}^{k} \Pr(B|A_i)\Pr(A_i)$$

[26]The identification of "classical" statistical inference with the frequentist interpretation of probability and of Bayesian inference with subjective probability is a simplification that glosses over differences in both camps. Such subtleties are well beyond the scope of this presentation.

- Imagine that a test for antibodies has been developed that never produces a false negative. Let P represent the event that a person tests *positive* for antibodies. The conditional probability that a person with antibodies correctly tests positive, called the *sensitivity* of the test, is then $\Pr(P|A) = 1$.

- Imagine further that the test has a false-positive rate of 10%—that is, 10% of people who don't have antibodies to the virus nevertheless test positive (perhaps because they've been infected by a similar virus). The conditional probability that a person who doesn't have antibodies incorrectly tests positive is therefore $\Pr(P|\overline{A}) = .1$.[27]

- Imagine, finally, that *you* test positive. What is the probability that you actually have antibodies to the virus and are therefore immune to it—that is, what is $\Pr(A|P)$?[28] [*Hint:* $\Pr(A|P)$ is much smaller than $\Pr(P|A) = 1$.]

A Preliminary Example of Bayesian Inference

Consider the following simple (if contrived) situation: Suppose that you are given a gift of two "biased" coins, one of which produces heads with probability $\Pr(H) = .3$ and the other with $\Pr(H) = .8$. Each of these coins comes in a box marked with its bias, but you carelessly misplace the boxes and put the coins in a drawer; a year later, you do not remember which coin is which. To try to distinguish the coins, you pick one arbitrarily and flip it 10 times, obtaining the data *HHTHHHHTTHH*—that is, a particular sequence of seven heads and three tails. (These are the "data" used in a preliminary example of maximum-likelihood estimation in Section 6.3.)

Let A represent the event that the selected coin has $\Pr(H) = .3$; then $\overline{A}$ is the event that the coin has $\Pr(H) = .8$. Under these circumstances, it seems reasonable to take as prior probabilities $\Pr(A) = \Pr(\overline{A}) = .5$. Calling the data

---

[27]The probability that a person who doesn't have antibodies correctly tests negative, called the *specificity* of the test, is $\Pr(\overline{P}|\overline{A}) = 1 - .1 = .9$, but this probability isn't needed for the problem.

[28]A strict frequentist would object to referring to the probability that a specific individual, like you, has antibodies to the virus because, after all, either you have antibodies or you don't. $\Pr(A|P)$ is therefore a subjective probability, reflecting your ignorance of the true state of affairs. $\Pr(A|P)$ can be given an objective frequentist interpretation as the long-run *proportion* (i.e., the relative frequency) of individuals testing positive who are actually positive.

B, the likelihood of the data under A and $\overline{A}$ is

$$\Pr(B|A) = .3^7(1-.3)^3 = .0000750$$
$$\Pr(B|\overline{A}) = .8^7(1-.8)^3 = .0016777$$

As is typically the case, the likelihood of the observed data is small in both cases, but the data are much more likely under $\overline{A}$ than under A. (The likelihood of these data for *any* value of $\Pr(H)$ between 0 and 1 was shown previously in Figure 6.10 on page 166.)

Using Bayes's theorem (Equation 6.13), you find the posterior probabilities

$$\Pr(A|B) = \frac{.0000750 \times .5}{.0000750 \times .5 + .0016777 \times .5} = .0428$$
$$\Pr(\overline{A}|B) = \frac{.0016777 \times .5}{.0000750 \times .5 + .0016777 \times .5} = .9572$$

suggesting that it is much more probable that the selected coin has $\Pr(H) = .8$ than $\Pr(H) = .3$.

6.4.2 Extending Bayes's Theorem

Bayes's theorem extends readily to situations in which there are more than two hypotheses A and $\overline{A}$: Let the various hypotheses be represented by $H_1, H_2, \ldots, H_k$, with prior probabilities $\Pr(H_i)$, $i = 1, \ldots, k$, that sum to one[29]; and let D represent the observed data, with likelihood $\Pr(D|H_i)$ under hypothesis H_i. Then the posterior probability of hypothesis H_i is

$$\Pr(H_i|D) = \frac{\Pr(D|H_i)\Pr(H_i)}{\sum_{j=1}^{k} \Pr(D|H_j)\Pr(H_j)} \tag{6.14}$$

The denominator in Equation 6.14 ensures that the posterior probabilities for the various hypotheses sum to 1. It is sometimes convenient to omit this normalization, simply noting that

$$\Pr(H_i|D) \propto \Pr(D|H_i)\Pr(H_i)$$

that is, that the posterior probability of a hypothesis is proportional to the product of the likelihood under the hypothesis and its prior probability. If

---

[29]To employ Bayesian inference, your prior beliefs must be consistent with probability theory, and so the prior probabilities must sum to 1.

necessary, we can always divide by $\sum \Pr(D|H_i)\Pr(H_i)$ to recover the posterior probabilities.

Bayes's theorem is also applicable to random variables: Let α represent a parameter of interest, with prior probability distribution or density $p(\alpha)$, and let $L(\alpha) \equiv p(D|\alpha)$ represent the likelihood function for the parameter α. Then,

$$p(\alpha|D) = \frac{L(\alpha)p(\alpha)}{\sum_{\text{all } \alpha'} L(\alpha')p(\alpha')}$$

when the parameter α is discrete, or

$$p(\alpha|D) = \frac{L(\alpha)p(\alpha)}{\int_A L(\alpha')p(\alpha')\,d\alpha'}$$

when, as is more common, α is continuous (and where A represents the set of all values of α). In either case,

$$p(\alpha|D) \propto L(\alpha)p(\alpha)$$

That is, the posterior probability or density is proportional to the product of the likelihood and the prior probability or density. As before, we can if necessary divide by $\sum L(\alpha)p(\alpha)$ or $\int L(\alpha)p(\alpha)\,d\alpha$ to recover the posterior probabilities or densities.[30]

The following points are noteworthy:

- We require a prior distribution $p(\alpha)$ over the possible values of the parameter α (the *parameter space*) to set the machinery of Bayesian inference in motion.

- In contrast to a frequentist statistician, a Bayesian treats the parameter α as a *random variable* rather than as an unknown *constant*. We retain Greek letters for parameters, however, because unlike the data, parameters are never known with certainty—even after collecting data.

Conjugate and Other Priors

The mathematics of Bayesian inference is especially simple when the prior distribution is selected so that the likelihood and prior combine to produce a

---

[30]The statement is glib, in that it may not be easy in the continuous case to evaluate the integral $\int L(\alpha)p(\alpha)\,d\alpha$. This potential difficulty motivates the use of conjugate priors, discussed immediately below, and the more generally applicable MCMC methods described later in the chapter (Section 6.4.6).

posterior distribution that is in the same family as the prior. In this case, we say that the prior distribution is a *conjugate prior*.

At one time, Bayesian inference was only practical when conjugate priors were employed, radically limiting its scope of application. Advances in computer software and hardware, however, make it practical to approximate mathematically intractable posterior distributions by simulated random sampling. Such MCMC methods (which are described in Section 6.4.6) have produced a flowering of Bayesian applied statistics. Nevertheless, the choice of prior distribution can be an important one.

6.4.3 An Example of Bayesian Inference

Continuing the previous example, suppose more realistically that you are given a coin and wish to estimate the probability ϕ that the coin turns up heads, but cannot restrict ϕ in advance to a small number of discrete values; rather, ϕ could, in principle, be any number between 0 and 1. To estimate ϕ, you plan to gather data by independently flipping the coin 10 times. We know from our previous work that the Bernoulli likelihood for this experiment is

$$L(\phi) = \phi^h (1 - \phi)^{10-h} \tag{6.15}$$

where h is the observed number of heads. You conduct the experiment, obtaining the data $HHTHHHHTTHH$, and thus $h = 7$.

The conjugate prior for the Bernoulli likelihood in Equation 6.15 is the beta distribution (see Section 5.2.9),

$$p(\phi) = \frac{\phi^{a-1}(1-\phi)^{b-1}}{B(a,b)} \text{ for } 0 \le \phi \le 1 \text{ and } a, b \ge 0$$

When you multiply the beta prior by the likelihood, you get a posterior density of the form

$$p(\phi|D) \propto \phi^{h+a-1}(1-\phi)^{10-h+b-1} = \phi^{6+a}(1-\phi)^{2+b}$$

that is, a beta distribution with shape parameters $h + a = 7 + a$ and $10 - h + b = 3 + b$. Put another way, the prior in effect adds a heads and b tails to the likelihood.

How should you select a and b? One approach would be to reflect your subjective assessment of the plausible values of ϕ. For example, you might confirm that the coin has both a head and a tail, and that it seems to be reasonably well balanced, suggesting that ϕ is probably close to .5. Picking $a = b = 16$ would in effect confine your estimate of ϕ to the range between .3 and .7 (see Figure 5.15 on page 141). If you are uncomfortable with this restriction, then you could select smaller values of a and b: When $a = b = 1$, all values of ϕ are equally likely—a so-called flat or uninformative prior distribution, reflecting complete ignorance about the value of ϕ.[31]

Figure 6.13 shows the posterior distributions for ϕ under these two priors. Under the flat prior, the posterior is proportional to the likelihood, and therefore if you take the mode of the posterior as your estimate of ϕ, you get the MLE $\widehat{\phi} = .7$.[32] The posterior for the *informative prior* $a = b = 16$, in contrast, has a mode at $\phi \approx .55$, which is much closer to the mode of the prior distribution $\phi = .5$.

It may be disconcerting that the conclusion should depend so crucially on the prior distribution, but this result is a consequence of the very small sample in the example: Recall that using a beta prior in this case is like adding $a + b$ observations to the data. As the sample size grows, the likelihood comes to dominate the posterior distribution, and the influence of the prior distribution fades.[33] In the current example, if the coin is flipped n times, then the posterior distribution takes the form

$$p(\phi|D) \propto \phi^{h+a-1}(1-\phi)^{n-h+b-1}$$

and the numbers of heads h and tails $n - h$ will grow with the number of flips. It is intuitively sensible that your prior beliefs should carry greater weight when the sample is small than when it is large.

---

[31] In this case, the prior is a rectangular density function, with the parameter ϕ bounded between 0 and 1. In other cases, such as estimating the mean μ of a normal distribution, which is unbounded, a flat prior of the form $p(\mu) = c$ (for any positive constant c) over $-\infty < \mu < \infty$ does not enclose a finite probability and, hence, cannot represent a density function. When combined with the likelihood, such an *improper prior* can nevertheless lead to a proper posterior distribution—that is, to a posterior density that integrates to 1.

A more subtle point is that a flat prior for one parametrization of a probability model for the data need not be flat for an alternative parametrization: For example, suppose that you take the odds $\omega \equiv \phi/(1-\phi)$ as the parameter of interest, or the logit (i.e., log-odds) $\Lambda \equiv \log_e[\phi/(1-\phi)]$; a flat prior for ϕ is not flat for ω or for Λ.

[32] An alternative is to take the mean or median of the posterior distribution as a point estimate of ϕ. In most cases, however, the posterior distribution will approach a normal distribution as the sample size increases, and the posterior mean, median, and mode will therefore be approximately equal if the sample size is sufficiently large.

[33] An exception to this rule occurs when the prior distribution assigns zero density to some values of the parameter; such values will necessarily have posterior densities of zero regardless of the data.

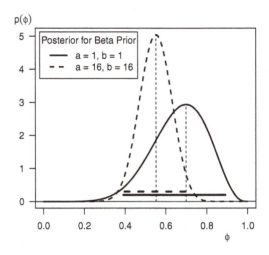

Figure 6.13   Posterior distributions for the probability of a head ϕ under two prior distributions: the flat beta prior with $a = 1, b = 1$ (the posterior for which is shown as a solid curve), and the informative beta prior with $a = 16, b = 16$ (the broken curve). The data contain seven heads in 10 flips of a coin. The two horizontal lines near the bottom of the graph show 95% central posterior intervals corresponding to the two priors.

6.4.4 Bayesian Interval Estimates

As in classical frequentist statistical inference, it is desirable not only to provide a point estimate of a parameter but also to quantify uncertainty in the estimate. The posterior distribution of the parameter displays statistical uncertainty in a direct form, and the standard deviation of the posterior distribution is a Bayesian analog of the frequentist standard error. One can also compute various kinds of Bayesian interval estimates (termed *credible intervals* and analogous to frequentist confidence intervals) from the posterior distribution.

A very simple choice of Bayesian interval estimate is the *central posterior interval*: The $100a\%$ central posterior interval runs from the $(1-a)/2$ to the

$(1+a)/2$ quantile of the posterior distribution. Unlike a classical confidence interval, however, the interpretation of which is famously convoluted (to the confusion of innumerable students of basic statistics), a Bayesian credible interval has a simple interpretation as a probability statement: The probability is .95 that the parameter is in the 95% posterior interval. This difference reflects the Bayesian interpretation of a parameter as a random variable, with the posterior distribution expressing subjective uncertainty about the value of the parameter after observing the data.

Ninety-five percent central posterior intervals for the example are shown for the two posterior distributions in Figure 6.13.

6.4.5   *Bayesian Inference for Several Parameters*

Bayesian inference extends straightforwardly to the simultaneous estimation of several parameters $\boldsymbol{\alpha} \equiv [\alpha_1, \alpha_2, \ldots, \alpha_k]'$. In this case, it is necessary to specify a *joint prior distribution* for the parameters, $p(\boldsymbol{\alpha})$,[34] along with the *joint likelihood*, $L(\boldsymbol{\alpha})$. Then, as in the case of one parameter, the *joint posterior distribution* is proportional to the product of the prior distribution and the likelihood,

$$p(\boldsymbol{\alpha}|D) \propto p(\boldsymbol{\alpha})L(\boldsymbol{\alpha}) \tag{6.16}$$

or

$$p(\boldsymbol{\alpha}|D) = \frac{p(\boldsymbol{\alpha})L(\boldsymbol{\alpha})}{\int_{\mathbf{A}} p(\boldsymbol{\alpha}^*)L(\boldsymbol{\alpha}^*)d^k\boldsymbol{\alpha}^*} \tag{6.17}$$

where $\mathbf{A}$ is the set of all values of the parameter vector $\boldsymbol{\alpha}$. Inference typically focuses on the *marginal posterior distribution* of each parameter, $p(\alpha_i|D)$.

6.4.6   *Markov-Chain Monte Carlo*

To find $p(\boldsymbol{\alpha}|D)$ explicitly is simple for a conjugate prior. More generally, however, we must integrate over all values $\mathbf{A}$ of $\boldsymbol{\alpha}$, and the integral in the denominator of Equation 6.17 is usually intractable analytically. *Markov-chain Monte Carlo (MCMC)* is a set of methods for drawing random samples from—and hence approximating—the posterior distribution $p(\boldsymbol{\alpha}|D)$ without having explicitly to evaluate the denominator of Equation 6.17. MCMC methods, coupled with the increasing power of computer hardware, have rendered Bayesian inference practical for a broad range of statistical problems.

---

[34] It's typically the case in practice that prior distributions are specified independently for the various parameters, so that the joint prior is the product of the separate (marginal) priors.

There are three common (and related) MCMC methods: the Metropolis–Hastings algorithm, the Gibbs sampler, and Hamiltonian Monte Carlo:

- What's come to be called the *Metropolis–Hastings algorithm* was originally formulated by Metropolis, Rosenbluth, Rosenbluth, Teller, and Teller (1953) and subsequently generalized by Hastings (1970). I'll explain the more general version of the algorithm, but will use the original, simpler version in an initial example and in an application to Bayesian inference.

- The *Gibbs sampler* is an MCMC algorithm developed for applications in image processing by Geman and Geman (1984), who named it after the American physicist Josiah Gibbs (1839–1903). Gelfand and Smith (1990) pointed out the applicability of the Gibbs sampler to statistical problems. The Gibbs sampler is based on the observation that the joint distribution of an n-dimensional vector random variable $\mathbf{x}$ can be composed from the conditional distribution of each of its elements given the others, that is $p(X_j|\mathbf{x}_{-j})$ for $j = 1, 2, \ldots, n$ (where $\mathbf{x}_{-j} = [X_1, X_2, \ldots, X_{j-1}, X_{j+1}, \ldots, X_n]'$ is $\mathbf{x}$ with the jth element removed). Although it was developed independently, in this basic form the Gibbs sampler turns out to be a special case of the general Metropolis–Hastings algorithm (see Gelman et al., 2013, page 281). The popular Bayesian statistical software *BUGS* (Lunn, Spiegelhalter, Thomas, & Best, 2009) is based on the Gibbs sampler, and indeed its name is an acronym for *B*ayesian inference *U*sing *G*ibbs *S*ampling.

- *Hamiltonian Monte Carlo* (*HMC*), introduced to statistics by Neal (1996), is an improvement to the Metropolis–Hastings algorithm that, when properly tuned, provides more efficient sampling from a target distribution. Hamiltonian Monte Carlo is named after the Irish mathematician and physicist William Rowan Hamilton (1805–1865), who reformulated the mathematics of classical Newtonian mechanics. HMC exploits an analogy between exploring the surface of a probability density function and the motion of an object along a frictionless surface, propelled by its initial momentum and gravity. HMC is considered the best current method of MCMC for sampling from continuous distributions, and is the basis for the state-of-the-art *Stan* Bayesian software (Carpenter et al., 2017).

In the interest of brevity, neither the Gibbs sampler nor Hamiltonian Monte Carlo is developed in this chapter (but see the references in the Preface, page xx).

The Metropolis–Hastings Algorithm

Here's the problem that the Metropolis–Hastings algorithm addresses: We have a continuous vector random variable $\mathbf{x}$ with n elements and with density function $p(\mathbf{x})$. We don't know how to compute $p(\mathbf{x})$, but we do have a function proportional to it, $p^*(\mathbf{x}) = c \times p(\mathbf{x})$, where $c = \int_{\mathbf{X}} p^*(\mathbf{x}) d\mathbf{x}$. We don't know the *normalizing constant* c, which makes $p(\mathbf{x})$ integrate to 1, or we'd know $p(\mathbf{x})$. We nevertheless want to draw a random sample from the *target distribution* $p(\mathbf{x})$. One way this situation might arise is in Bayesian inference, where $p^*(\cdot)$ could be the *unnormalized posterior*, computed (as in Expression 6.16 on page 186) as the product of the prior density and the likelihood.

The Metropolis-Hastings algorithm starts with an arbitrary value $\mathbf{x}_0$ of $\mathbf{x}$, and proceeds to generate a sequence of m realized values $\mathbf{x}_1, \mathbf{x}_2, \ldots, \mathbf{x}_{i-1}$, $\mathbf{x}_i, \ldots, \mathbf{x}_m$. Each subsequent realization is selected randomly based on a *candidate* or *proposal distribution*, with conditional density function $f(\mathbf{x}_i|\mathbf{x}_{i-1})$, from which we know how to sample. The proposal distribution $f(\cdot)$ is generally distinct from the target distribution $p(\cdot)$.

As the notation implies, the proposal distribution employed depends only on the immediately preceding value of $\mathbf{x}$. The next value of $\mathbf{x}$ sampled from the proposal distribution may be accepted or rejected, hence the term *proposal* or *candidate*. If the proposed value of $\mathbf{x}_i$ is rejected, then the preceding value is retained; that is, $\mathbf{x}_i$ is set to $\mathbf{x}_{i-1}$. This procedure—where the probability of transition from one "state" to another (i.e., one value of $\mathbf{x}$ to the next) depends only on the previous state—defines a *Markov process*[35] yielding a *Markov chain* of sampled values.

Within broad conditions, the choice of proposal distribution is arbitrary. For example, it's necessary that the proposal distribution and initial value $\mathbf{x}_0$ lead to a Markov process capable of visiting the complete support of $\mathbf{x}$— that is, all values of $\mathbf{x}$ for which the density $p(\mathbf{x})$ is nonzero. And different choices of proposal distributions may be differentially desirable, for example, in the sense that they are more or less efficient—that is, tend to require, respectively, fewer or more generated values to cover the support of $\mathbf{x}$ thoroughly.

With this background, the Metropolis–Hastings algorithm proceeds as follows. For each $i = 1, 2, \ldots, m$:

1. Sample a candidate value $\mathbf{x}^*$ from the proposal distribution $f(\mathbf{x}_i|\mathbf{x}_{i-1})$.

---

[35]Named after the Russian mathematician Andrey Andreevich Markov (1856–1922).

2. Compute the *acceptance ratio*

$$a = \frac{p(\mathbf{x}^*)f(\mathbf{x}^*|\mathbf{x}_{i-1})}{p(\mathbf{x}_{i-1})f(\mathbf{x}_{i-1}|\mathbf{x}^*)} \tag{6.18}$$

$$= \frac{p^*(\mathbf{x}^*)f(\mathbf{x}^*|\mathbf{x}_{i-1})}{p^*(\mathbf{x}_{i-1})f(\mathbf{x}_{i-1}|\mathbf{x}^*)}$$

The substitution of $p^*(\cdot)$ for $p(\cdot)$ in the second line of Equation 6.18 is justified because the unknown normalizing constant c (recall, the number that makes the density integrate to 1) cancels in the numerator and denominator, making the *ratio* in the equation computable even though the numerator and denominator in the first line of the equation are not separately computable. Calculate $a' = \min(a, 1)$.

3. Generate a uniform random number u on the unit interval, $U \sim \text{Unif}$ $(0, 1)$. If $u \leq a'$, set the ith value in the chain to the proposal, $\mathbf{x}_i = \mathbf{x}^*$; otherwise retain the previous value, $\mathbf{x}_i = \mathbf{x}_{i-1}$. In effect, the proposal is accepted with certainty if it is "at least as probable" as the preceding value, taking into account the possible bias in the direction of movement of the proposal function from the preceding value. If the proposal is less probable than the preceding value, then the probability of accepting the proposal declines with the ratio a, but isn't zero. Thus, the chain will tend to visit higher-density regions of the target distribution with greater frequency but will still explore the entire target distribution. It can be shown (e.g., Chib & Greenberg, 1995) that the *limiting distribution* of the Markov chain (the distribution to which the sample tends as $m \to \infty$) is indeed the target distribution, and so the algorithm should work if m is big enough.

The Metropolis–Hastings algorithm is simpler when the proposal distribution is symmetric, in the sense that $f(\mathbf{x}_i|\mathbf{x}_{i-1}) = f(\mathbf{x}_{i-1}|\mathbf{x}_i)$. This is true, for example, when the proposal distribution is multivariate-normal (see Section 5.2.5) with mean vector $\mathbf{x}_{i-1}$ and some specified covariance matrix $\mathbf{S}$ (adapting Equation 5.6 on page 132):

$$f(\mathbf{x}_i|\mathbf{x}_{i-1}) = \frac{1}{(2\pi)^{n/2}\sqrt{\det \mathbf{S}}} \times \exp\left[-\frac{1}{2}(\mathbf{x}_i - \mathbf{x}_{i-1})'\mathbf{S}^{-1}(\mathbf{x}_i - \mathbf{x}_{i-1})\right]$$

$$= f(\mathbf{x}_{i-1}|\mathbf{x}_i) \tag{6.19}$$

Then, a in Equation 6.18 becomes

$$a = \frac{p^*(\mathbf{x}^*)}{p^*(\mathbf{x}_{i-1})} \tag{6.20}$$

which (again, because the missing normalizing constant c cancels) is equivalent to the ratio of the target density at the proposed and preceding values of **x**. This simplified version of the Metropolis–Hastings algorithm, based on a symmetric proposal distribution, is the version originally introduced by Metropolis et al. (1953).

By construction, the Metropolis–Hastings algorithm generates statistically *dependent* successive values of **x**. If an approximately independent sample is desired, then the sequence of sampled values can be *thinned* by discarding a sufficient number of intermediate values of **x**, retaining only every kth value. Additionally, because of an unfortunately selected initial value $\mathbf{x}_0$, it may take some time for the sampled sequence to approach its limiting distribution—that is, the target distribution. It may therefore be advantageous to discard a number of values at the beginning of the sequence, termed the *burn-in period*.

Example: Sampling From the Bivariate-Normal Distribution

I'll demonstrate the Metropolis algorithm by sampling from a bivariate-normal distribution (introduced in Section 5.2.5) with the following (arbitrary) mean vector and covariance matrix:

$$\boldsymbol{\mu} = [1, 2]' \tag{6.21}$$

$$\boldsymbol{\Sigma} = \begin{bmatrix} 1 & 1 \\ 1 & 4 \end{bmatrix}$$

It's not necessary to use MCMC in this case, because it's easy to approximate bivariate-normal probabilities or to draw samples from the distribution directly, but the bivariate-normal distribution provides a simple setting in which to demonstrate the Metropolis algorithm, and for pedagogical purposes it helps to know the right answer in advance—that is, the example is selected for its transparency.

Let's pretend that we know the bivariate-normal distribution only up to a constant of proportionality. To this end, I omit the normalizing constant, which for this simple example works out to $2\pi \times \sqrt{3}$ (see Equation 5.6 on page 132).

To illustrate that the proposal distribution and the target distribution are distinct, I use a bivariate-rectangular proposal distribution centered at the preceding value $\mathbf{x}_{i-1}$ with half-extent $\delta_1 = 2$ in the direction of the coordinate x_1 and $\delta_2 = 4$ in the direction of x_2, reflecting the relative sizes of the standard deviations of the two variables. This distribution is symmetric, as required by the simpler Metropolis algorithm. Clearly, because it has finite support, the rectangular proposal distribution doesn't cover the entire support of the bivariate-normal target distribution, which extends infinitely in each direction, but because the proposal distribution "travels" (i.e., moves in the $\{x_1, x_2\}$ plane) with $\mathbf{x}_i$, it can generate a valid Markov chain.

I arbitrarily set $\mathbf{x}_0 = [0,0]'$, and sample $m = 10^5$ values of $\mathbf{x}$. As it turns out, 41.7% of proposals are accepted. To get a sense of how Metropolis sampling proceeds, I show the first 50 accepted proposals, along with the duplicated points corresponding to rejected proposals (of which there are 75), in Figure 6.14. The 95% concentration ellipse for the bivariate-normal distribution (see Section 5.2.5) is also shown on the graph.

How well does the Metropolis algorithm approximate the bivariate-normal distribution? Here are the mean vector and covariance matrix of the sampled points, which are quite close to the parameters in Equation 6.21:

$$\widehat{\mu} = [1.003, 1.987]'$$
$$\widehat{\Sigma} = \begin{bmatrix} 0.989 & 0.972 \\ 0.972 & 3.963 \end{bmatrix}$$

Figure 6.15 shows all of the 10^5 sampled points together with several theoretical elliptical contours of constant density and corresponding empirical density contours.[36] Clearly, the Metropolis algorithm does a good job of recovering the bivariate-normal density.

As mentioned, the Metropolis algorithm doesn't produce an independent random sample from the target distribution. One way to measure the dependence among the sampled values is to compute their *autocorrelations*. Focus, for example, on the vector of jth sampled coordinates, say $\mathbf{x}_j = [x_{1j}, x_{2j}, \ldots, x_{mj}]'$, with mean $\bar{x}_j$. The sample autocorrelation at *lag t* is defined as

$$r_t = \frac{\sum_{i=t+1}^{m} (x_{ij} - \bar{x}_j)(x_{i-t,j} - \bar{x}_j)}{\sum_{i=1}^{m} (x_{ij} - \bar{x}_j)^2}$$

Figure 6.16 shows autocorrelations at lags $t = 0, 1, \ldots, 50$, for the coordinates $\mathbf{x}_1$ and $\mathbf{x}_2$ in the example (where the autocorrelation at Lag 0, r_0, is necessarily 1). The autocorrelations are large at small lags, but decay to near zero by around Lag 25, which suggests thinning by selecting, say, every 25th value to produce an approximately independent sample

---

[36] The empirical density contours are computed by a 2D *kernel-density estimator*; see Silverman (1986, Chapter 4).

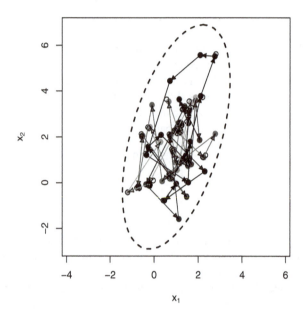

Figure 6.14   First 50 accepted proposals and duplicated points representing rejected proposals, sampling from the bivariate-normal distribution in Equation 6.21, which is represented by its 95% concentration ellipse. The solid dots represent the 50 distinct points, corresponding to accepted proposals, starting out as light gray and getting progressively darker, with the arrows showing the transitions. Duplicated points corresponding to rejected proposals, shown as hollow dots, are slightly randomly "jittered" so that they don't precisely overplot the accepted proposals.

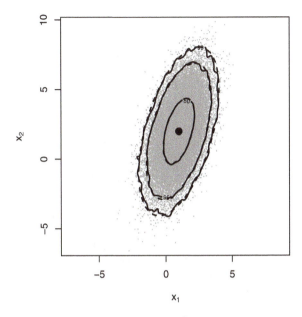

Figure 6.15   The gray dots show $m = 10^5$ values sampled from the
bivariate-normal distribution in Equation 6.21 by the
Metropolis algorithm. The slightly irregular solid lines
represent estimated density contours enclosing 50%, 95%,
and 99% of the sampled points. The broken lines are the
corresponding elliptical density contours of the
bivariate-normal distribution.

A Simple Application to Bayesian Inference

I'll illustrate the application of MCMC to Bayesian inference by considering
a simple and familiar single-parameter problem: estimating a probability (or
population proportion) ϕ, a problem that we previously encountered in this
chapter (in Section 6.4.3).

To recapitulate briefly, the likelihood for this problem comes from the
Bernoulli distribution. As before, I'll use a prior distribution from the beta
family, the conjugate prior to the Bernoulli likelihood. The posterior distribution is also beta, and it's therefore not necessary to approximate it by
MCMC. Doing so, however, allows us to compare the results of MCMC with
the known right answer.

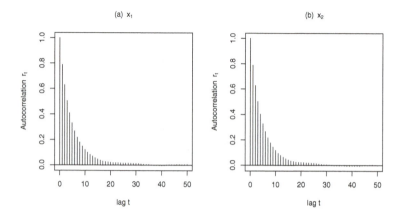

Figure 6.16   Autocorrelations of the sampled values of (a) x_1 and (b) x_2 produced by the Metropolis algorithm applied to the bivariate-normal distribution in Equation 6.21.

Recall our coin-flipping experiment, which produced $h = 7$ heads in $n = 10$ independent flips of a coin, with Bernoulli likelihood $L(\phi|h=7) = \phi^h(1 - \phi)^{n-h} = \phi^7(1 - \phi)^3$. As in Section 6.4.3, I'll consider two prior distributions: a flat prior, in which the parameters of the Beta(α, β) distribution (Equation 5.7 on page 139) are set to $\alpha = \beta = 1$, and an informative prior centered on the population proportion $\phi = 0.5$ (representing a "fair" coin) in which $\alpha = \beta = 16$. In the first case, the posterior is Beta$(8,4)$, and in the second case, it is Beta$(23, 19)$. These priors and posteriors appeared in Figure 6.13 (page 185).

For the first simulation—with a flat prior—I set the standard deviation of the normal proposal distribution $N(\phi_{i-1}, s^2)$ in the Metropolis algorithm to $s = 0.1$, starting arbitrarily from $\phi_0 = 0.5$ and sampling $m = 10^5$ values from the posterior distribution of ϕ, with an acceptance rate of 77.5%. An estimate of the resulting posterior density function is shown in Panel (a) of Figure 6.17, along with the true Beta$(8,4)$ posterior density; Panel(b) shows a *quantile-comparison* (*QQ*) *plot* of the sampled values versus the Beta$(8,4)$ distribution: If the values were sampled from Beta$(8,4)$, then the points would lie approximately on a $45°$ straight line (shown on the QQ plot), within the bounds of sampling error.[37]

The agreement between the approximate posterior produced by the Metropolis algorithm and the true posterior distribution is very good, except at the extreme left of the distribution, where the sampled values are slightly shorter-tailed than the Beta$(8,4)$ distribution. The results for the second simulation, employing the informative Beta$(16,16)$ prior, for which the true posterior is Beta$(23,19)$ (shown in Panels (c) and (d) of Figure 6.17), are similarly encouraging. The acceptance rate for the Metropolis algorithm in the second simulation is 63.2%. In both cases (but particularly with the flat prior), the Metropolis samples of ϕ are highly autocorrelated and would require thinning to produce an approximately independent sample; see Figure 6.18.

In the first case, using the flat Beta$(1,1)$ prior, an estimate of ϕ based on the median of the true Beta$(8,4)$ posterior distribution is $\widehat{\phi} = 0.676$, and the 95% Bayesian credible interval for ϕ from the 0.025 and 0.975 quantiles of the posterior is $0.390 < \phi < 0.891$. In comparison, using the median and 0.025 and 0.975 quantiles of the Metropolis sample, we have $\widehat{\phi} = 0.677$ and $0.392 < \phi < 0.891$.

The analogous results for the second case, with the informative Beta$(16,16)$ prior, are $\widehat{\phi} = 0.548$ and $0.397 < \phi < 0.693$ based on the true Beta$(23,19)$ posterior, and $\widehat{\phi} = 0.549$ and $0.396 < \phi < 0.692$ based on the Metropolis sample.

---

[37]See, e.g., Fox (2016, Section 3.1.3) for an explanation of QQ plots.

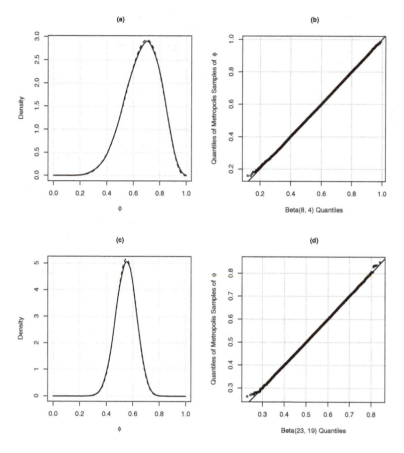

Figure 6.17   Comparing the results produced by the Metropolis algorithm to the true posterior distribution of the population proportion of heads ϕ, based on an independent sample of size $n = 10$ with $h = 7$ heads, and a prior distribution in the conjugate beta family. For Panels (a) and (b), the flat prior $\text{Beta}(1,1)$ is used, producing the true posterior $\text{Beta}(8,4)$; in Panels (c) and (d), the informative prior $\text{Beta}(16,16)$ is used, producing the true posterior $\text{Beta}(23,19)$. Panels (a) and (c) show nonparametric density estimates (solid lines) for the Metropolis samples, comparing these to the true posterior densities (broken lines); Panels (b) and (d) are quantile-comparison plots for the samples versus the true posterior distributions.

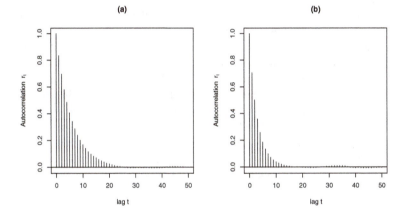

Figure 6.18   Autocorrelations of the Metropolis samples from the two posterior distributions: (a) based on the flat Beta(1, 1) prior, and (b) based on the informative Beta(16, 16) prior.

CHAPTER 7. PUTTING THE MATH TO WORK: LINEAR LEAST-SQUARES REGRESSION

As explained in the preface, this book aims to introduce mathematics useful for social statistics, and it does not focus on statistical methods themselves. Nevertheless, I feel that it is helpful to convey some sense of how the math is employed to develop statistical methods. This is the purpose of the last chapter of the book.

First, however, an important caveat: I describe some of the mathematics of linear least-squares regression in this chapter, but that tells only part of the larger statistical story. Although mathematics plays an important role in applied statistics, statistics is not exclusively mathematical and extends, for example, to methodological issues. Moreover, the application of statistical methods to data analysis is partly a craft.

Linear least-squares regression (a topic that I assume is at least cursorily familiar to the reader) is in several respects the central method in applied statistics: It appears frequently in applications; extends readily to the general linear model, to generalized linear models, and beyond; and provides a computational basis for many statistical methods. Consequently, adequately explaining the role of linear least-squares regression in data analysis requires a much more extensive development of the topic than is possible in this chapter. This is the proper task of texts on applied regression analysis (such as my own: Fox, 2016).

Linear least-squares regression is mathematically rich, and the current chapter makes use of material in Chapters 1 and 2 on matrices and linear algebra, including matrix rank, the solution of linear simultaneous equations, and the elliptical geometry of quadratic forms; in Chapter 3 on matrix differential calculus for optimization problems; and in Chapters 4, 5, and 6 on probability, statistical distributions, properties of estimators, and maximum-likelihood estimation.

7.1 Least-Squares Fit

A linear regression equation can be written as

$$Y_i = A + B_1 x_{i1} + B_2 x_{i2} + \cdots + B_k x_{ik} + E_i \tag{7.1}$$

where Y_i is the value of a quantitative *response variable* (or "dependent variable") for the *i*th of *n* observations; $x_{i1}, x_{i2}, \ldots, x_{ik}$ are the values of k quantitative *explanatory variables* (or "independent variables") for observation

$i; A, B_1, B_2, \ldots, B_k$ are *regression coefficients*—the first of these, A, is the regression *intercept* or *constant* and the Bs are *partial slope coefficients*; and E_i is the regression *residual*, reflecting the departure of Y_i from the corresponding point on the linear regression surface,

$$\widehat{Y}_i = A + B_1 x_{i1} + B_2 x_{i2} + \cdots + B_k x_{ik}$$

$\widehat{Y}_i$ is called the *fitted value* for observation i.

I use uppercase letters for Y_i and E_i because the response and the residuals are random variables: Were we to draw a different sample of n observations, the values of the response variable and the residuals would change. Similarly, because the values of the regression coefficients also change from sample to sample, they are also represented by uppercase letters. Conversely, I use lowercase letters for the explanatory variables to indicate that their values are fixed with respect to repeated sampling, a situation that typically occurs only in designed experiments, where the xs are under the direct control of the researcher and need not change if the study is replicated. Treating the xs as fixed produces simpler mathematics and turns out to be nearly inconsequential (at least formally); I will briefly consider random Xs later in the chapter (Section 7.6).

The least-squares regression coefficients are the values of A and the Bs that minimize the sum of squared residuals, considered as a function of the regression coefficients:

$$
\begin{aligned}
S(A, B_1, \ldots, B_k) &= \sum_{i=1}^{n} E_i^2 \\
&= \sum_{i=1}^{n} (Y_i - \widehat{Y}_i)^2 \\
&= \sum_{i=1}^{n} (Y_i - A - B_1 x_{i1} - \cdots - B_k x_{ik})^2
\end{aligned}
$$

Although we could continue with the linear regression equation in scalar form, it is advantageous to work instead with matrices. Let us therefore rewrite Equation 7.1 as

$$\underset{(n \times 1)}{\mathbf{y}} = \underset{(n \times k+1)}{\mathbf{X}} \underset{(k+1 \times 1)}{\mathbf{b}} + \underset{(n \times 1)}{\mathbf{e}}$$

where $\mathbf{y} \equiv [Y_1, Y_2, \ldots, Y_n]'$ is a vector of observations on the response variable,

$$\mathbf{X} \equiv \begin{bmatrix} 1 & x_{11} & \cdots & x_{1k} \\ 1 & x_{21} & \cdots & x_{2k} \\ \vdots & \vdots & & \vdots \\ 1 & x_{n1} & \cdots & x_{nk} \end{bmatrix}$$

called the *model* (or *design*) *matrix*, contains the values of the explanatory variables, with an initial column of 1s (called the *constant regressor*) for the regression constant; $\mathbf{b} \equiv [A, B_1, \ldots, B_k]'$ contains the regression coefficients; and $\mathbf{e} \equiv [E_1, E_2, \ldots, E_n]'$ is a vector of residuals. Then the sum of squared residuals is

$$\begin{aligned} S(\mathbf{b}) &= \mathbf{e}'\mathbf{e} \qquad\qquad\qquad\qquad\qquad\qquad (7.2) \\ &= (\mathbf{y} - \mathbf{Xb})'(\mathbf{y} - \mathbf{Xb}) \\ &= \mathbf{y}'\mathbf{y} - \mathbf{y}'\mathbf{Xb} - \mathbf{b}'\mathbf{X}'\mathbf{y} + \mathbf{b}'\mathbf{X}'\mathbf{Xb} \\ &= \mathbf{y}'\mathbf{y} - 2\mathbf{y}'\mathbf{Xb} + \mathbf{b}'\mathbf{X}'\mathbf{Xb} \end{aligned}$$

The transition to the last line of Equation 7.2 is justified by noticing that $\mathbf{y}'\mathbf{Xb}$ is (1×1) and, consequently, is necessarily equal to its transpose, $\mathbf{b}'\mathbf{X}'\mathbf{y}$.

To minimize the sum-of-squares function $S(\mathbf{b})$, differentiate it with respect to the regression coefficients $\mathbf{b}$, a process facilitated by the recognition that Equation 7.2 consists of a constant (with respect to $\mathbf{b}$), a linear term in $\mathbf{b}$, and a quadratic form in $\mathbf{b}$; thus,

$$\frac{\partial S(\mathbf{b})}{\partial \mathbf{b}} = \mathbf{0} - 2\mathbf{X}'\mathbf{y} + 2\mathbf{X}'\mathbf{Xb}$$

Setting the vector partial derivative to $\mathbf{0}$ and rearranging produces the so-called *normal equations* for linear least-squares regression[1]:

$$\underset{(k+1 \times k+1)}{\mathbf{X}'\mathbf{X}} \underset{(k+1 \times 1)}{\mathbf{b}} = \underset{(k+1 \times 1)}{\mathbf{X}'\mathbf{y}} \qquad\qquad (7.3)$$

---

[1] That the normal equations are called "normal" has nothing to do with the normal distribution: As explained in Section 1.3.1 on orthogonal projections, the vector of residuals $\mathbf{e}$ in least-squares regression is orthogonal to—in the language of geometry, *normal to*—the subspace spanned by the columns of the model matrix $\mathbf{X}$.

This is a system of $k+1$ linear equations in the $k+1$ unknown regression coefficients $\mathbf{b}$. The coefficient matrix for the system of equation,

$$\mathbf{X'X} = \begin{bmatrix} n & \sum x_{i1} & \sum x_{i2} & \cdots & \sum x_{ik} \\ \sum x_{i1} & \sum x_{ik}^2 & \sum x_{i1}x_{i2} & \cdots & \sum x_{i1}x_{ik} \\ \sum x_{i2} & \sum x_{i2}x_{i1} & \sum x_{i2}^2 & \cdots & \sum x_{i2}x_{ik} \\ \vdots & \vdots & \vdots & \ddots & \vdots \\ \sum x_{ik} & \sum x_{ik}x_{i1} & \sum x_{ik}x_{i2} & \cdots & \sum x_{ik}^2 \end{bmatrix}$$

contains sums of squares and cross-products among the columns of the model matrix, while the right-hand-side vector $\mathbf{X'y} = [\sum Y_i, \sum x_{i1}Y_i, \sum x_{i2}Y_i, \ldots, \sum x_{ik}Y_i]'$ contains sums of cross products between each column of the model matrix and the vector of responses. The sums of squares and products $\mathbf{X'X}$ and $\mathbf{X'y}$ can be calculated directly from the data.

The $\mathbf{X'X}$ matrix is of full rank, and hence nonsingular, if the model matrix $\mathbf{X}$ is of full-column rank, $k+1$—that is, if no explanatory variable is a perfect linear function of the others.[2] Under these circumstances, the normal equations have the unique solution

$$\mathbf{b} = \left(\mathbf{X'X}\right)^{-1}\mathbf{X'y} \tag{7.4}$$

That this solution represents a minimum of $S(\mathbf{b})$ is supported by the fact that if $\mathbf{X'X}$ is nonsingular, it is also positive-definite. Alternatively, if any of the columns of the model matrix are perfectly collinear with others, then the normal equations are underdetermined, and there are infinitely many coefficient vectors $\mathbf{b}$ that minimize the sum of squared residuals.

7.1.1 Computing the Least-Squares Solution by the QR and SVD Decompositions

The rationale for computing the vector of least-squares coefficients by Equation 7.4 is straightforward, but using this formula is numerically disadvantageous: In certain circumstances, for example, when some of the Xs are highly correlated, computing the matrices $\mathbf{X'X}$ and $\mathbf{X'y}$ of sums of squares and products and then inverting $\mathbf{X'X}$ is prone to serious rounding errors. And when there are *perfect* collinearities among the Xs, the matrix $\mathbf{X'X}$ has no inverse.

---

[2]This condition excludes invariant Xs, which are multiples of the constant regressor. The condition also implies that the number of observations must be at least as large as the number of regression coefficients, $n \geq k+1$; in typical (but not all) applications of linear regression, n is much larger than $k+1$.

There are better approaches to calculating the least-squares regression coefficients than directly solving the normal equations, including methods that use the QR and SVD decompositions of the $\mathbf{X}$ matrix.[3]

Least-Squares Regression by the QR Decomposition

The QR decomposition of the $(n \times k + 1)$ model matrix is $\mathbf{X} = \mathbf{QR}$. I'll assume initially that $\mathbf{X}$ is of full-column rank $k + 1$, relaxing this assumption later in the section. If $\mathbf{X}$ is of full rank, then $\mathbf{Q}$ is an orthonormal matrix of order $(n \times k + 1)$, and hence of rank $k + 1$, and $\mathbf{R}$ is an upper-triangular of order $(k + 1 \times k + 1)$ with nonzero diagonal elements, thus also of rank $k + 1$.

Let's return to the least-squares normal equations (Equation 7.3), substituting $\mathbf{QR}$ for $\mathbf{X}$:

$$\mathbf{X}'\mathbf{X}\mathbf{b} = \mathbf{X}'\mathbf{y} \tag{7.5}$$
$$(\mathbf{QR})'\mathbf{QR}\mathbf{b} = (\mathbf{QR})'\mathbf{y}$$
$$\mathbf{R}'\mathbf{Q}'\mathbf{QR}\mathbf{b} = \mathbf{R}'\mathbf{Q}'\mathbf{y}$$
$$\mathbf{R}'\mathbf{R}\mathbf{b} = \mathbf{R}'\mathbf{Q}'\mathbf{y}$$

The transition to the last line in Equation 7.5 is justified because $\mathbf{Q}$ is orthonormal and so $\mathbf{Q}'\mathbf{Q} = \mathbf{I}_{k+1}$. Then multiplying both sides of the equation on the left by $\mathbf{R}'^{-1}$ simplifies the result to

$$\mathbf{R}\mathbf{b} = \mathbf{Q}'\mathbf{y} \tag{7.6}$$

This is a system of $k + 1$ linear equations in $k + 1$ unknowns. The right-hand side of the equations, $\mathbf{Q}'\mathbf{y}$, can be stably calculated from the data, and because the matrix $\mathbf{R}$ is upper-triangular, the system of equations is very easily solved (*Reader:* Can you see why?).

If there are perfect collinearities among the columns of $\mathbf{X}$, so that it is of rank $r < k + 1$, then $k + 1 - r$ columns of $\mathbf{Q}$ will be zero, as will the corresponding $k + 1 - r$ rows of $\mathbf{R}$. If we eliminate the zero columns from $\mathbf{Q}$ and the zero rows from $\mathbf{R}$, and delete the corresponding elements of $\mathbf{b}$ (in effect setting these regression coefficients to zero), then the remaining values in $\mathbf{b}$ produced by Equation 7.6 are *an arbitrary* solution to the least-squares problem—that is, one among the infinite number of full vectors $\mathbf{b}$ that minimize the sum of squared residuals. In some circumstances, an arbitrary solution is all that we need.

---

[3]The QR and SVD decompositions of a matrix were introduced in Sections 2.3 and 2.1.2, respectively.

Least-Squares Regression by the SVD Decomposition

The rationale for least-squares regression by the SVD decomposition is a bit more involved, and so I'll simply present the result here, for the general case where the rank of the model matrix $\mathbf{X}$ is $r \leq k+1$. Applying the compact form of the SVD to the model matrix, adapting Equation 2.7 (on page 47):

$$\underset{(n \times k+1)}{\mathbf{X}} = \underset{(n \times r)(r \times r)(r \times k+1)}{\mathbf{B}^* \ \mathbf{\Lambda} \ \mathbf{C}^{*\prime}}$$

Recall that $\mathbf{B}^*$ and $\mathbf{C}^*$ are both orthonormal matrices.

Then the vector of least-squares coefficients is

$$\mathbf{b} = \mathbf{C}^* \mathbf{\Lambda}^{-1} \mathbf{B}^{*\prime} \mathbf{y} \tag{7.7}$$

Because the matrix $\mathbf{\Lambda}$ is diagonal, its inverse is simply the diagonal matrix $\mathbf{\Lambda}^{-1} = \{1/\lambda_i\}$, where the λ_is are the singular values of $\mathbf{X}$. If $\mathbf{X}$ is of full-column rank $r = k+1$, then Equation 7.7 provides the usual (unique) vector of least-squares coefficients; if, alternatively, $r < k+1$, then $\mathbf{b}$ is an arbitrary least-squares solution.

7.2 A Statistical Model for Linear Regression

A common statistical model for linear regression is

$$Y_i = \alpha + \beta_1 x_{i1} + \beta_2 x_{i2} + \cdots + \beta_k x_{ik} + \varepsilon_i$$

where, as before, Y_i represents the value of the response variable for the ith of n sample observations; also as before, $x_{i1}, x_{i2}, \ldots, x_{ik}$ are the values of the k fixed explanatory variables; $\alpha, \beta_1, \beta_2, \ldots, \beta_k$ are *population* regression coefficients to be estimated from the sample data; and ε_i is an *error variable* associated with observation i. A Greek letter is used for the error, even though it is a random variable, because the errors (unlike the least-squares residuals, E_i) are not directly observable. It is assumed that the errors are normally distributed with zero means and constant variance σ^2,

$$\varepsilon_i \sim N(0, \sigma^2)$$

and that errors from different observations are independent of one another.

Equivalently, in matrix form,

$$\underset{(n \times 1)}{\mathbf{y}} = \underset{(n \times k+1)(k+1 \times 1)}{\mathbf{X} \ \boldsymbol{\beta}} + \underset{(n \times 1)}{\boldsymbol{\varepsilon}} \tag{7.8}$$

where $\mathbf{y}$ is the response vector and $\mathbf{X}$ is the model matrix, assumed to be of full-column rank, as in the preceding section; $\boldsymbol{\beta} \equiv [\alpha, \beta_1, \ldots, \beta_k]'$ is the vector of population regression coefficients; and $\boldsymbol{\varepsilon} \equiv [\varepsilon_1, \varepsilon_2, \ldots, \varepsilon_n]'$ is the vector of errors. The error vector is multivariately normally distributed with a scalar covariance matrix, $\boldsymbol{\varepsilon} \sim N_n(\mathbf{0}, \sigma^2 \mathbf{I}_n)$. Because they are independent, different errors are uncorrelated.[4]

The distribution of the response vector $\mathbf{y}$ follows from the distribution of $\boldsymbol{\varepsilon}$:

$$
\begin{aligned}
\boldsymbol{\mu} \equiv E(\mathbf{y}) &= E(\mathbf{X}\boldsymbol{\beta} + \boldsymbol{\varepsilon}) \\
&= \mathbf{X}\boldsymbol{\beta} + E(\boldsymbol{\varepsilon}) \\
&= \mathbf{X}\boldsymbol{\beta} \\
V(\mathbf{y}) &= E\left[(\mathbf{y} - \boldsymbol{\mu})(\mathbf{y} - \boldsymbol{\mu})'\right] \\
&= E\left[(\mathbf{X}\boldsymbol{\beta} + \boldsymbol{\varepsilon} - \mathbf{X}\boldsymbol{\beta})(\mathbf{X}\boldsymbol{\beta} + \boldsymbol{\varepsilon} - \mathbf{X}\boldsymbol{\beta})'\right] \\
&= E(\boldsymbol{\varepsilon}\boldsymbol{\varepsilon}') \\
&= \sigma^2 \mathbf{I}_n \\
\mathbf{y} &\sim N_n(\mathbf{X}\boldsymbol{\beta}, \sigma^2 \mathbf{I}_n)
\end{aligned}
$$

Thus, for example, the assumption that $E(\boldsymbol{\varepsilon}) = \mathbf{0}$ implies that $E(\mathbf{y})$ is a linear function of $\mathbf{X}$.

7.3   The Least-Squares Coefficients as Estimators

The least-squares regression coefficients $\mathbf{b}$ from Equation 7.4 (page 201) may be used to estimate the coefficients of the linear regression model of Equation 7.8. Because $\mathbf{b}$ results from a linear transformation of the response vector $\mathbf{y}$, the properties of the least-squares estimator are easily established:

$$
\mathbf{b} = (\mathbf{X}'\mathbf{X})^{-1}\mathbf{X}'\mathbf{y} = \mathbf{My}
$$

where the transformation matrix $\mathbf{M} \equiv (\mathbf{X}'\mathbf{X})^{-1}\mathbf{X}'$. Because the model matrix $\mathbf{X}$ is fixed with respect to repeated sampling, so is $\mathbf{M}$. Then,

$$
E(\mathbf{b}) = \mathbf{M}E(\mathbf{y}) = (\mathbf{X}'\mathbf{X})^{-1}\mathbf{X}'\mathbf{X}\boldsymbol{\beta} = \boldsymbol{\beta}
$$

---

[4]As a general matter, independence implies uncorrelation, but uncorrelated random variables are not necessarily independent (see Section 4.2). In the multivariate-normal distribution, however, independence and uncorrelation coincide.

demonstrating that **b** is an unbiased estimator of $\boldsymbol{\beta}$. This conclusion depends only on the assumption that $E(\mathbf{y}) = \mathbf{X}\boldsymbol{\beta}$ (i.e., the assumption of linearity).

The covariance matrix of **b** is also simply derived from the assumptions of constant error variance and uncorrelated errors—that is, that $V(\mathbf{y}) = \sigma^2 \mathbf{I}_n$:

$$
\begin{aligned}
V(\mathbf{b}) &= \mathbf{M}V(\mathbf{y})\mathbf{M}' \\
&= [(\mathbf{X}'\mathbf{X})^{-1}\mathbf{X}']\sigma^2\mathbf{I}_n[(\mathbf{X}'\mathbf{X})^{-1}\mathbf{X}']' \\
&= \sigma^2(\mathbf{X}'\mathbf{X})^{-1}\mathbf{X}'\mathbf{X}(\mathbf{X}'\mathbf{X})^{-1} \\
&= \sigma^2(\mathbf{X}'\mathbf{X})^{-1}
\end{aligned}
$$

Finally, from the assumption of normally distributed errors,

$$
\mathbf{b} \sim N_{k+1}\left[\boldsymbol{\beta}, \sigma^2(\mathbf{X}'\mathbf{X})^{-1}\right] \tag{7.9}
$$

It can be shown that the least-squares estimator **b** is not only an unbiased estimator of $\boldsymbol{\beta}$, but also that, under the assumptions of linearity, constant error variance, and independence, it is the minimum-variance unbiased estimator that is a linear function of the data. This result, called the *Gauss–Markov theorem*,[5] is often taken as justification for least-squares estimation, but it does not lend strong support to the least-squares estimator: When the error distribution is nonnormal, other unbiased estimators that are *nonlinear* functions of the data (so-called *robust-regression* estimators) can be much more efficient than the least-squares estimator.[6] When the errors are normally distributed, however, the least-squares estimator is maximally efficient among *all* unbiased estimators—a much more compelling result.[7]

7.4 Statistical Inference for the Regression Model

Statistical inference for the population regression coefficients $\boldsymbol{\beta}$, beyond point estimation, is complicated by the fact that we typically do not know the error variance σ^2 and, therefore, cannot directly apply Equation 7.9 for

---

[5]The Gauss–Markov theorem is named after the great 18th- to 19th-century German mathematician Carl Friedrich Gauss, and the 19th- to 20th-century Russian probabilist Andrey Andreevich Markov.

[6]For example, the M-estimators of location discussed in Section 6.2.5 extend naturally to linear regression.

[7]For proofs of the results mentioned in this paragraph, see, for example, Rao (1973).

the distribution of the least-squares estimator $\mathbf{b}$. We must instead estimate σ^2 along with $\boldsymbol{\beta}$. An unbiased estimator of σ^2 is given by

$$S^2 = \frac{\sum_{i=1}^{n} E_i^2}{n-k-1} = \frac{\mathbf{e}'\mathbf{e}}{n-k-1}$$

where $n-k-1$ are the degrees of freedom for error (having "lost" $k+1$ degrees of freedom as a consequence of estimating the $k+1$ elements of $\boldsymbol{\beta}$). Then the *estimated* covariance matrix for the least-squares coefficients is

$$\widehat{V}(\mathbf{b}) = S^2(\mathbf{X}'\mathbf{X})^{-1}$$

and the square roots of the diagonal entries of $\widehat{V}(\mathbf{b})$ are the standard errors of the regression coefficients, $SE(A)$, $SE(B_1), \ldots, SE(B_k)$.

Inference for individual regression coefficients is based on the t-distribution (see Section 5.2.3). For example, to test the hypothesis $H_0\colon \beta_j = \beta_j^{(0)}$ that a population slope coefficient is equal to the particular value $\beta_j^{(0)}$ (typically zero), we compute the test statistic

$$t_0 = \frac{B_j - \beta_j^{(0)}}{SE(B_j)}$$

which is distributed as t_{n-k-1} under H_0. Similarly, to construct a 95% confidence interval for β_j, we take

$$\beta_j = B_j \pm t_{.975, n-k-1} SE(B_j)$$

where $t_{.975, n-k-1}$ is the .975 quantile of t with $n-k-1$ degrees of freedom.

More generally, we can test the *linear hypothesis*

$$H_0\colon \underset{(q \times k+1)}{\mathbf{L}} \underset{(k+1 \times 1)}{\boldsymbol{\beta}} = \underset{(q \times 1)}{\mathbf{c}}$$

where $\mathbf{L}$ and $\mathbf{c}$ contain prespecified constants, and the *hypothesis matrix* $\mathbf{L}$ is of full row rank $q \leq k+1$. The resulting F-statistic,

$$F_0 = \frac{(\mathbf{Lb} - \mathbf{c})' [\mathbf{L}(\mathbf{X}'\mathbf{X})^{-1}\mathbf{L}']^{-1} (\mathbf{Lb} - \mathbf{c})}{qS^2} \tag{7.10}$$

follows an F-distribution (see Section 5.2.4) with q and $n-k-1$ degrees of freedom if H_0 is true.

Suppose, for example, that we wish to test the "omnibus" null hypothesis $H_0\colon \beta_1 = \beta_2 = 0$ in a regression model with two explanatory variables; we can take

$$\mathbf{L} = \begin{bmatrix} 0 & 1 & 0 \\ 0 & 0 & 1 \end{bmatrix}$$

and $\mathbf{c} = [0,0]'$. To test the hypothesis that the two population partial regression coefficients are equal, H_0: $\beta_1 = \beta_2$, which is equivalent to H_0: $\beta_1 - \beta_2 = 0$, we can take $\mathbf{L} = [0, 1, -1]$ and $\mathbf{c} = [0]$.[8]

As I have shown, under the assumptions of the regression model, the least-squares regression coefficients are multivariately normally distributed. Consequently, if the sample size is sufficiently large, then we can employ the delta method (Section 6.3.5) to derive the standard error of a *nonlinear* function of the regression coefficients.

Consider, for example, the quadratic regression model

$$Y = \beta_0 + \beta_1 x + \beta_2 x^2 + \varepsilon \qquad (7.11)$$

Although the expectation of Y is not a straight-line function of x, this model can be fit by the linear least-squares regression of Y on x and x^2 because the model is linear in the parameters β_0, β_1, and β_2. Suppose that we are interested in determining the x-value at which the regression equation reaches its maximum or minimum.[9] Taking the expectation of both sides of Equation 7.11 and differentiating with respect to x, we get

$$\frac{dE(Y)}{dx} = \beta_1 + 2\beta_2 x$$

Setting the derivative to zero and solving for x produces the x-value at which the function reaches a minimum (if β_2 is positive) or a maximum (if β_2 is negative),

$$x = -\frac{\beta_1}{2\beta_2}$$

which is a nonlinear function of the regression coefficients β_1 and β_2.

To apply the delta method, we need the partial derivatives of $\gamma = f(\beta_1, \beta_2) \equiv -\beta_1/(2\beta_2)$ with respect to the regression coefficients:

$$\frac{\partial \gamma}{\partial \beta_1} = -\frac{1}{2\beta_2}$$

$$\frac{\partial \gamma}{\partial \beta_2} = \frac{\beta_1}{2\beta_2^2}$$

---

[8] For this hypothesis to be sensible, the two explanatory variables x_1 and x_2, would have to be measured in the same units.

[9] The application of the delta method to this problem is suggested by Weisberg (2014, Section 6.1.2).

Now suppose that we compute least-squares estimates B_1 of β_1 and B_2 of β_2, along with the estimated variances of the coefficients, $\widehat{V}(B_1)$ and $\widehat{V}(B_2)$, and their covariance, $\widehat{C}(B_1, B_2)$. An estimate of γ is $\widehat{\gamma} = -B_1/(2B_2)$,[10] and the delta-method variance of $\widehat{\gamma}$ is

$$\widehat{\mathscr{V}}(\widehat{\gamma}) = \widehat{V}(B_1)\left(-\frac{1}{2B_2}\right)^2 + \widehat{V}(B_2)\left(\frac{B_1}{2B_2^2}\right)^2 + 2\widehat{C}(B_1, B_2)\left(-\frac{1}{2B_2}\right)\left(\frac{B_1}{2B_2^2}\right)$$

Thus, an asymptotic 95% confidence interval for γ is given by $\widehat{\gamma} \pm 1.96\sqrt{\widehat{\mathscr{V}}(\widehat{\gamma})}$.

7.5   Maximum-Likelihood Estimation of the Regression Model

As I have explained, under the assumptions of the linear model, the distribution of the response is $\mathbf{y} \sim N_n(\mathbf{X}\boldsymbol{\beta}, \sigma^2\mathbf{I}_n)$. Thus, for the ith observation, $Y_i \sim N(\mathbf{x}_i'\boldsymbol{\beta}, \sigma^2)$, where $\mathbf{x}_i'$ is the ith row of the model matrix $\mathbf{X}$. In equation form, the probability density for observation i is (from the formula for the normal distribution, Equation 5.2 on page 127)

$$p(y_i) = \frac{1}{\sigma\sqrt{2\pi}}\exp\left[-\frac{(y_i - \mathbf{x}_i'\boldsymbol{\beta})^2}{2\sigma^2}\right]$$

Because the n observations are independent, their joint probability density is the product of their marginal densities:

$$\begin{aligned}
p(\mathbf{y}) &= \frac{1}{\left(\sigma\sqrt{2\pi}\right)^n}\exp\left[-\frac{\sum(y_i - \mathbf{x}_i'\boldsymbol{\beta})^2}{2\sigma^2}\right] \qquad (7.12)\\
&= \frac{1}{(2\pi\sigma^2)^{n/2}}\exp\left[-\frac{(\mathbf{y} - \mathbf{X}\boldsymbol{\beta})'(\mathbf{y} - \mathbf{X}\boldsymbol{\beta})}{2\sigma^2}\right]
\end{aligned}$$

Although this equation also follows directly from the multivariate-normal distribution of $\mathbf{y}$, the development from $p(y_i)$ to $p(\mathbf{y})$ will prove helpful when we consider random Xs (in the next section).

From Equation 7.12, the log likelihood is

$$\log_e L(\boldsymbol{\beta}, \sigma^2) = -\frac{n}{2}\log_e 2\pi - \frac{n}{2}\log_e \sigma^2 - \frac{1}{2\sigma^2}(\mathbf{y} - \mathbf{X}\boldsymbol{\beta})'(\mathbf{y} - \mathbf{X}\boldsymbol{\beta}) \quad (7.13)$$

---

[10]As shown immediately below, under the assumptions of the regression model, the least-squares coefficients are maximum-likelihood estimators of the population regression coefficients, and so $\widehat{\gamma}$ is the MLE of γ.

To maximize the likelihood, we require the partial derivatives of Equation 7.13 with respect to the parameters $\boldsymbol{\beta}$ and σ^2. Differentiation is simplified when we notice that $(\mathbf{y} - \mathbf{X}\boldsymbol{\beta})'(\mathbf{y} - \mathbf{X}\boldsymbol{\beta})$ is the sum of squared errors:

$$\frac{\partial \log_e L(\boldsymbol{\beta}, \sigma^2)}{\partial \boldsymbol{\beta}} = -\frac{1}{2\sigma^2}(2\mathbf{X}'\mathbf{X}\boldsymbol{\beta} - 2\mathbf{X}'\mathbf{y})$$

$$\frac{\partial \log_e L(\boldsymbol{\beta}, \sigma^2)}{\partial \sigma^2} = -\frac{n}{2}\left(\frac{1}{\sigma^2}\right) + \frac{1}{2\sigma^4}(\mathbf{y} - \mathbf{X}\boldsymbol{\beta})'(\mathbf{y} - \mathbf{X}\boldsymbol{\beta})$$

Setting these partial derivatives to zero and solving for the maximum-likelihood estimators $\widehat{\boldsymbol{\beta}}$ and $\widehat{\sigma}_\varepsilon^2$ produces

$$\widehat{\boldsymbol{\beta}} = (\mathbf{X}'\mathbf{X})^{-1}\mathbf{X}'\mathbf{y}$$

$$\widehat{\sigma}^2 = \frac{(\mathbf{y} - \mathbf{X}\widehat{\boldsymbol{\beta}})'(\mathbf{y} - \mathbf{X}\widehat{\boldsymbol{\beta}})}{n} = \frac{\mathbf{e}'\mathbf{e}}{n}$$

The maximum-likelihood estimator $\widehat{\boldsymbol{\beta}}$ is therefore the same as the least-squares estimator $\mathbf{b}$. In fact, this identity is clear directly from Equation 7.12, without formal maximization of the likelihood: The likelihood is large when the negative exponent is small, and the numerator of the exponent contains the sum of squared errors; minimizing the sum of squared residuals, therefore, maximizes the likelihood.

The maximum-likelihood estimator $\widehat{\sigma}^2$ of the error variance is biased; consequently, we prefer the similar, unbiased estimator $S^2 = \mathbf{e}'\mathbf{e}/(n-k-1)$, described previously. As n increases, however, the bias of $\widehat{\sigma}^2$ shrinks toward zero: As a maximum-likelihood estimator, $\widehat{\sigma}^2$ is consistent.

7.6 Random Xs

The theory of linear regression analysis developed in this chapter has proceeded from the premise that the model matrix $\mathbf{X}$ is *fixed*. If we repeat a study, we expect the response-variable observations $\mathbf{y}$ to change, but if $\mathbf{X}$ is fixed, then the explanatory-variable values are constant across replications of the study. This situation is realistically descriptive of an experiment, where the explanatory variables are manipulated by the researcher. Most research in the social sciences, however, is observational rather than experimental; and in an observational study (e.g., survey research), we would typically obtain different explanatory-variable values on replication of the study. In observational research, therefore, $\mathbf{X}$ is *random* rather than fixed.

It is remarkable that the statistical theory of linear regression applies even when $\mathbf{X}$ is random, as long as certain conditions are met. For fixed explanatory variables, the assumptions underlying the model take the form $\boldsymbol{\varepsilon} \sim N_n(\mathbf{0},\ \sigma^2\mathbf{I}_n)$. That is, the distribution of the error is the same for all observed combinations of explanatory-variable values represented by the distinct rows of the model matrix. When $\mathbf{X}$ is random, we need to assume that this property holds for *all possible* combinations of explanatory-variable values in the population that is sampled: That is, $\mathbf{X}$ and $\boldsymbol{\varepsilon}$ are assumed to be independent, and thus the *conditional* distribution of the error for a sample of explanatory variable values $\boldsymbol{\varepsilon}|\mathbf{X}_0$ is $N_n(\mathbf{0}, \sigma^2\mathbf{I}_n)$, regardless of the *particular* sample $\mathbf{X}_0 = \{x_{ij}\}$ that is chosen.

Because $\mathbf{X}$ is random, it has some (multivariate) probability distribution. It is not necessary to make assumptions about this distribution, however, beyond (1) requiring that $\mathbf{X}$ is measured without error, (2) assuming that $\mathbf{X}$ and $\boldsymbol{\varepsilon}$ are independent (as just explained), (3) assuming that the distribution of $\mathbf{X}$ does not depend on the parameters $\boldsymbol{\beta}$ and σ^2 of the regression model, and (4) stipulating that the population covariance matrix of the Xs is nonsingular (i.e., that no X is invariant or a perfect linear function of the others in the population). In particular, we need *not* assume that the Xs (as opposed to the *errors*) are normally distributed. This is fortunate, for many Xs are highly nonnormal—dummy regressors and polynomial regressors come immediately to mind, not to mention many quantitative explanatory variables.[11]

It would be unnecessarily tedious to recapitulate the entire argument of this chapter for random Xs, but I will show that some key results still hold under the new assumptions when the explanatory variables are random. The other results of the chapter can be established for random Xs in a similar manner.

---

[11]To say that the previous results hold with random Xs under these new assumptions is not to assert that the new assumptions are necessarily unproblematic. Most explanatory variables are measured with error, and to assume otherwise can, in certain circumstances, seriously bias the estimated regression coefficients. Similarly, under certain (causal) interpretations of regression equations, the assumption that the errors are independent of the explanatory variables is tantamount to assuming that the aggregated omitted prior determinants of Y are unrelated to the determinants of Y that are included in the model. Finally, the assumptions of linearity, constant error variance, and normality are also potentially problematic. Dealing satisfactorily with these issues is the difference between regression analysis as a mathematical abstraction and as a practical tool for data analysis, and, possibly, causal inference.

For a particular sample of X-values, $\mathbf{X}_0$, the conditional distribution of $\mathbf{y}$ is

$$\begin{aligned} E(\mathbf{y}|\mathbf{X}_0) &= E\left[(\mathbf{X}\boldsymbol{\beta} + \boldsymbol{\varepsilon})|\mathbf{X}_0\right] \\ &= \mathbf{X}_0\boldsymbol{\beta} + E(\boldsymbol{\varepsilon}|\mathbf{X}_0) \\ &= \mathbf{X}_0\boldsymbol{\beta} \end{aligned}$$

Consequently, the conditional expectation of the least-squares estimator is

$$\begin{aligned} E(\mathbf{b}|\mathbf{X}_0) &= E\left[(\mathbf{X}'\mathbf{X})^{-1}\mathbf{X}'\mathbf{y}|\mathbf{X}_0\right] \\ &= (\mathbf{X}_0'\mathbf{X}_0)^{-1}\mathbf{X}_0'E(\mathbf{y}|\mathbf{X}_0) \\ &= (\mathbf{X}_0'\mathbf{X}_0)^{-1}\mathbf{X}_0'\mathbf{X}_0\boldsymbol{\beta} \\ &= \boldsymbol{\beta} \end{aligned}$$

Because we can repeat this argument for *any* value of $\mathbf{X}$, the least-squares estimator $\mathbf{b}$ is conditionally unbiased for any and every such value; it is therefore *unconditionally* unbiased as well, $E(\mathbf{b}) = \boldsymbol{\beta}$.

Suppose now that we use the procedures described earlier in this chapter to perform statistical inference for $\boldsymbol{\beta}$. For concreteness, imagine that we calculate a p-value for the omnibus null hypothesis $H_0: \beta_1 = \cdots = \beta_k = 0$. Because $\boldsymbol{\varepsilon}|\mathbf{X}_0 \sim N_n(\mathbf{0}, \sigma^2\mathbf{I}_n)$, as was required when we treated $\mathbf{X}$ as fixed, the p-value obtained is correct for $\mathbf{X} = \mathbf{X}_0$ (i.e., for the sample at hand). There is, however, nothing special about a particular $\mathbf{X}_0$: The error vector $\boldsymbol{\varepsilon}$ is independent of $\mathbf{X}$, and so the distribution of $\boldsymbol{\varepsilon}$ is $N_n(\mathbf{0}, \sigma^2\mathbf{I}_n)$ for any and every value of $\mathbf{X}$. The p-value, therefore, is *unconditionally* valid.

Finally, I will show that the maximum-likelihood estimators of $\boldsymbol{\beta}$ and σ^2 are unchanged when $\mathbf{X}$ is random, as long as the new assumptions hold: When $\mathbf{X}$ is random, sampled observations consist not just of response-variable values $(Y_1, \ldots, Y_n)$ but also of explanatory-variable values $(\mathbf{x}_1', \ldots, \mathbf{x}_n')$. The observations themselves are denoted $[Y_1, \mathbf{x}_1'], \ldots, [Y_n, \mathbf{x}_n']$. Because these observations are sampled independently, their joint probability density is the product of their marginal densities:

$$p(\mathbf{y}, \mathbf{X}) \equiv p\left([y_1, \mathbf{x}_1'], \ldots, [y_n, \mathbf{x}_n']\right) = p(y_1, \mathbf{x}_1') \times \cdots \times p(y_n, \mathbf{x}_n')$$

Now, the probability density $p(y_i, \mathbf{x}_i')$ for observation i can be written as $p(y_i|\mathbf{x}_i')p(\mathbf{x}_i')$. According to the linear model, the conditional distribution of Y_i given $\mathbf{x}_i'$ is normal:

$$p(y_i|\mathbf{x}_i') = \frac{1}{\sigma\sqrt{2\pi}}\exp\left[-\frac{(y_i - \mathbf{x}_i'\boldsymbol{\beta})^2}{2\sigma^2}\right]$$

Thus, the joint probability density for all observations becomes

$$p(\mathbf{y}, \mathbf{X}) = \prod_{i=1}^{n} p(\mathbf{x}_i') \frac{1}{\sigma\sqrt{2\pi}} \exp\left[-\frac{(y_i - \mathbf{x}_i'\boldsymbol{\beta})^2}{2\sigma^2} \right]$$

$$= \left[\prod_{i=1}^{n} p(\mathbf{x}_i') \right] \frac{1}{(2\pi\sigma^2)^{n/2}} \exp\left[-\frac{(\mathbf{y} - \mathbf{X}\boldsymbol{\beta})'(\mathbf{y} - \mathbf{X}\boldsymbol{\beta})}{2\sigma^2} \right]$$

$$= p(\mathbf{X}) p(\mathbf{y}|\mathbf{X})$$

As long as $p(\mathbf{X})$ does not depend on the parameters $\boldsymbol{\beta}$ and σ^2, we can ignore the joint density of the Xs in maximizing $p(\mathbf{y}, \mathbf{X})$ with respect to the parameters. Consequently, the maximum-likelihood estimator of $\boldsymbol{\beta}$ is the least-squares estimator, as was the case for fixed $\mathbf{X}$.

7.7 The Elliptical Geometry of Linear Least-Squares Regression

7.7.1 Simple Regression

I developed the general relationship between quadratic forms and ellipses in Section 2.2.1, and then applied these results to the bivariate-normal distribution in Section 5.2.5, visualizing properties of the covariance matrix of the two variables as an ellipse (see in particular Figure 5.10 on page 135). A remarkably similar elliptical representation applies to the sample covariance matrix for *any* two variables, whether or not they are drawn from a bivariate-normal population, and this representation helps us visualize linear least-squares simple regression, where there is a single explanatory variable.

In simple regression, the regression model is $Y = \alpha + \beta X + \varepsilon$, where the errors are independently and normally distributed with zero means and constant variance, $\varepsilon \sim N(0, \sigma^2)$. For concreteness, I randomly generated $n = 100$ values of X from the rectangular distribution on the interval $[0, 5]$ (to emphasize that the ideas to be developed don't depend on bivariate normality), and then used the simple-regression model, with $\alpha = 1.5$, $\beta = 0.5$, and $\sigma^2 = 1$ to randomly generate corresponding observations for Y by sampling the errors from the distribution $\varepsilon \sim N(0, 1)$.[12]

The data are graphed in the scatterplot in Figure 7.1, along with the *standard data ellipse*, a close analog of the standard concentration ellipse for

---

[12]I usually prefer to illustrate regression analysis with real data, but, in the general spirit of this book, the focus here is on the mathematics rather than on data analysis.

the bivariate-normal distribution (cf. Figure 5.10 on page 135). The sample statistics depicted in Figure 7.1 are the means $\overline{X} = 2.547$ and $\overline{Y} = 2.922$, standard deviations $S_X = 1.504$ and $S_Y = 1.316$, and correlation $r = .5056$; the sample covariance of X and Y is therefore $S_{XY} = rS_XS_Y = .5056 \times 1.504 \times 1.316 = 1.001$. The standard data ellipse shown in the graph is the locus of points (x,y) satisfying the equation

$$[x-\overline{X}, y-\overline{Y}]S^{-1}[x-\overline{X}, y-\overline{Y}]'$$
$$= [x-2.547, y-2.922]\begin{bmatrix} 1.504 & 1.001 \\ 1.001 & 2.547 \end{bmatrix}^{-1}\begin{bmatrix} x-2.547 \\ y-2.922 \end{bmatrix} = 1$$

where S is the sample covariance matrix of X and Y.

The standard data ellipse is centered at the point of means $(\overline{X}, \overline{Y})$, and the shadows of the ellipse on the two axes mark off twice the standard deviation of each variable. The line drawn on the graph between the two points of vertical tangency to the ellipse is the least-squares line for the regression of Y on X.[13] The distance between a horizontal line drawn through one of the points of vertical tangency and a horizontal line through the point of means is the product of the absolute value of the correlation coefficient (which in the example is positive) and the standard deviation of the response. When the ellipse is "sliced" vertically above the mean of X, the length of the slice is twice the standard deviation of the residuals (i.e., the conditional standard deviation of Y given X).[14]

7.7.2 Multiple Regression

Ellipses also illuminate statistical inference in multiple regression analysis. I focus here on a multiple regression for two explanatory variables, $Y = \alpha + \beta_1 X_1 + \beta_2 X_2 + \varepsilon$ with normally and independently distributed errors with constant variance, $\varepsilon \sim N(0, \sigma^2)$. As in the preceding simple-regression example, I generated data according to this model, first sampling $n = 100$ values of the Xs from a bivariate-normal distribution with $E(X_1) = \mu_1 = 5$, $E(X_2) = \mu_2 = 6$, $V(X_1) = \sigma_1^2 = 1.5^2$, $V(X_2) = \sigma_2^2 = 3^2$, and $C(X_1, X_2) = \sigma_{12} = 2.25$. Thus, the population correlation between X_1 and X_2 is $\rho_{12} = 2.25/(1.5 \times 3) = .5$. I then sampled errors from the distribution $\varepsilon \sim N(0, 5^2)$

---

[13]The least-squares line for the regression of X on Y (not shown on the graph) goes through the two points of *horizontal* tangency to the ellipse.

[14]There is slight slippage here due to degrees of freedom: S_E in the graph is implicitly computed using $n-1$ in the denominator of the residual variance, rather than the residual degrees of freedom, $n-2$.

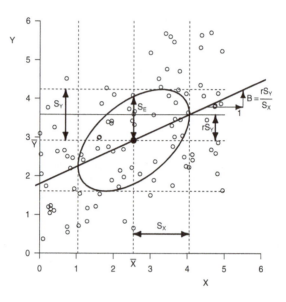

Figure 7.1 The elliptical geometry of simple regression: The standard
data ellipse is centered at the point of means $(\overline{X}, \overline{Y})$; the
shadows of the ellipse on the horizontal and vertical axes are
respectively twice the standard deviations of the variables, S_X
and S_Y; and the distance between the horizontal lines through
the point of means and the point of vertical tangency is the
product of the absolute value of the correlation coefficient
and the standard deviation of the response, $|r|S_Y$. The
least-squares line goes through the points of vertical tangency
to the ellipse, and so its slope is $B = rS_Y/S_x$. The vertical
distance between the point of means and the ellipse is the
standard deviation of the residuals, S_E.

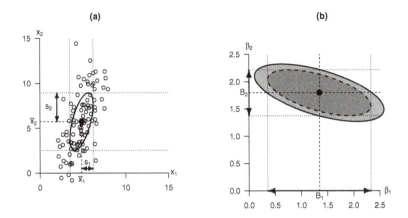

Figure 7.2 (a) The scatterplot and standard data ellipse for X_1 and X_2 and
(b) confidence ellipses for the regression coefficients B_1 and
B_2 in the regression of Y on X_1 and X_2. The larger (solid-line)
ellipse marks the 95% joint confidence region for the
population regression coefficients β_1 and β_2; the smaller
(broken-line) ellipse is the confidence interval–generating
ellipse, whose projections on the axes are the individual 95%
confidence intervals for β_1 and β_2. The confidence ellipses
are rescaled clockwise 90° rotations of the data ellipse.

and constructed the response variable according to the population regression
equation $Y = 3 + 1.5X_1 + 2X_2 + \varepsilon$.

Figure 7.2(a) shows the scatterplot and standard data ellipse for the generated sample of values of X_1 and X_2. Because the Xs were sampled from a
bivariate-normal distribution,[15] the data ellipse estimates the standard concentration ellipse for the population. As usual, the data ellipse is centered at
the point of sample means of the two variables, $(\overline{X}_1, \overline{X}_2)$, and the shadows
of the ellipse on the axes give twice the standard deviations of the variables,
S_1 and S_2.

---

[15]The standard data ellipse for X_1 and X_2 would still represent their sample standard deviations
and covariance (or correlation) even if the variables were *not* sampled from a bivariate-normal
distribution. Recall that the regression model doesn't make distributional assumptions about the
Xs (other than independence from the errors).

Turning around the F-test for a general linear hypothesis given in Equation 7.10 (on page 206), and setting the hypothesis matrix to the identity matrix, produces a *joint confidence region* (say at the 95% level of confidence) for the $k+1$ regression coefficients in a linear least-squares regression with k explanatory variables:

$$(\mathbf{b} - \boldsymbol{\beta})'\widehat{V}(\mathbf{b})^{-1}(\mathbf{b} - \boldsymbol{\beta}) \leq (k+1)F_{.95,k+1,n-k-1} \tag{7.14}$$

where $\mathbf{b}$ is the vector of least-squares regression coefficients, $\widehat{V}(\mathbf{b})$ is the estimated covariance matrix of the coefficients, and $F_{.95,k+1,n-k-1}$ is the .95 quantile of F with $k+1$ and $n-k-1$ degrees of freedom. Vectors of the population regression coefficients $\boldsymbol{\beta} = [\alpha, \beta_1, \ldots, \beta_k]'$ that satisfy Inequality 7.14 are jointly acceptable at the 95% level of confidence and define a hyperellipsoidal region in the $k+1$-dimensional parameter space. For $k = 2$ (i.e., for $k+1 = 3$ regression coefficients), this is an ellipsoid in 3D space.

I'll use a trick to reduce the dimensionality of the parameter space from three to two when there are $k = 2$ explanatory variables: Because the least-squares regression plane goes through the point of means $(\overline{X}_1, \overline{X}_2, \overline{Y})$, subtracting the means from the three variables eliminates the intercept A from the regression equation (*Reader:* Why?):

$$Y - \overline{Y} = (X_1 - \overline{X}_1)B_1 + (X_2 - \overline{X}_2)B_2 + E$$
$$Y^* = X_1^* B_1 + X_2^* B_2 + E$$

The regression slope coefficients B_1 and B_2 are unchanged when the variables are centered at their means, as are the residuals E. For compactness, I've marked the variables in mean-deviation form with asterisks.

Using this result, focusing on the joint confidence region for β_1 and β_2, and adapting Inequality 7.14 produces a *confidence ellipse* for the slopes:

$$(\mathbf{b}^* - \boldsymbol{\beta}^*)'\widehat{V}(\mathbf{b}^*)^{-1}(\mathbf{b}^* - \boldsymbol{\beta}^*) \leq 2F_{.95,2,n-3} \tag{7.15}$$

where $\mathbf{b}^* = [B_1, B_2]'$ and $\boldsymbol{\beta}^* = [\beta_1, \beta_2]'$. A subtle point here is that we still have $n - k - 1 = n - 3$ denominator degrees of freedom for F, having "lost" 1 degree of freedom by subtracting the mean from Y, which corresponds to the degree of freedom for the intercept A.

Recall that the covariance matrix of the least-squares regression coefficients is $\widehat{V}(\mathbf{b}) = S^2(\mathbf{X'X})^{-1}$. Applying this formula to the explanatory variables in mean-deviation form, we have

$$\widehat{V}(\mathbf{b}^*) = S^2(\mathbf{X}^{*'}\mathbf{X}^*)^{-1} = \frac{S^2}{n-1}\widehat{V}(\mathbf{X})^{-1} \tag{7.16}$$

because the covariance matrix of the explanatory variable is $\widehat{V}(\mathbf{X}) = \frac{1}{n-1}\mathbf{X}^{*\prime}\mathbf{X}^*$ (and where $\mathbf{X}$ now represents the uncentered matrix of explanatory variables *without* a column of 1s for the intercept). Substituting Equation 7.16 into Inequality 7.15 produces

$$(\mathbf{b}^* - \boldsymbol{\beta}^*)'\widehat{V}(\mathbf{X})(\mathbf{b}^* - \boldsymbol{\beta}^*) \leq \frac{2S^2}{n-1}F_{.95,2,n-3} \qquad (7.17)$$

Compare the joint confidence ellipse for $\mathbf{b}^* = [\beta_1, \beta_2]'$ in Inequality 7.17 to the equation of the standard data ellipse for X_1 and X_2, which we can write as $\mathbf{x}^{*\prime}\widehat{V}(\mathbf{X})^{-1}\mathbf{x}^* = 1$. Apart from the constant on the right-hand side (and the fact that one is an inequality and the other an equation), the two differ only in that the covariance matrix at the center of the quadratic form is inverted for the data ellipse. That implies that the confidence ellipse is a 90° rescaled clockwise rotation of the data ellipse (see the discussion of the elliptical geometry of quadratic forms in Section 2.2.1), as is apparent in Figure 7.2 for the example.

Because the data ellipse and the confidence ellipse are in this sense inverses of each other, the more spread out the Xs are and the larger the sample size, the more precisely the regression coefficients will be estimated; and the more highly correlated the Xs are, the less precisely the coefficients will be estimated. Similarly, if, as in the example, the Xs are *positively* correlated (reflected in the positive tilt of the data ellipse), the regression coefficients are *negatively* correlated.[16]

In Figure 7.2(b), the larger ellipse is the 95% joint confidence region for β_1 and β_2. The projections of this ellipse onto the β_1 and β_2 axes give individual confidence intervals for the two slope coefficients, but at a *higher* level of confidence than 95%. To produce individual 95% confidence intervals, we can use the smaller ellipse defined by

$$(\mathbf{b}^* - \boldsymbol{\beta}^*)'\widehat{V}(\mathbf{X})(\mathbf{b}^* - \boldsymbol{\beta}^*) \leq \frac{S^2}{n-1}F_{.95,1,n-3}$$

---

[16]The negative correlation of B_1 and B_2 is a *sampling correlation*, implying therefore that in samples where B_1 is unusually large, B_2 will tend to be unusually small, and vice-versa.

which is also shown in Figure 7.2(b), and which is called the *confidence interval–generating ellipse*.[17] The smaller ellipse corresponds to a *joint* confidence level of approximately 85%.

---

[17]The larger ellipse generates so-called *Scheffé* confidence intervals for the coefficients, named for the American statistician Henri Scheffé (see Scheffé, 1959, Chapter 3). The wider Scheffé intervals reflect a "penalty" for simultaneous inference about two regression coefficients. This idea generalizes straightforwardly to $k > 2$. Scheffé's exposition relies heavily ellipses and ellipsoids but without any diagrams!

REFERENCES

Aldrich, J. (1997). R. A. Fisher and the making of maximum-likelihood 1912–1922. *Statistical Science*, *12*, 162–176.

Barndorf-Nielsen, O. E., & Cox, D. R. (1994). *Inference and asymptotics*. Boca Raton: Chapman & Hall/CRC Press.

Binmore, K., & Davies, J. (2001). *Calculus: Concepts and methods*. Cambridge UK: Cambridge University Press.

Carpenter, B., Gelman, A., Hoffman, M. D., Lee, D., Goodrich, B., Betancourt, M., . . . Riddell, A. (2017). Stan: A probabilistic programming language. *Journal of Statistical Software*, *76*(1), 1–32.

Casella, G., & George, E. J. (1992). Explaining the Gibbs sampler. *The American Statistician*, *46*(3), 167–174.

Chib, S., & Greenberg, E. (1995). Understanding the Metropolis-Hastings algorithm. *The American Statistician*, *49*, 327–335.

Cox, D. R., & Hinkley, D. V. (1974). *Theoretical statistics*. London.

Davis, P. J. (1965). *Mathematics of matrices: A first book of matrix theory and linear algebra*. New York: Blaisdell.

Engle, R. (1984). Wald, likelihood ratio, and Lagrange multiplier tests in econometrics. In Z. Griliches & M. D. Intriligator (Eds.), *Handbook of econometrics* (Vol. II, pp. 775–879). Amsterdam: North-Holland.

Fieller, N. (2016). *Basics of matrix algebra for statistics with R*. Boca Raton: Chapman & Hall/CRC Press.

Fisher, R. A. (1922). On the mathematical foundations of theoretical statistics. *Philosophical Transactions of the Royal Society of London, A*, *222*, 309–368.

Fox, J. (2008). *Applied regression analysis and generalized linear models* (2nd ed.). Thousand Oaks CA: Sage.

Fox, J. (2016). *Applied regression analysis and generalized linear models* (3rd ed.). Thousand Oaks, CA: Sage.

Francis, J. G. F. (1961). The QR transformation: A unitary analogue to the LR transformation—part 1. *The Computer Journal*, *4*, 265–271.

Francis, J. G. F. (1962). The QR transformation—part 2. *The Computer Journal*, *4*, 332–345.

Friendly, M., Monette, G., & Fox, J. (2013). Elliptical insights: Understanding statistical methods through elliptical geometry. *Statistical Science*, *28*, 1–39.

Gelfand, A. E., & Smith, A. F. M. (1990). Sampling-based approaches to calculating marginal densities. *Journal of the American Statistical Association*, *85*, 398–409.

Gelman, A., Carlin, J. B., Stern, H. S., & Rubin, D. B. (2013). *Bayesian data analysis* (3rd ed.). Boca Raton FL: Chapman & Hall/CRC Press.

Gelman, A., & Hill, J. (2007). *Data analysis using regression and multilevel/hierarchical models*. Cambridge UK: Cambridge University Press.

Geman, S., & Geman, D. (1984). Stochastic relaxation, Gibbs distributions, and the Bayesian restoration of images. *IEEE Transactions on Pattern Analysis and Machine Intelligence*, *6*, 721–742.

Graybill, F. A. (1983). *Introduction to matrices with applications in statistics* (2nd ed.). Belmont CA: Wadsworth.

Green, P. E., & Carroll, J. D. (1976). *Mathematical tools for applied multivariate analysis*. New York: Academic Press.

Hastings, W. K. (1970). Monte Carlo sampling methods using Markov chains and their applications. *Biometrika, 57*, 97–109.

Healy, M. J. R. (1986). *Matrices for statistics*. Oxford UK: Clarendon Press.

Johnston, J. (1972). *Econometric methods* (2nd ed.). New York: McGraw-Hill.

Kennedy, W. J., Jr., & Gentle, J. E. (1980). *Statistical computing*. New York: Dekker.

Lancaster, T. (2004). *An introduction to modern Bayesian econometrics*. Oxford UK: Blackwell.

Lunn, D., Spiegelhalter, D., Thomas, A., & Best, N. (2009). The BUGS project: Evolution, critique and future directions (with discussion). *Statistics in Medicine, 28*, 3049–3082.

McCallum, B. T. (1973). A note concerning asymptotic covariance expressions. *Econometrica, 41*, 581–583.

McElreath, R. (2020). *Statistical rethinking: A Bayesian course with examples in R and Stan* (second ed.). Boca Raton: Chapman & Hall/CRC Press.

Metropolis, N., Rosenbluth, A. W., Rosenbluth, M. N., Teller, A. H., & Teller, E. (1953). Equation of state calculations by fast computing machines. *Journal of Chemical Physics, 21*, 1087–1092.

Monahan, J. F. (2001). *Numerical methods of statistics*. Cambridge UK: Cambridge University Press.

Namboodiri, K. (1984). *Matrix algebra: An introduction*. Beverly Hills: Sage.

Nash, J. C. (2014). *Nonlinear parameter optimization using R tools*. Chichester UK: Wiley.

Neal, R. M. (1996). *Bayesian learning for neural networks*. New York: Springer.

Neal, R. M. (2011). MCMC using Hamiltonian dynamics. In S. Brooks, A. Gelman, G. L. Jones, & X.-L. Meng (Eds.), *Handbook of Markov chain Monte Carlo* (pp. 113–162). Boca Raton FL: Chapman & Hall/CRC Press.

Nelder, J. A., & Wedderburn, R. W. M. (1972). Generalized linear models. *Journal of the Royal Statistical Society, Series A (General), 135*, 370–384.

Rao, C. R. (1973). *Linear statistical inference and its applications* (2nd ed.). New York: Wiley.

Rao, C. R. and Mitra, S. K. (1971). *Generalized Inverse of Matrices and Its Applications*. New York: Wiley.

Scheffé, H. (1959). *The analysis of variance*. New York: Wiley.

Searle, S. R. (1982). *Matrix algebra useful for statistics*. New York.

Silverman, B. W. (1986). *Density estimation for statistics and data analysis*. Boca Raton FL: Chapman & Hall/CRC.

Stewart, J. (2016). *Calculus* (eighth ed.). Boston: Cengage Learning.

Theil, H. (1971). *Principles of econometrics*. New York: Wiley.

Thompson, S. P., & Gardner, M. (1998). *Calculus made easy*. New York: St. Martin's.

Weisberg, S. (2014). *Applied linear regression* (4th ed.). Hoboken, NJ: Wiley.

Wolfram, S. (2003). *The Mathematica book* (5th ed.). Champaign IL: Wolfram Research.

Wonnacott, T. H., & Wonnacott, R. J. (1990). *Introductory statistics* (5th ed.). New York: Wiley.

Zellner, A. (1983). Statistical theory and econometrics. In Z. Griliches & M. D. Intriligator (Eds.), *Handbook of econometrics* (Vol. 1, pp. 67–178). Amsterdam: North-Holland.

INDEX